Take it to the Cross

Prayer that Destroys the Root of your Problems

Dr. Elijah Akpan

Take it to the Cross

Prophet Dr. Elijah Akpan

THE HEALING HOUSE MINISTRIES
P. O. BOX 36773
LAS VEGAS, NV 89133-6773
Web: www.the-healinghouse.com
Email: info@the-healinghouse.com

TAKE IT TO THE CROSS

by Prophet Dr. Elijah Akpan
Published by The Healing House Ministries, Inc.

Unless otherwise noted, all biblical quotations and all references are taken from the New King James Version Holy Bible.
Copyright ©1982, by Thomas Nelson, Inc., Publishers. Used by permission.

Scriptural quotations marked AMP are taken from the Amplified Bible.
Copyright © 1954, 1958, 1962, 1964, 1965, 1987 by the Lockman Foundation. Used by permission.

Other Scriptural quotations are taken from God's Word Translation Bible.
Copyright © 1995 by God's Word to the Nations, Baker Publishing Group.
Used by permission.

This book or parts thereof may not be reproduced in any form, stored in a retrieval system, or transmitted in any form by any means—electronic, mechanical, photocopy, recording, or otherwise—without prior written permission of the publisher, except as provided by United States of America copyright law.

Cover design by Jessica Akpan, Crossing Bridge Productions
Los Angeles, California
Photographer: Huan Manton
Models: Jessica Akpan, Jasmine Pringle, Matthew Peter Murphy, Rand Kurdi, Brian Spengel

Copyright ©2014 by Prophet Dr. Elijah Akpan
All Rights Reserved

ISBN: 069226809X
ISBN 13: 9780692268094

Acknowledgments

I AM MOST grateful to our Lord and Savior Jesus Christ for giving me the inspiration and strength to write this prayer book. Lord Jesus, You have never broken Your promises nor Your word. Today, You have fulfilled that which You declared concerning my life. May glory and honor be unto Your name forever. I know that the prayers in this book will truly set the captives free, heal the sick, and deliver the oppressed, in Your Mighty precious name. Amen.

My appreciation also goes to the Holy Spirit, my Friend and Teacher, who led and inspired me day and night to write this book and bring it to completion. Without the Holy Spirit, this project would not have been possible today. Thank You my Friend.

I also want to thank my Heavenly Father for His grace and mercy upon our lives, and for standing by us through the stormy days when the world rejected us. I thank Him from the bottom of my heart for His faithful guidance and protection over us from the beginning to the completion of this project. To You O Lord, be all the glory and honor. Amen.

To my dearest friend and wife, Ini Akpan, I say thank you for enduring with me throughout the trying periods. I feel overly blessed to have you as a wife, a partner, and my best friend. Thank you for the countless hours of encouragement, support, and contribution to the completion of this edition of **TAKE IT TO THE CROSS**. May the Almighty God bless and keep you for me. Amen.

To my dearest children, Jessica, Rebecca, Angel, Elijah Jr., and Victoria, I thank you all. I am very proud of you for all your sacrifices and understanding since the Lord called me into His field. Thank you for being exceptional by setting yourselves apart, being trustworthy, caring, and loving, and for praying with us throughout the stormy times. You all have brought us tremendous joy and blessings. Thank you.

To my dear brother and his wife, John and Ekaette Tom, thank you for all your support, prayer, and dedication. May God continue to bless you immensely.

To all our ministers and leaders, DaWanda Thomas, Patrice Gray, Vernon and Patricia Barbee, Manny and Linda Dot Dot, and Kay Agwara, thank you for all your dedication, faithfulness, and support to this ministry. May God continue to bless you all.

To the entire staff and members of the International Ministry of Salvation & Praise (IMSP) and the Healing House Ministries (HHM), thank you for laboring day and night with us, and for standing in the gap for us to this day. I am very grateful for your dedication and for the unwavering love you have shown to us over the past years. Know that this project would not have been possible without you. Thank you for being our friends and partners in the ministry.

I also want to give my special thanks to Dr. Daniel K. Olukoya of the Mountain of Fire and Miracles Ministries in Nigeria, West Africa, for giving me the inspiration to write this prayer book. He has been a tremendous blessing to me, my family, and the kingdom of God through his work.

My special thanks also go to Sr. Apostle Dr. David Udo Udo of the Apostolic Mount Olive Church, Nigeria, for standing in agreement with us during this project. Thank you for letting God used you to bless us and partner with our ministry to spread the gospel of our Lord Jesus Christ to the world.

To our friends, Drs. Richard and Renee Durfield, I say thank you for all your support, love, and kindness. May God bless you for standing behind us and supporting us over these past months.

To Pastors Isaac and Mayen Usen of the Apostolic District Head Quarters, Calabar, Cross River State, Nigeria, thank you for all your prayers and support. Be blessed.

Introduction

IT IS THE farmer's hope that when he plants crops in his farmland, it will yield him a great harvest during harvest time. In order to see this hope and dream come true, the farmer begins to clear the field, removes all weeds, and removes shrubs and trees from the roots prior to planting his crops. In the third-world countries where there are no mechanized systems of farming, the farmer uses cutlasses and shovels to clear the farm, allows the grass, weeds, or trees to dry up, and then sets the whole land on fire to burn out and destroy the weeds, shrubs, and trees. This whole process is applied to make the farm become more useful again.

The farmer then begins to water the farm regularly before and after planting his crops. The weeds are removed from this point on as they grow, manures are applied, and pesticides and insecticides are applied to keep off insect and pest infestations. All these are done to routinely ensure a great harvest at the end of the harvest season. Once the crops have been harvested, the farmer begins the process again in the new season.

Prayer requires time, effort, and patience to see it come to pass. Just as the farmer needs time to implement the necessary steps in his farming process to see a great harvest in the end, prayer also needs to be given time, commitment, faith, and hope to see our petitions to God come to pass. Many Christians believe in persistent and aggressive prayers. Some do not believe in persistent prayers, but believe that once they have prayed, they don't have to repeat themselves or pray anymore for the same things because their prayers were answered from the moment they prayed. Some have even told me that they don't have to pray at all, because Christ has already provided solutions to their needs on the cross. They claim that they are resting and receiving from the Lord as their blessings have already been made available beyond the cross.

This is true but not always realistically so, because we need God daily in our lives. Should God allow us to have everything we want when we want, and how we want it, then we would not need Him anymore. All over the world people go to church and remain there for as long as they can, from the time they join the church until they receive what they desired from God. The moment God gives them what they wanted they walk out of the church and never look back. Sometimes this does not happen intentionally. It is part of that human struggle with the flesh that tells these people "You don't have to be in church to serve God." Effective and successful prayer takes dedication, passion, commitment, and constant reminding from God about His promises for you. This does not mean that God will forget your prayer after you have prayed or break His promises to you. It is impossible for God to lie against His word, and it is impossible for God to breach His oath. God uses His oath to guarantee His agreement with us. Since God is Unchanging, All Knowing, and All Powerful, He will not lie but fulfill His promises to you. You need to pray always and daily, and believe in your heart that He will do what you ask Him to do for you.

Effective prayer requires precision and targeting by faith. You must use your mustard seed faith to activate God's faith to provide answers to your targeted petitions. That's all the faith you need in this process. Just as one trains to develop strength and stamina in sports, so are we to train ourselves spiritually to pray. Prayer therefore is a spiritual exercise that requires fervent and effective effort. You must know what to ask or pray for, and be persistent toward it until you have received answers from God. Above all, you must trust

God to do what you ask Him to do for you. Otherwise, your effort will be in vain. It is impossible to please God or move God to do what you want Him to do on your behalf without faith.

Over time, many have built up much faith in God because He repeatedly provides solutions to their problems such that when they pray, they see results right there. They do not have to struggle with faith any longer, but just ask and receive. Sometimes, God still has to stress their patience so they can depend on Him more and more, and trust in Him more and more to fulfill their petitions. This is how we form a trusting relationship with God. At this point, we do not have to think about whether our petitions shall be done or not, because we know that they shall be established by the Lord. We have mastered and embraced patience and become one with God. It is the absence of patience that creates doubts in our minds, causing us to lose hope and trust in God. Oftentimes, many people do not even understand what it means to trust God and believe in Him by faith to receive their petitions. When they do, they don't exercise patience and wait on the Lord to fulfill His promises to them. However, by His grace, we can see God providing for us and supplying our daily needs even when we do not pray for them.

Take It To The Cross, is written to teach you how to pray effectively and fervently. The book starts by breaking down to your understanding what prayer is all about and why you need to pray this way always. It also gives you instruction on how to water your prayers at the root and not on the surface. The book will also teach you how to destroy your problems from the roots. Once the roots of your problems are destroyed, the problems themselves will disappear and you will be free. The process by which your problems are uprooted from your life is called deliverance, and the process by which they disappear from your life is called healing. You will see a clear distinction between healing and deliverance in my *"Healing and Deliverance* book" coming out soon. I want you to realize that the prayer points in this book are guaranteed to set your problems on fire, just like the farmer sets his farm on fire to kill the weeds. Once the weeds are destroyed, the crops can grow healthily and the farmer is assured a great harvest. God will turn your destiny around, heal you, deliver you, and bring restoration to you as you persistently and aggressively pray the prayer points in any chosen chapter.

This book will teach you step-by-step how to pray and receive answers to your petitions. It will also address why your prayers may not be answered when you pray, and teach you what you must avoid in order to receive answers to your prayers from God. The prayer points are intentionally formulated to be strong and effective simply because the enemy does not understand mild to soft-spoken prayer language. The enemy also does not understand love, affection, grace, forgiveness, blessing, mercy, or compassion. So the prayer points are intended and targeted to break down the devil's stronghold in your life and set you free from his yoke and burden.

Also, the prayer points in this book are written from a kingdom mindset and not a democratic mindset. The devil was created and raised from a kingdom and thrown out of that kingdom into our world. Thus he operates with kingdom mentality and understands kingdom declarations, commands, and decrees. Anything outside of that will not move him from you. That is why you must pray the prayer points exactly as they are written, and with the same authority as expressed in the prayer points. No prayer point is targeted to destroy any human being, but the spirits behind the human beings they use. When we pray against a strongman or a strongwoman, we do not mean your wicked father or mother or brother or sister or mother in-law, father in-law, neighbor, or friend.

Finally, you must realize that God will heal whomever He wants to heal, bless whomever He wants to bless, and deliver whomever He wants to deliver by His grace. Regardless of your position and opinion when it comes to prayer, His word says that we should ask and it shall be given, that we should seek and we shall find, that we should knock and it shall be opened. Your faith is the key to unlocking God's faith to activate your faith to produce the desired results for you. If you don't ask, how will you receive and how will you know that God listens to you? Let's go to war against the devil and claim back what is yours, in Jesus Mighty name. Amen.

Table of Contents

Acknowledgments -- v

Introduction --- ix

1 What Is Prayer? ------------------------------------ 1

2 Steps to Effective Prayers for Beginners, Prayer Warriors, and Prayer Champions ---------------------------- 15

3 Why Are Your Prayers Not Answered by God? --------- 26

4 Be Divinely Aligned with God - Part 1 -------------- 43

5 Be Divinely Alligned with God - Part 2 ------------- 50

6 Closing Evil Portals from Your Destiny ------------- 56

7 Overcoming Pervasive Sexual Desires ---------------- 63

8 Receive Divine Protection Today Part 1 ------------- 72

9 Receive Divine Protection Today Part 2 ------------- 78

10 Take Control of Your Marriage - Part 1 ------------ 84

11	Take Control of Your Marriage - Part 2	92
12	Claim Back Your Financial Potential - Part 1	99
13	Claim Back Your Financial Potential - Part 2	107
14	O Lord, Send Your Revival Now - Part 1	113
15	O Lord, Send Your Revival Now - Part 2	123
16	Reversing Evil Covenants in Your Destiny - Part 1	128
17	Reversing Evil Covenants in Your Destiny - Part 2	133
18	Destroy Territorial Powers and Claim Back Your Blessings	136
19	This Is My Time to Shine	144
20	Victory over Satanic Conflict in Your Home	152
21	Power to Change Spiritual Lanes in Your Life - Part 1	158
22	Power to Change Spiritual Lanes in Your Life - Part 2	164
23	Receive Breakthrough in Your Storm	170
24	My Darkness and Storms Are Over	178
25	Victory over Unsound Minds	187
26	Take Back Your Destiny by Fire	193
27	Uproot Satanic Yokes from Your Destiny	201

28 Lord, Restore My Wasted Years — 207

29 Lord, Turn My Mourning into Dancing — 214

30 O Lord, Let My Giants Become Grasshoppers before Me — 220

31 My Angels Must Work for Me — 226

32 Holy Ghost Fire, Destroy Them — 231

33 Be Delivered from Evil Contracts in Your Entertainment Career — 239

34 Be Delivered from Demonic Powers and Curses in Your Entertainment Career - Part 1 — 246

35 Be Delivered from Demonic Powers and Curses in Your Entertainment Career - Part 2 — 254

36 Arise and Dwell in God's Glory Today — 260

37 Victory over Repeated Problems - Part 1 — 266

38 Victory over Repeated Problems - Part 2 — 271

39 Receive Healing by Confessing the Word of God - Part 1 — 276

40 Receive Healing by Confessing the Word of God - Part 2 — 285

41 Defeat Obsessive-Compulsive Disorder and Receive Healing for Your Mind — 297

42 Change Poverty Codes in Your Life to Blessings — 303

References ---313

About the Author ---------------------------------------315

1

What Is Prayer?

1) TELLING GOD THAT you are depending on Him for solutions to your problems

When we pray, we are either communicating our problems to God or thanking Him for what He's done for us or expressing our love to Him for who He is. In other words, to pray simply means to dialogue with God concerning our issues, our afflictions, our hurts, and our pains, and to expect Him to solve these problems for us. It is a way of bringing our complaints to God instead of man, and asking Him to look at these bad situations and provide solutions for us because we are incapable of solving them by ourselves. Prayer is also a way of thanking God and appreciating Him for who He is, and for what He's already done and will do for us. The Psalmist said, "I called on the Lord in distress; the Lord answered me and set me in a broad place" (Ps. 118:5). The whole process of prayer is a dialogue because you have to talk to God and wait for Him to talk back to you with a yes or no answer.

God requires you to expect Him to do what He says He will do for you. Otherwise, you make His word untrue. Since the word of God is truth and must surely come to pass (Ps. 33:4; John 17:17; Isa. 55:10–11), you must believe that God will fulfill His promises to you no matter how long it takes. The act of believing and waiting for God to fulfill His promises to you is called faith, and it is a major component of what I call our "Relationship" with God. To trust the God that you cannot see and believe that He will unfailingly solve your problems by supplying and meeting your needs whether now or in the future are the footprints of your relationship with God. That relationship is always tested by faith and hope, which are products of patience. As your faith increases in God, so does your hope. It is impossible to have faith without hope. Faith walks with time, and hope, which is your expectation, also walks with time. This is patience, and the more patience you have with God, the more intimate you become with Him.

It is hard to trust in someone or believe in someone you have no relationship with. And if you must have a relationship with someone, then you must trust and believe in that individual; otherwise, he or she will not take you seriously. You might also be considered deceitful and untrustworthy. If you cannot trust God and believe in Him by faith to provide solutions to your problems, then He cannot do anything uncommon for you because you have no relationship with Him. Therefore, faith plus trust in God equals your relationship with Him. Prayer by faith and trust will create the relationship between us and our Heavenly Father, and open the heavenly portal through which God channels His resources and answers to our petitions.

Many have lost connection with God because they could not trust and have faith in Him to take care of them, supply their needs, and provide solutions to their problems. No matter how much we claim to have a relationship with God, such a relationship shall remain boneless, deceitful, and weak, and shall lead to unfaithfulness, rebellion, and disloyalty against God without faith and trust. By believing and trusting in God when you pray, you stand to be reconciled and restored to Him as a legitimate son or daughter. It is impossible to please God without your faith (Hebrew 11:6). At this point, I encourage you to acknowledge God to be who He is to you, your Father, and not a counterfeit through unbelief and doubt. When we do not doubt, He sees us as sons and daughters, princes and princesses, and commands victory for us perpetually. The sons of Korah said, "You are my King, O God; command victories for Jacob" (Ps. 44:4).

2) **Prayer is relating to God in the most humble and submissive attitude.**

We often hear that "pride goes before a fall." God despises the proud and gives grace to the humble. It is hard for anyone to approach the Almighty God, the one and only true God, with pride and arrogance and expect to receive anything from Him. In relating to God, you must do so with a contrite and a broken heart. The word of God says that a broken and a contrite heart He will not despise. Your ability and willingness to come before God in humility and submission is the only way you can receive anything from Him. Can a man force God to do something for him if and when God says no? Can anyone challenge God to a fight and win? Has anyone ever seized His goods or claimed God's blessings by force? The answer to these questions is no—it is impossible.

Our God is not delighted in burnt offering. His sacrifice is a broken spirit, for a broken spirit and a contrite heart He will not despise. Obedience and submission before God are staircases that bring you to Him. Your ability to say, "Lord, I am yours. I am inadequate. As your son or daughter I have sinned. Forgive me and help me," and then to go to Him with great expectation, knowing that He will not turn you back, but receive and attend to you, are the only ways you can approach and receive what you ask from Him. In Psalm 51, David said to God, "For You do not desire sacrifice, or else I would give it; You do not delight in burnt offering. The sacrifices of God are a broken spirit, a broken and a contrite heart—these, O God, You will not despise."

Here we see that God's pleasure was not in the animals David sacrificed for Him. No matter how many animals David sacrificed to God, they would not please Him or change His position on any situation. God's desire is to find pleasure in you as you come before His presence in obedience and humility. He found pleasure in David because he was humble and submissive before God. This pleased God, and He received David's sacrifices. You must realize that God is not interested in your deeds and playing church. He is looking for the restored and changed man from inside out, so He can have fellowship with him. Though God demanded animal sacrifices from David and Israel, His chosen, He was never going to accept any sacrifice that wasn't accompanied by a broken and a contrite heart. Our brokenness is what pleases God. He spoke to Solomon and said, "If My people who are called by My name will humble themselves, and pray and seek My face, and turn from their wicked ways, then I will hear from heaven, and will forgive their sin and heal their land. Now My eyes will be open and My ears attentive to prayer made in this place" (2 Chron. 7:14–15).

God's people needed to humble themselves before Him by confessing their sins. They needed to pray to God and repent for their sins. They also needed to turn back to God and serve Him only. As a Christian, you need to remain humble, pray daily, and turn to God. In return, He will hear, forgive, and heal you. God wants you to be sober and humble, and to approach Him with a repentant heart and not with an arrogant or prideful mindset. When you come before Him in humility, He will attend to you and answer you.

Psalm 34:18 *The* Lord *is near to those who have a broken heart, And saves such as have a contrite spirit.*

3) Prayer is a medium of inviting God into your life.

Jesus said in Revelation 3:20, "Behold, I stand at the door and knock. If anyone hears My voice and opens the door, I will come in to him and dine with him, and he with Me."

It is impossible for God to force Himself into your life if you do not open your mouth to confess and receive Him. You have to invite Him into your life, an act that must be voluntarily done because you love, appreciate, and acknowledge Jesus Christ for what He did for you on the cross. Jesus Christ is always knocking at the door of an unbeliever's heart so He would come in. Paul said,

Romans 10:9-10 [9] that if you confess with your mouth the Lord Jesus and believe in your heart that God has raised Him from the dead, you will be saved. [10] For with the heart one believes unto righteousness, and with the mouth confession is made unto salvation.

First, you must open your mouth and confess and believe in your heart that God raised Jesus Christ from the dead. This is the most important prayer of faith for any unbeliever coming to Christ to receive salvation. It is the only medium to invite Jesus Christ into our lives so we can walk in the fullness of God's blessings through Christ Jesus, our Lord and Savior. Note that the Scripture does not tell us to *meditate* in our hearts unto righteousness and *meditate* confession unto salvation. It simply says that you must believe in your heart and confess with your mouth. To invite Jesus Christ into your life, you must believe in Him and then speak up. Only a weak prince or princess would stand before the Father and not speak up. Christ died so you would have the boldness to come before the Father as a free man through Him.

4) A medium of commanding God's presence for help in an immediate situation

Our God is merciful and will not allow anything to happen to His children without His permission. He asks in Jeremiah 32:27, "Behold, I am the Lord, the God of all flesh. Is there anything too hard for Me?" Jeremiah responded to this question in Jer. 32:17 and said, "Ah, Lord God! Behold, you have made the heavens and the earth by your great power and outstretched arm. There is nothing too hard for you."

There is no bad situation in your life in which God cannot and will not intervene for you. He will deliver you from impending dangers if you call upon Him. He is strong and mighty in battle. He will show you a way of escape and teach you the secrets of overcoming. This can only be done through prayers.

In Jeremiah 33:3, the Lord says, "Call to Me, and I will answer you, and show you great and mighty things, which you do not know."

Psalm 86:15 says, "But you, O Lord, are a God full of compassion, and gracious, Long-suffering and abundant in mercy and truth."

Psalm 103:8–13 also say, "The Lord is merciful and gracious, Slow to anger, and abounding in mercy. He will not always strive with us, Nor will He keep His anger forever. He has not dealt with us according to our sins, Nor punished us according to our iniquities. For as the heavens are high above the earth So great is His mercy toward those who fear Him; As far as the east is from the west, So far has He removed our transgressions from us. As a father pities his children, So the Lord pities those who fear Him."

- your God is very compassionate
- Full of grace
- Has lasting patience
- Has abundant and dumbfounding mercies
- He does not contend, struggle, or pick a fight with you
- He forgives and forgets your sins
- He does not deal with you or punish you according to your sins
- He is extremely merciful to those who fear Him
- He is extremely forgiving to those who fear Him
- As a Father, He pities those who fear Him

Fearing God by submission and obedience will put us in favor with Him to help us in times of need and when we call on Him.

In Acts, chapter 16, Paul and Silas were imprisoned—locked and secured with iron bars so they could not escape. In addition, prison guards were positioned to watch and make sure they did not escape. At midnight, they began to pray and sing to God in their prison cell, and behold, God caused a great earthquake to shake the foundations of the prison and forced all doors to open. Every prisoner's chain was broken and loosened at that instance, and they were all freed (Acts 16:25–26). Only the power of prayer could have done this miracle. When you submit yourself to God in prayer, you immediately put yourself under God's direct supervision and protection. "He who dwells in the secret place of the Most High shall abide under the shadow of the Almighty" (Ps. 91:1). Prayer gives us the assurance that we will have God's divine protection and intervention in times of our trouble.

A lady who used to attend our regular prayer sessions once brought a case before the Lord. Her son was incarcerated and faced many years in prison for a crime he had not committed. He was accused of rape, but he firmly maintained that he was innocent. We then presented the matter before God and asked Him, the God of Justice, to review the case again. The Lord spoke right there and told me that her son would be freed, and I informed her of the same. Three months later, she received a call from her son in Reno, who said that he had been released and wanted to return home. According to her son, the person who had committed that rape had been caught in another crime and confessed to committing the rape that he was falsely accused of. So, after spending three years in prison, God released him and set him free.

Another young man was brought to one of our prayer sessions and was to be sentenced to many years in prison for a crime he had committed. We then called him out and gathered around him, and started asking God to have mercy and to intervene in the case for him. When he went to court the following morning, the judge handling the case dismissed the case and sent him home just like that. We have had so many situations where God pities His people and forgives them of their sins. God will intervene for you because of your prayers.

5) A tool for establishing and maintaining friendship with God

A married couple whose relationship is healthy will always find it difficult to stay apart for any length of time without communication. Close friends communicate more often than non-close friends. People who are passionate about each other always find a way to stay in touch and connect at the slightest opportunity they have. A good father or mother will not remain for long without seeking to know the welfare of his or her children. All these scenarios point to relationships that are healthy and desirable. Your relationship with God is not different and should NOT be different. God is not only your Father, but your Friend. He wants you to get closer to Him in every way and every day.

In John 15:12–15, Jesus said, "Greater love has no one than this, than to lay down one's life for his friends. You are My friends if you do whatever I command you. No longer do I call you servants, for a servant does not know what his master is doing; but I have called you friends, for all things that I heard from My Father I have made known to you."

Prayer draws you closer to God. It establishes and maintains your relationship with Him. When you stay connected to God through prayers, you are bound to know more about Him. He will reveal Himself and His secrets to you in ways you can never imagine.

In 2 Chronicles 15:1–2, we read, "Now the Spirit of God came upon Azariah the son of Oded. And he went out to meet Asa, and said to him: 'Hear me, Asa, and all Judah and Benjamin. The Lord is with you while you are with Him. If you seek Him, He will be found by you; but if you forsake Him, He will forsake you.'"

Through prayers we are able to seek His face, commune with Him, dialogue with Him, and maintain our relationship with Him. It is hard to be a friend of God and not do the things friends do for each other. This is what made David "a man after God's own heart." He loved God and served God, and God loved him and cared for him and met his needs. In the same manner, God loves you so much and wants you to stay closely connected to Him, so He can care for you and meet all your needs the way He did for David.

6) **Prayer is a meeting place between divinity and humanity, the point where earth connects with heaven.**

Nothing brings heaven down to earth more than prayer. Through prayer, we are able to speak the word of God back to Him, and the word is established for us. Prayer puts the Holy Spirit in position to act for us, and brings miracles, signs, and wonders down from heaven to us. This is why Jesus seized every opportunity He had to pray, because He needed to stay connected and remain one with the Father through His Spirit at all times. Prayer keeps us joined together with the spirit of Christ so we are not disconnected from Him. In Ezekiel 22:30 God said, "So I sought for a man among them who would make a wall, and stand in the gap before Me on behalf of the land, that I should not destroy it; but I found no one."

It is sad that God could not find intercessors, people to connect with heaven and bring it down to earth, so as to make peace and not destroy the land. The word says that "many are called but few are chosen" (Matthew 22:14). Out of the chosen few, only the willing are used by God. Are you willing to be a person God can trust and use as a conduit of peace between heaven and earth? If your answer is yes, then you must be a prayer champion, an intercessor.

Isaiah 62:6–7 says, "I have set watchmen on your walls, O Jerusalem; They shall never hold their peace day or night. You who make mention of the Lord, do not keep silent, And give Him no rest till He establishes And till He makes Jerusalem a praise in the earth."

7) **Prayer is the source of your healing from God.**

One of the major ways we receive healing from God is through prayer. Prayer plus faith equals power, and this power is driven by the word of God. Therefore, praying the word of God produces a kind of power that will uproot, shatter, and destroy every form of satanic affliction against our lives. In Luke 9:1, Jesus gave His disciples authority and power to cast out demons and to heal diseases. You have this authority and power at your disposal at all times through prayer. You must pray and exercise this authority by faith to see great results. When you pray with mustard seed faith, it is enough to activate God's faith to move mountains (Matthew 17:20) in the area you are seeking help from God. The power generated by your prayers with faith is capable of raising the dead, destroying cancers, breaking and removing satanic chains and oppressions, healing every form of sickness, and uprooting satanic arrows and yokes from your life. In James 5:13–16, Apostle James said,

> Is anyone among you suffering? Let him pray. Is anyone cheerful? Let him sing psalms. Is anyone among you sick? Let him call for the elders of the church, and let them pray over him, anointing him with oil in the name of the Lord. And the prayer of faith will save the sick, and the Lord will raise him up. And if he has committed sins, he will be forgiven. Confess your trespasses to one another, and pray for one another, that you may be healed. The effective, fervent prayer of a righteous man avails much.

Here, Apostle James advises that…

- You must pray when you are suffering and in pain.
- When you are happy you should sing songs or psalms to the Lord.
- When you are sick you should go to the elders in the church and get prayed for, because of your bodily weaknesses.
- When you pray, you must pray by faith and believe that God is able to heal you.
- Prayer for forgiveness will make God forgive your sins.
- As you make your confessions to each other by forgiving one another and praying for one another, your healing will surely come. This will facilitate or ensure your healing faster
- You must pray targeted prayers as shown in this book and be persistent to see good results.

8) Prayer is a way of knowing God's secrets.

Prayer helps you know the Lord's position about events that happen in your life. It unfolds God's secrets to us and places us in a better position with Him. David said, "The secret of the Lord is with those who fear Him, And He will show them His covenant" (Ps. 25:14). God does not hide His secrets from those who truly love Him. If you desire to know what God is doing in the earth or what His will is for your life and for a particular situation in your life, begin to pray about those situations and watch Him reveal each situation to you: "Surely the Lord God does nothing, Unless He reveals His secret to His servants the prophets" (Amos 3:7).

God is constantly looking for loyal partners with Him, so He can use them to show His power and glory in the earth. God has to test and approve you in order to use you for any significant assignment. He has to know what's in your heart and your intentions. He has to know your integrity toward Him, and He must humble you in the process (Deut. 8:2–4). Obedience to the word of God guarantees us this access to the Father, and through prayer we become one with Him.

John 14:23 Jesus answered and said to him, "If anyone loves Me, he will keep My word; and My Father will love him, and We will come to him and make Our home with him."

9) Prayer is a way of interceding for the kingdom of God and God's people.

Prayer is the only medium by which we are able to speak to God on behalf of our family members, saved and unsaved friends, churches, neighborhoods, cities, nations, and this world. A prayer that we pray not for ourselves, but for others, is called an intercessory prayer. By intercession, we voluntarily and unconditionally allow ourselves to stand in the gap due to a burden God has placed upon us, and we pray for that person or family or church about the situation at hand.

In my former church in Las Vegas, my wife and I used to fast and pray for our pastor and the church six to eight months every year for many years. The Lord placed this burden on us to fast and pray this way, and we did so to please Him and to His glory. We did not discuss this with anyone in the church except with our children. Whenever our pastor travelled and for as long as he was gone, we were always in prayer and fasting for him, his family, his staff, and the church. Over the years, we watched our church grow astronomically in membership, and became more and more spiritually powerful as the true presence of God was seen at all times.

As intercessors, we must pray for our pastors, our leaders, our churches, and our governments. This should be our daily devotion to God. Intercessors are ones that will change our families, governments, and nations, and turn them to God through prayers. As an intercessor, God has given you the ability to sit in your bedroom and control the affairs of nations, situations, and events around the world through prayers. God loves His intercessors, and I have personally come to bear witness that He will reveal His secrets to you before executing His plans under your watch if you give Him no rest. Ever since I came to the United States, there has been no president that has won an election from that time on that God did not reveal to me before it happened. In addition, God always reveals many other events that take place around the world before they happen so I can pray about them. He will reveal His secrets to you if you have interest in knowing them. But you must pray.

10) Prayer is the weapon of all spiritual warfare.

All spiritual warfare is fought through prayer. Our prayer releases arrows, bullets, and explosions that bring down satanic strongholds, and establishes peace within us, our homes, and our environments. Prayer strengthens our walk with God and empowers our spiritual beings to steer through life amid many obstacles. A praying Christian is a victor and a conqueror, and will always remain at the top and not the bottom. It is the will of Satan to stop us from praying so he can gain control and take over our lives so we may fall short.

When you pray, you are disrupting satanic schemes and conspiracies against your life. You are also on the offense and not the defense. Prayer makes you see yourself becoming spiritually sensitive and discerning of the presence of the enemy and his deception around you. As you unceasingly continue to pray, your faith and trust in God increase so that fear, rejection, discouragement, offense, depression, pride, and rebellion are removed from your life. You must realize that spiritual battle is not physical, because you cannot see evil spirits with your physical eyes to battle physically. Everything that happens when we pray is spiritual, and Jesus Christ is the one who fights for us through the Holy Spirit.

Ephesians 6:10–13: "Finally, my brethren, be strong in the Lord and in the power of His might. Put on the whole armor of God, that you may be able to stand against the wiles of the devil. For we do not wrestle against flesh and blood, but against principalities, against powers, against the rulers of the darkness of this age, against spiritual hosts of wickedness in the heavenly places. Therefore take up the whole armor of God that you may be able to withstand in the evil day, and having done all, to stand."

Intercessors are equipped with special anointing from God. God anoints them with power, miracles, signs, and wonders to do spiritual warfare. This is the anointing that break the yokes and burdens Satan puts upon us. Jesus was and still is the uttermost intercessor, and we know that His ministry while on this earth was highlighted by miracles, signs, and wonders.

Our daily intercession should include the following:

- Praying for breakthrough in our daily battles (Matt. 6:13)
- Praying for our families and friends (Eph. 6:1–2)
- Praying for the sick and the oppressed (James 5:13–18)
- Praying for world salvation, especially for our loved ones (Ps. 2:8)

- Praying for our churches or the body of Christ (Eph. 1:15–18)
- Praying for missions and missionaries (Isa. 55:5)
- Praying for the peace of our changing world (Jer. 29:5; Phi. 4:6–8; Rom. 15:13)
- Praying for our communities and cities (Jer. 29:5; Isa. 62:6)

2

Steps to Effective Prayers for Beginners, Prayer Warriors, and Prayer Champions

THE FOLLOWING STEPS will help you navigate your prayers and direct you to pray effectively for your breakthrough. I have discovered that very many Christians still don't know how to pray effectively and how to use proper prayer language to command victories into their lives. David was a true prayer champion, and most of the prayer points written in this book originate from his early prayer languages, as God directed him by His spirit. Whether you are a beginner or a seasoned prayer champion, I recommend that you use the following steps to pray effectively and aggressively.

1) **Know what to pray ahead of time, write it down, be prepared, and be organized.**

   Knowing what to pray ahead of time can be very helpful in keeping you and your thoughts in order before God. You don't just walk before God unprepared, not knowing what to ask or request from Him. Though God knows all your thoughts and needs, you must still be prepared and ready to communicate your thoughts and needs to Him. This is where prayer brings you into a relationship with God. Through this relationship, you can laugh, cry, jump, express your emotions, express your frustrations, ask for mercy and forgiveness, and equally ask for your needs to be met by Him.

When you start to pray, the devil may come to battle against your mind and make you forget about what you came to request from God. He may remind you of the bills that need to be paid, though you don't have the money to do so right away. He may send a phone call at that moment of prayer through your best friend or family member and cause serious distraction to get you off-track. No matter how much distraction the enemy brings across while you are praying, knowing what to pray about ahead of time will always put you back on track. The devil knows what button to push to make you forget about important points of your prayer. My advice is to write them down before you come to His presence. If you already know what you want from God, then you don't have to write anything down. Just proceed to the next step.

2) Start with praise and worship, and engage yourself with clapping of hands to the glory of God.

The best way to start your prayer is with praise and worship, by singing and clapping your hands and rejoicing before the Lord. This helps to prepare you to physically and spiritually engage in the prayer. Praise and worship will make you focus on God and open up heavenly portals for your prayers to be received. It is always good to sanitize the atmosphere with praise and worship before engaging in any spiritual battle. Know that demons cannot withstand praises offered to God when you are praising and worshipping God. David said, "Bless the Lord Oh! my Soul, and all that is within me, praise His Holy name" (Ps. 103:1). Because David knew how to sing and praise the Lord, he became a man after God's own heart. As you worship and praise His name, you shall surely be recognized as the man or woman after God's own heart by heaven.

Psalm 146:1–2 Praise the Lord! Praise the Lord, O my soul! While I live I will praise the Lord; I will sing praises to my God while I have my being.

3) Read your Bible—preferably the Book of Psalms, or whatever book, chapter, or portions of the Bible the Holy Spirit leads you to read in that hour.

Nothing paralyzes the enemy with fear more than to hear you speak the word of God. The word of God is the greatest weapon of destruction against the enemy. It is living and powerful (Hebrews 4:12). Jesus said, "The words that I speak are spirits and they are life" (John 6:63). The word of God is the sword that destroys demonic yokes, and the fire that breaks satanic chains and bonds. Without using the word of God in prayer, it is almost impossible to have victory over the enemy. This is why I recommend that you read the word before prayer, because it will truly set you apart for desired victory.

4) Begin to thank God for His goodness and for all He has done for you.

It feels good to hear someone say thank you when you have done something good for him or her. God is pleased and happy when we thank Him for His faithfulness and kindness to us. He is merciful and always forgiving us of our sins. He does not punish us according to our sins, nor reward us according to our iniquities. He constantly blesses you as His son or daughter even when you walk away from Him sometimes. He knows your strengths and weaknesses, and has unquestionable patience to tolerate your shortcomings. His love for you is unconditionally and factually proven. Thanking Him before starting to pray would not be bad idea after all. Psalm 136 says, "Oh, give thanks to the Lord, for He is good! For His mercy endures forever. Oh, give thanks to the God of gods! For His mercy endures forever. Oh, give thanks to the Lord of lords! For His mercy endures forever."

5) Begin to ask God for forgiveness for all your wrongs to Him.

When you go before God in prayer, it is important to ask Him to forgive all your sins. I once heard a brother say, "You are not supposed to keep confessing your sins after you have already received Christ." This statement would be justified if everyone would stay out of sin after receiving Christ. However, there are Christians who still allow flesh to control their emotions, thereby falling into sin and starting all over again.

If you were to fall into mud wearing a white suit or gown, I can assure you that such a suit or gown would be muddy and dirty, and would definitely need to be cleaned again. This is what sin does to a Christian who has been saved at one point but returns to old lifestyles. You may have to wash that suit or gown again, or take it to the dry cleaner's for cleaning prior to wearing it again. A man or woman who has become a Christian but returned to committing adultery will not enter God's glory unless he or she repents and reconciles with God. As a sinner who hasn't received Jesus Christ before, and as a fallen Christian who has received Christ in the past, but fell back into sin and is now returning to make confessions to God and ask for forgiveness, the sinner will be cleansed with His blood by the Lord Jesus, who will forgive him of his sins and receive him again to Himself. Here, we see the grace of God in action. By His grace, the Lord justifies the sinner. He is no longer condemned but restored. By reason of the blood of Jesus Christ, the restored Christian is qualified to enter God's presence with boldness and claim his inheritance from God.

The greatest hindrance to salvation is not knowing and believing that God will forgive your sins once you come before Him and confess them. Another hindrance is taking the sufferings of Christ on the cross for granted by refusing to repent after sinning by reason of grace. You are under grace outside of sin. In sin, you are not protected by grace, but are on your own. This is why Apostle Paul says that, "There is therefore now no condemnation to those who are in Christ Jesus, who do not walk according to the flesh, but according to the Spirit (Romans 8:1). People condemn themselves because they think God will not forgive them of their sins. You might have heard people say, "God will never forgive me," or, "I have done so many bad things in my life, and I don't think God will ever forgive me." Says who? This is what the grace of God is for and about: to ensure that you will always be reconciled with God, provided you confess your sins to Him. However, if you are walking according to the flesh, and allow flesh to rule over your life and stop you from confessing your sins to God, then you have allowed your sins to judge you. It will condemn you and keep you from salvation while grace still abounds even more for you.

You can come to God as many times as you have walked according to the flesh (sinned) and ask God for forgiveness. By His grace, you shall be forgiven and purified by the blood of Jesus Christ. This is why we must take time to ask God to forgive our sins before praying. So long as we are in this body called the flesh, fleshly desires will always knock on our doors. This is a constant battle and trial that you as a Christian must go through until the flesh dies and you are free from sin forever. This is why Paul said, "Where sin abounds, grace also abounds much more" (Romans 5:20). Otherwise, you will be standing before God with that muddy and dirty garment. It is not God who condemns, it is the sin, that dirty suit or gown you are wearing, that condemns you before Him.

The Christian that feels he should not confess his sins knowingly or unknowingly before God, because he was once saved, is taking a serious risk against his eternal salvation. While grace abounds and guarantees us constant or continuous justification as we come to Him in repentance, sin also abounds and fights against us in order to displace us from His righteousness. Sin has consequences, and the wages of sin are death. To tell a lie and not repent before God, because I am already born again and walk under grace, is a risk I am not willing to take. I will repent a million times more if I have to—because I am broken for Him and also understand the risk of not telling God I am sorry for my sins.

6) **Ask for the sins of your family and generational sins to be forgiven and be flushed away by the blood of Jesus Christ.**

So many Christians have suffered from the consequences of the sins their fathers and mothers committed without knowing the sources of the afflictions. Generational sins are real and must be confronted by prayers; otherwise they will destroy the lives of many within the family.

Many afflictions we experience in our families, such as poverty, sickness, addictions, psychological issues, incest, abuse, divorce, witchcraft, occultism, and many other afflictions are generational problems. From the moment you receive Jesus Christ into your life, your soul is saved, and if you should die, you will enter His eternal rest. However, your physical or mortal body still has to deal with sin in the flesh, and must be delivered from the consequences of these generational sins committed by your parents and your ancestors. This explains why Jane now has the same type of cancer her mother had while she was alive, or why Tom is now addicted to alcohol just like his father was addicted to alcohol while he was alive. Every sickness has a spiritual origin and oftentimes comes from generational curses. For this reason, Reverend John or Apostle Tom may have cancers and high blood pressure as their parents or grandparents had, or they may be living in poverty as their parents or grandparents lived in poverty, though Reverend John or Apostle Tom are doing the work of God—because the curses were not broken by deliverance. Every Christian needs to go through deliverance from the consequences of generational curses after being saved. Some may find it difficult to agree with this recommendation. If you are that person, then don't worry about going through deliverance, because all is well with you. After being in deliverance ministry and seeing what generational curses or evil powers of the father's house have done to devoted and faithful Christians, I can't help but recommend deliverance for struggling Christians and their families. We have seen and received so many testimonies on freedom from people and families that were plagued with drug and alcohol addiction, divorce, cancer, poverty, incest, abuse, illness, psychological problems, social disorders, and so on, due to generational curses.

When you go to the doctor's office, they always ask you about family medical history to determine your health status. Have you ever wondered what family medical history is? It is the history of generational curses in your family that doctors try to find out about. The spiritual enforcers (demonic spirits) of these curses can only be eradicated through prayers by repentance and deliverance in the name of Jesus Christ. Healing of the physical manifestations in your body will also be possible through prayers in the name of Jesus Christ.

This is why you must ask God to forgive your generational sins and remove their curses and limitations from you by the blood of Jesus Christ, regardless of whether you are saved or not. Some Christian leaders have chosen to live in denial and become ignorant of the havoc generational curses can bring upon their congregations. They believe that once you are saved, old things have passed away and all things have become new. Yes, this is true. Christ redeemed us from the curse of the law, having become a curse for us (Gal. 3:10) and wiped out the handwriting of requirements that was against us (Col. 3:14). However, you must repent and be delivered from generational curses in the name of Jesus Christ. It is not automatic that once you receive Christ you are no longer susceptible to the consequences of generational curses. If that were so, no one would be sick and no one would suffer from the same afflictions that affected his or her parent after being saved. We all need deliverance from our generational sins and curses, in the name of Jesus Christ.

7) Ask God for His divine protection for you and for your family.

You are covered by the blood of Jesus Christ. The Lord is the one who protects and shields you from demonic attacks and from the devil's wicked devices. Unless the Lord watches over a man, his armed bodyguards cannot stop the enemy when he comes to strike.

Since the battle between you and the enemy is not a physical one but spiritual, you must cover your children, your family, friends, and loved ones with the blood of Jesus Christ through your prayers. David said, "But You, O Lord, are a shield for me, My glory and the One who lifts up my head" (Ps. 3:3).

You must know that when you cannot get help from anywhere, God will always be your helper and shield. He will protect you in time of trouble. I could have been dead many times in the past if not for the mercy and protection of the Almighty. Know that you have nothing to lose by asking Him to protect you: "He who dwells in the secret place of the Most High Shall abide under the shadow of the Almighty. I will say of the Lord, 'He is my refuge and my fortress; My God, in Him I will trust'" (Ps. 91:1–2).

Many years ago in Los Angeles, I was driving a taxi cab, and at about 2:00 a.m. in the night, I was dispatched to go pick up a passenger. As soon as I crossed the intersection of Wilshire Boulevard and Western Avenue, at the bus stop, I saw a man standing and pointing something like a gun at my taxi. Within seconds, I heard a loud gunshot coming from that direction. Before I could realize what was happening, a bullet had flown and hit my right front passenger window. To my amazement, the bullet did not shatter the glass nor hit me. There was not even a scratch on the glass despite the intensity of the hit on the glass. The bullet would have gone straight through my head if it had broken through that glass. I was very scared that night because I could have easily lost my life just like that. God saved me from death. He protected me when there was no one to help.

Prayer for protection may save you from fatal accidents. It may save you from impending disaster. It may save you from burglary, from being fired from your job, from sustaining injuries, from being sick, or from satanic attacks. It may save your children while they are away in school or save you while travelling. God will protect you while coming in and going out. It is Him who saves and protects.

8) **Ask God to release His peace upon your home, neighborhood, and city.**

We all need the peace of God in our lives, our homes, our families, our businesses, our jobs, our neighborhoods, our cities, our nations, and in this world. Without peace, we will all live in a state of conflict, strife, and hate. People commit suicide because they do not have peace of mind. Paul said, "For God has not given us a spirit of fear, but of power and of love and of a sound mind" (2 Timothy 1:7). It is the peace of God that gives us self-control to go through life, to appreciate one another and our changing world. You need His peace upon your life and your family. Ask God for His peace and it shall be given to you.

9) **Take authority and bind the powers of the second heaven to give way for your petitions to rise before God.**

Some Christians are so afraid to say the word "bind" when they pray. You only bind something that is loosened and obstructing you from getting ahead. You may have to bind an obstacle in your way or move it out of your way so you don't get stuck. Your enemy in the second heaven does not want your prayer to rise to the third heaven. So he and his demons position themselves to intervene or obstruct your prayers from crossing over to the third heaven. It is possible for a person to pray and pray and still his prayer does not rise. This is because the enemy is contending against his prayer and breakthrough in the second heaven. The good news is that you have been given the authority to bind and loose on earth (the first heaven), and the same will be done for you in the third heaven. Daniel prayed and God heard his prayer from the first day, but the prince of the kingdom of Persia withstood the angel who brought answers to Daniel in the second heaven for twenty-one days. Our Lord Jesus Christ has given you power to bind these principalities in the second heaven in His name so you can pray to God and receive answers to your prayers instantaneously. Use your God-given power to take authority and subdue your enemies.

10) Begin to direct God's attention to your problems and the reasons for praying at this hour.

At this point, begin to go through your list and declare what you want God to do for you. God is very patient and will listen to all you have to petition. He is never bored and never will be. Do not think that you are asking Him for too much. I hear people say, "I don't want to ask too much from God." Has God ever complained that you've asked Him for too much? I don't think so. He knows exactly what you need and how to or when to give it to you, along with all the extras you did not ask for. If you don't ask, you will still receive what everyone is receiving and probably more. However, when you ask, you may receive the uncommon blessing, which would have never come to you in this life. Asking demonstrates to God that you have a relationship with Him. Some people have maintained the idea that they should only rest and receive from the Lord. Yes, I want you to enter God's rest and receive all His benefits. However, while we are still here on earth, many are battling with curses, personal afflictions, self-induced curses, sins, and other limitations. We need God's intervention and provision daily in our lives. Asking God to attend to my problems keeps me in touch with God. It makes me know that He is in control and that I must surrender to Him daily. It gives me hope and faith to continue to wait for Him to bless me while I rest upon Him. I cannot take a chance to rest upon the Lord and not dialogue with Him on a daily basis. That to me would be disastrous. His word says, "Ask, and it will be given to you; seek, and you will find; knock, and it will be opened to you. For everyone who asks receives, and he who seeks finds, and to him who knocks it will be opened." (Matthew 7:7-8).

11) Ask Our Lord Jesus Christ to cover you and your prayers with His precious blood.

I always cover my prayers with the blood of Jesus Christ, the protection I need to secure my request and blessings against spiritual robbers and thieves in the heavenly places. You might ask, are there spiritual robbers and thieves? Yes, my friend, I will answer. The thief comes to steal, kill, and destroy (John 10:10). Spiritual robbers are impoverished spirits that come to drain, devour, and plunder God's children. They fight against your promotion and success. Their goal is to keep you stagnant and to stop all your progress. They may come by bewitchments against your life from household members, neighbors, unfriendly friends, coworkers, evil associations, generational curses, spells cast on you, exposure to the occult, exposure to demonic deities, and so on. Pleading for the blood of Jesus Christ over your prayers will keep poverty spirits away and protect your gains and blessings (Revelation 12:11).

12) Thank God for answering all your prayers in a timely manner.

It is good to thank God after praying, because He will answer your prayers and give you satisfaction. You may not see the result right there and then, but rest assured that He will fulfill His promises to you. God does not know how to disappoint and lie to you. He is different from your earthly father or mother or friend who may disappoint you or even lie to you. God is not man that He should lie (Num. 23:19).

Believe that your prayers have been answered. Amen.

3

Why Are Your Prayers Not Answered by God?

1) Lack Of Faith

YOU MUST BELIEVE, trust, and have faith in God to supply your needs. Without you believing that God has the power to supply your needs, how can He respond to your prayers when you call on Him? It is impossible to please God without faith. You must go to Him with full recognition and reverence and believe that He has power to fight your battles and restore all your stolen blessings to you (Phil. 4:19; Eph. 6:13–18; Heb. 11:1–3, 6, 32–34; Josh. 10:12–14).

2) Rebellion against God

Rebellion simply means that you are turning your back against God and His will for your life. Rebellion brings curses and invokes God's anger and judgment against us. A rebellious child is less likely to receive a blessing from his or her parents. When people rebel, they do not always reflect at that moment or remember any good thing that God or anyone has done for them. At the moment of rebellion, the rebellious one is driven by a strong passion to fulfill his desires or achieve his selfish aims regardless of the consequences.

Rebellion could be triggered by disappointment, jealousy, offense, hatred, betrayal, or failure. God hates rebellion, and Satan uses this tool to deceive and destroy a majority of people by displacing them from God and from their destinies (Gen. 3:1–24; Isaiah 14:12–17; Numbers 16:1–50). We must be careful not to walk in rebellion or welcome it among us as Christians. God will not honor anything that is birthed out of rebellion, including our prayers.

3) Being ashamed of the name of Jesus Christ

You cannot claim to love God or be a follower of Christ and deny His name. Many Christians would rather go to church to pray and declare the name of Jesus Christ but deny Him outside of the church. We must constantly pray against the spirit of the Antichrist, which makes us deny our Lord and Savior Jesus Christ and rob Him of His glory when we should rightly render to Him all the glory due to His name. An Antichrist spirit is the spirit that opposes Christ. Even Christians can be susceptible to the devastating effects of this spirit if they do not pray. We should assess or checklist ourselves to make sure we do not carry the spirit of the Antichrist and denounce Christ when the opportunity arises for us to speak of Him and win more souls to the kingdom of God.

Jesus said, "Therefore whoever confesses Me before men, him I will also confess before My Father who is in heaven. But whoever denies Me before men, him I will also deny before My Father who is in heaven" (Matthew 10:32–33).

This is a very strong statement from our Lord Jesus Christ. He knew that there were many in the body of Christ that would deny Him when an opportunity came for them to speak and declare His name as witnesses to unbelievers. Christ was not referring to unbelievers when He made this statement, but to believers.

The question you should ask yourself is this: What would make me deny Christ or become ashamed of mentioning His name at work, in school, in the marketplace, on the streets, or wherever an opportunity prevails for me to speak of Him? I believe the number-one answer to this question is fear. Satan uses fear to prevent Christians from speaking about Christ in front of colleagues, unbelievers, and people unknown to them. He manipulates Christians into wondering what people would think of them if they spoke about Christ in public. By so doing, some Christians pay more attention to their reputations than to Christ. They become more entangled by self-image and identity preservation than by proclaiming the Lord's name and sharing His "good news gospel."

In areas where Christianity is not a popular religion or belief, the fear of death becomes the number-one tool that Satan uses to limit Christians from speaking openly about Christ, as they fear that they will be persecuted. Jesus said, "And do not fear those who kill the body but cannot kill the soul. But rather fear Him who is able to destroy both soul and body in hell" (Matthew 10:28).

Again He said, "Blessed are those who are persecuted for righteousness' sake, For theirs is the kingdom of heaven. Blessed are you when they revile and persecute you, and say all kinds of evil against you falsely for My sake. Rejoice and be exceedingly glad, for great is your reward in heaven, for so they persecuted the prophets who were before you" (Matthew 5:10–12).

Some so-called born-again Christians today are partially committed to Christianity and partially committed to the occult, witchcraft, deities, and other forms of religion. If we must be in Christ, we must totally surrender to Him and carry our crosses and follow Him. We must give Jesus Christ our all or nothing, and remain faithful to Him at all times. Being ashamed of the name of Jesus Christ will hinder our prayers and stop our blessings from God (Ps. 119:6, 80; Acts 19:11–15; I John 2:21–23; Rev. 3:20–22).

4) Living a sinful lifestyle

Sin will stop us from entering into God's presence when we pray. Our bodies are the temple of God, and we must keep them holy to ensure God's continuous presence and permanent inhabitation of the Holy Spirit within us. The Old Testament reminds us that God would not receive any sacrifice to Him that was defective or unclean. Today a defective sacrifice is an impure vessel or a defiled vessel standing before God to praise Him or petition Him for help without repentance.

In 1 Peter 1:14–16, it says, "As obedient children, not conforming yourselves to the former lusts, as in your ignorance; but as He who called you is holy, you also be holy in all your conduct, because it is written, 'Be holy, for I am holy.'"

Sin is simply disobedience to God. In Genesis 3 we have learned that God rejected Adam and Eve by sending them out of the Garden of Eden because they disobeyed His commandment not to eat the fruit from the tree that He had forbidden them. Saul was also rejected by God for disobeying His commandment to completely destroy the Amalekites when he spared Agag, the king of the Amalekites, and the best of the animals and brought them to Israel (1 Samuel 15:8–9). Sin does not only make us face rejection from God, but also separates us from Him, placing us in danger of facing His righteous judgment and condemnation to fire. But when we repent and confess our sins to God, and receive Jesus Christ into our lives as our Lord and Savior, we are forgiven and cleansed by His precious blood. Then we receive salvation and enter His grace.

When we are in Christ Jesus, we are no longer under condemnation, because we are not walking according to our flesh but according to the Spirit of Christ that is in us. If we are still involved in sinful acts and behave like nonbelievers in Christ, then we are not in Christ Jesus and are subject to condemnation. We cannot be covered by the grace of God if we are still under condemnation. Sin will separate us from God and hinder our prayers unless we repent and enter His grace

(Isa. 1:18–20;Rom. 1:24–32; Rom. 6:23; 1 Pet. 4:17; 2 Thess. 1:8; Ps. 9:17; Ps. 11:6; 2 Cor. 5:11).

5) Un-Forgiveness

Un-forgiveness is sin against ourselves and will separate us from God and further cut off His blessings from us. We forgive others to release ourselves from the burden and yoke of the bondage that we find ourselves due to offenses we experience from our loved ones or people we don't like. Forgiveness is really about us and for us, and not so much about the people who offended us.

    Colossians 3:13: "Bearing with one another, and forgiving one another, if anyone has a complaint against another; even as Christ forgave you, so you also must do."
    Matthew 6:12: "And forgive us our debts, As we forgive our debtors."
    Matthew 6:14: "For if you forgive men their trespasses, your heavenly Father will also forgive you."
    Mark 11:25–26: "And whenever you stand praying, if you have anything against anyone, forgive him, that your Father in heaven may also forgive you your trespasses. But if you do not forgive, neither will your Father in heaven forgive your trespasses."
    Offense, rejection, betrayal, hatred, quarrels, disagreements, misunderstandings, insults, disregard for one another, and unresolved conflict will result in un-forgiveness if not properly managed. Un-forgiveness brings serious limitation to our spiritual lives. We have to forgive one another in order to be forgiven by God. Holding on to an offense, hurt, hatred, or any unresolved conflict will hinder our prayers, minimize our spiritual growth, and hinder us from receiving our blessings from God. Our hearts must remain pure for us to be in God's presence. Our Lord Jesus Christ taught us to reconcile every conflict between us before praying to our heavenly Father. He knew our prayers would not be answered if we went before Him with filthy hearts full of un-forgiveness. We must repent for un-forgiveness and be ready to forgive others from any wrong brought against us, whether we are justified or unjustified.

    I held on to an offense because someone in my past had offended me badly beyond forgiveness. I never thought forgiving this individual was possible because I felt justified in every aspect when I reviewed the situation that led to the offense. However, upon going to sleep every night after aggressive prayer and intercession, I found myself walking barefooted in very dirty and filthy toilets that seemed to have been unclean for years. I got tired of this sight, such that I decided to ask the Lord what it meant, and why I was visiting dirty and filthy, nasty-looking toilets every night. The Lord then said to me, "This is the condition of your heart. You are carrying an offense and an un-forgiveness. You must set yourself free by letting go of the offense and forgiving them."

When I woke up from sleep, I was upset as to why the Lord asked me to forgive this individual. To make myself feel good, I decided to hold on to the offense just a little longer. As we were worshipping in church a year later, on a Sunday morning, my wife turned around and said to me, "Honey, God wants you to forgive-- person." I said to her, "Again?" I thought He had forgotten about this issue and given me permission to hold on to this offense, as I had never heard back from Him. That day, I did the unthinkable. I forgave that individual right there before the altar and felt the heaviest weight lifted off my body. My blood pressure dropped automatically. My eyesight improved instantaneously. My severely painful and swollen knees were healed instantly as I felt my knee bones shifted into position as the pains disappeared. As I went to sleep that night, I saw a clean and sparkling bathroom in my dream. It was like a seven-star hotel bathroom. It was so clean and beautiful that I had to sit down on the shiny marble floor doing nothing.

Brethren, forgiveness is for you and not anyone else. The Lord knew I was going to die if I still held on to that offense which was rightfully mine to keep. Meanwhile, the person who offended me was having fun and probably never knew or cared about the fact that I was offended by his actions and which he should call to apologize to correct his wrongs against me. My prayers to God were hindered, as I could never understand why everything was wrong in my life.

The condition of your heart during prayer will determine whether God will answer your prayer or not. Even the slightest offense will hinder your relationship with God and distort your interaction with Him. Learn to forgive and don't take too long like I did, waiting until death became imminent before I could forgive. Forgiveness is for you, your physical and spiritual well-being. Forgiveness is needed to improve your relationship with God and to ensure that the Lord's blessings for you and your destiny will not be shortened.

6) Ungratefulness to God

As children of God, we must always remember the goodness of God in our lives and pronounce it to Him. We must constantly remind Him of His former and continuous blessings in our lives. We must continuously testify to His infinite benefits and goodness to us in our congregations, our gatherings, at work, at our homes, and wherever we are led to fellowship. David said, "I will speak of your testimonies also before kings, And will not be ashamed" (Ps. 119:46).

Our testimonies make God bless us the more. We overcome the enemy by the blood of the lamb and by the word of our testimony (Rev. 12:11). Our testimonies will guarantee us continuous victory before God. We were created to praise, worship, and remain grateful to God. Some people are not able to appreciate others for what they do for them. Some consider ungratefulness their right and take advantage of others by not giving thanks for what has been done for them. We are constantly under God's sustaining grace and protection, yet we are not sufficiently thankful to Him. Jesus Christ offered His life by dying on the cross for us, yet we walk away from Him and betray Him daily. He healed ten lepers, yet only a Samaritan returned to give Him thanks (Luke 17:12–17). Jesus came to free His people, yet they rejected Him. "He came to His own, and His own did not receive Him" (John 1:11).

The psalmist by inspiration declared, "Blessed be the Lord, Who daily loads us with benefits, The God of our salvation! Selah" (Ps. 68:1). A person who continuously asks for favors and remains ungrateful for what he has received is less likely to receive the same or continuous blessings for too long. Though our God is very compassionate, gracious, long-suffering, and plenteous in mercy and truth, we must not take His loving kindness and patience lightly. We must be grateful to Him and give Him thanks at all times. We must continue in "giving thanks always for all things to God the Father in the name of our Lord Jesus Christ" (Ephesians 5:20).

Selfishness toward God and man can rob us of divine blessings. When we don't give thanks to God, we are being, self-centered, ungrateful, and prideful toward Him. This nonchalant attitude will block or hinder our prayers and answers to and from Him. We should be waking up every morning with great excitement and thanksgiving to God for His faithfulness toward us. Always remember that our ungratefulness to God destroys our relationship with Him, though His sustaining grace continues to keep us. The more grateful we are to God, the better our relationship with Him, and the more uncommon favor we receive from Him. Learn to say thank you, Lord.

7) Not being honest with God and living a deceitful life

Lack of honesty and truth will hinder our prayers from rising before God and stop God's blessings from coming to us. We must live transparently as Christians and recognize that nothing we do is hidden from God's eyes. In Psalm 10:11, the psalmist says, "He has said in his heart, 'God has forgotten; He hides His face; He will never see.'" But in Psalm 10 verse 14, the psalmist says, "But you have seen, for you observe trouble and grief, To repay it by your hand."

Also, we must be open before God and willingly confess our sins to Him and to one another. We must forgive one another so we might be forgiven by Him. Never live in denial and pretense, thinking you will fool God. His eyes can see through our minds, souls, and spirits. He knows our thoughts and actions before and after.

God hates injustice and corruption, and will not answer us with this attitude when we pray. "For I, the Lord, love justice; I hate robbery for burnt offering; I will direct their work in truth, And will make with them an everlasting covenant" (Isa. 61:8). He hates bribery and wants us to distaste it. We cannot say we love God and engage in bribery and corruption to bring glory to His name. This will truly hinder our prayers and rob us of His blessings. "He who is greedy for gain troubles his own house, But he who hates bribes will live" (Prov. 15:27).

I remember having heard people mention that they went to buy groceries from a store and the cashier gave them more money than necessary as change. In addition, they said that they never returned the excess change when they found out they had received more money from the cashier. I have also heard that someone picked up a wallet in the store and found some money inside. Instead of returning the wallet with the money to the store manager, this person decided to remove the cash, and returned only the wallet and noncash items to the manager.

In both situations, these people were happy at their gains at the expense of the error of the struggling store clerk or the single mom with five children who had just lost her wallet because she was busy trying to push her one-year-old child in the shopping cart while her three-year-old tossed the wallet on the floor. Whatever might have been the reason for any of these situations, keeping something that belongs to someone else is wrong before God, and will surely affect our prayers if we don't repent and correct our actions. God will never take pleasure in any form of corruption, no matter how little we think it is, because He is righteous and just.

Psalm 52:1–5: "Why do you boast in evil, O mighty man? The goodness of God endures continually. Your tongue devises destruction, Like a sharp razor, working deceitfully. You love evil more than good, Lying rather than speaking righteousness. Selah. You love all devouring words, you deceitful tongue. God shall likewise destroy you forever; He shall take you away, and pluck you out of your dwelling place, And uproot you from the land of the living. Selah."

Please, do not lie to the Lord. Be honest with Him. Remember, God knows our thoughts and also knows us better than we know ourselves. When we are honest to God, we will be honest to one another and our prayers will have no hindrance rising up to Him when we pray.

Isaiah 55:8–9 "For My thoughts are not your thoughts, Nor are your ways My ways," says the Lord. "For as the heavens are higher than the earth, So are My ways higher than your ways, And My thoughts than your thoughts."

8) Breaking your vows and commitments to God

God will never break His covenant and His vows with us because He honors His word. When we break our vows to God, we break His heart and make His word in us become powerless. A vow can be regarded as a covenant between two people, with the condition that one party first perform a duty, and that the second party perform his part of the duty based on his satisfaction as to the duty performed by the first party.

When Hannah asked God to give her a male child, she also vowed to give the child back to God and to let no razor touch his head. God fulfilled His part of the vow by blessing Hannah with a boy named Samuel (1 Samuel 1). Hannah redeemed that vow by returning the boy to Shiloh to serve God under Eli the prophet. Imagine that you were God in this case, though you were not: Should Hannah make another vow to you or petition you for something without a vow, would you hesitate to deny whatever request she asked of you? I think not. You would give her whatever she requested, provided it was within your ability to do so, because of her trustworthiness. God uses vows to test the integrity of our hearts, to see if we will do what we promise Him. Hannah went on to have more children because God validated her character and integrity when she redeemed her vows.

David said in Psalm 116:18 "I will pay my vows to the LORD, Now in the presence of all His people."
And in Psalm 105:8–11, David said, "He remembers His covenant forever, The word which He commanded, for a thousand generations, The covenant which He made with Abraham, And His oath to Isaac, And confirmed it to Jacob for a statute, To Israel as an everlasting covenant, Saying, 'To you I will give the land of Canaan, As the allotment of your inheritance.'"
God will never go back on His word. He expects us to be the same way, and keep to our words and promises to Him. Many Christians are quick to make a promise or a vow to God so He will

intervene for them when they or their loved ones are facing death due to illness or going through bad circumstances. The moment God executes His part of the agreement and they prevail in that situation, they forget about the vow or the covenant they made with God and move on. However, these people do not care to return to give thanks to God for what He has done for them. This attitude will surely hinder our prayers and stop further blessings from God if we intentionally refuse to redeem our vows to Him. King Solomon wrote in Ecclesiastes 5:4–5, "When you make a vow to God, do not delay to pay it; For He has no pleasure in fools. Pay what you have vowed—Better not to vow than to vow and not pay."

9) Curses

Curses affect our prayers negatively and, if not broken, can make us go through life miserable and unfulfilled. In Genesis, chapter 4, we see God pronouncing a curse on Cain for being angry and killing his brother, Abel, over receiving favor from God for his offering: "And He said, 'What have you done? The voice of your brother's blood cries out to Me from the ground. So now you are cursed from the earth, which has opened its mouth to receive your brother's blood from your hand. When you till the ground, it shall no longer yield its strength to you. A fugitive and a vagabond you shall be on the earth'" (Genesis 4:10–11).

In this life, you will see that either one is blessed or cursed. The blessings continue from one generation to another, and the curses also continue from one generation to another. Most of the sicknesses that afflict God's children are generationally transferred by their fathers and forefathers. Conversely, blessings are likewise handed down from one generation to another by the fathers and forefathers. What we do today will affect the future and the future generations either positively or negatively. The Bible has documented this in several scriptures, including 2 Sam. 12:1–15, 2 Sam 16:5–14, Deut. 27:11–26, Deut. 28:15–68.

There are three types of curses:

    a) Generational curses, which could be broken into
        i) Ancestral curses
        ii) Family curses
        iii) Father
        iv) Mother
        v) Sibling
        vi) Spousal
        vii) Individual

    b) Natural or universal curses (territorial, regional, national, country, states, county, local government, cities, neighborhood, etc.)

    c) Spiritual curses
        i) Biblical curses (rebellion, disobedience, sins against God, etc.)
        ii) Satanic curses such as bewitchments, occultism, evil covenants, money rituals, human sacrifices, worshipping of deities, idols, etc.

    I recommend all believers in Christ go through deliverance to break away from spiritual or generational or universal curses, as this will transform their lives forever and bring fulfillment to their destinies. Deliverance will lead us through proper repentance for the sins of our fathers, the sins of the land, territorial sins, national sins, and sins against God, and allow the blood of Jesus Christ to come in and flush away every curse accompanying each sin. Otherwise, you could still be a Christian and go through divorce as your father or mother went through it. You could still be a Christian and have cancer, become an alcoholic or a womanizer, be afflicted by high blood pressure or diabetes, or even become a drug addict just like your father or your mother or your forefathers, simply because the spirits enforcing these curses are still alive around you and need to be forced or cast out of your life, in the name of Jesus Christ.

Again, people have said that once you are in Christ Jesus, old things have passed away and all things have become new according to the word of God. Yes, this is true, but generational spirits or demons enforcing generational curses are still alive. Evil spirits don't die until Christ returns and hell is opened to condemn them to eternal death. The Bible never promised that these demons or spirits would leave us alone as we received Christ. Rather, we will overcome them by the power of Christ, in the name of Jesus Christ, because He conquered them and made a public spectacle of them.

HOW CAN WE GAIN ACCESS TO THE THRONE OF GOD WHEN WE PRAY?

- Start by commanding the spirit of the flesh to become obedient to the spirit of God inside of you.
- Acknowledge your sins before him. Repent for your sins and those of your fathers and forefathers (Ps. 51).
- Be a friend of the Holy Spirit.
- Love the Lord with a passion (Ps. 69:5; Ps. 119:139; Rom. 8:38–39).
- Commit the Lord to His word (John 15:7–8).
- Be sober and tender before the Lord (Ps. 51:17).
- Always bless the Lord with praise and worship (Ps. 104:33; Ps. 30:4; Ps. 147; Ps. 149).
- Be sincere in your prayers to God.
- Go before the Lord with a clean heart. Forgive those who offend you. Remember, un-forgiveness is a sin and therefore creates a barrier between you and God.
- Make a declaration before God.
- Trust in his word (Num. 23:19).

DOES GOD ANSWER MY REQUESTS THROUGH PRAYERS?

- Yes! When you ask sincerely from God and ask according to His will for you, He will answer your request through your prayers (1 John 5:14–15).

- You must trust God and know that He is able to do what you are asking Him to do for you (Josh. 1:9; 1 Chron. 16:11; Eph. 6:10; Prov. 3:5).

- We do not receive because we do not ask, and when we ask, we do not receive because we ask not for the kingdom but for our selfish interest. Ask not only for yourself, but also for the kingdom of God, and your request shall be granted (Matt. 7:7; James 4:3; 2 Chron. 1:7–12).

- Our God will supply all your *needs* according to His riches in glory by Christ Jesus. Ask for your needs first, not your wants (Phil. 4:19; Matt. 6:8, 11).

- Ask, and it will be given you; seek, and you will find; knock, and it will be opened to you (Matt. 7:7–11).

- Have faith in God and be diligent in seeking Him, for He is a rewarder of those who diligently seek him (Heb. 11:6).

- Love God and bless Him in the midst of your lack or your plenty so that He will rebuke the devourer for your sake and protect your harvest. And when affliction comes, He will remember your good work (Mal. 3:10–12; Luke 6:38; Mal. 3:16; Neh. 5:19; 2 Kings 20:3–7).

- Make and redeem your vows before the Lord. Do not withhold that which you have promised Him, for He will hold you accountable to your word. It is better not to promise than to promise without fulfilling (Eccles. 5:4–5).

- Be persistent in your prayers. Persistent prayers break demonic resistance, destroy their stronghold, empower your authority over them, and render them obedient to your commands (James 5:16).

- Pray through the four watches in the night, and through the four watches in the day. Choose at least one of these watches during the day and during the night and pray persistently, vehemently, and diligently. David said in Psalm 63:6, "When I remember you on my bed, I meditate on you in the night watches."

The Night Watches

1) **First Watch**   6:00 p.m. – 9:00 p.m.

This watch is clouded by the spirit of confusion, manipulation, deception, conspiracy, and indoctrination.

2) **Second Watch**   9:00 p.m. – 12:00 a.m.

This watch is clouded by the spirit of seduction, pornography, masturbation, suicide, loneliness, unholy thoughts, mind control, etc.

3) **Third Watch**   12:00 a.m. – 3:00 a.m.

This watch is clouded by demonic spirits, marine spirits and worshippers, seductive spirits and marriage breakers, witches and wizards, powers and principalities, occult powers, deities, conjuring spirits, powers of invocation, demonic sacrifice, sorceries, divinations, enchanted spirits, spirits of impersonation, projection spirits, manipulation spirits, and astral travelers. Curses and spells are cast more commonly during this watch, by enchanters, sorcerers, diviners, cultists, Satanists, and witch doctors to bewitch and destroy their victims.

4) **Fourth Watch**   3:00 a.m. – 6:00 a.m.

This watch is clouded by demonic spirit messengers who come to steal your dreams, visions, revelations, etc. The watch is also controlled by the spirit of infirmities, fatigue, discouragement, poverty, fear and deception. People wake up from bed tired, with fear and discouragement about the new day. They may forget their dreams easily as they wake up from bed because of these demonic enforcers.

The Day Watches

1) First Watch   6:00 a.m. – 9:00 a.m.
2) Second Watch   9:00 a.m. – 12:00 p.m.
3) Third Watch   12:00 p.m. – 3:00 p.m.
4) Fourth Watch   3:00 p.m. – 6:00 p.m.

God spoke to Job in chapter 38, verses 12 to 13, about one of the deepest kept secrets we must know in order to live victoriously in all our days. God asked Job if indeed he had ever commanded the morning to obey his voice, to do what he wanted done for him during the day and take control of the power of wickedness against him:

> New King James Version: "Have you commanded the morning since your days began, And caused the dawn to know its place, That it might take hold of the ends of the earth, And the wicked be shaken out of it?"

> The Amplified Bible: "Have you commanded the morning since your days began and caused the dawn to know its place, So that [light] may get hold of the corners of the earth and shake the wickedness [of night] out of it?"

> God's Word Translation Bible: "Have you ever given orders to the morning or assigned a place for the dawn so that it could grab the earth by its edges and shake the wicked people out of it?"

The morning is therefore the best time to rise up and command your day to align with the will of God for you that day. God has given you the power to declare His promises for you and see them come to pass. Many people do not believe in prayers, and when they finally decide to pray, they use the word of God to brush their teeth or mumble with the word of God in their mouths. You need to use the word of God to speak, call out, and declare and decree blessings and victories into your life.

If you are blessed with a mouth, a tongue, and a voice, then you are a good candidate to pray aggressively and declare blessings, good health, prosperity, provisions, growth, abundance, life, salvation, repentance, peace, favor, increase, expansion, wealth, riches, and victories not only into your life, but into your children's lives, your marriage, your business, your household, your family, your neighborhood, your city, and your nation. No one can do this better for you, except you.

I urge you to engage aggressively in the prayer topics below, and I assure you that you will receive your victory according to James 5:16. May God bless you and lead you in every prayer session below until you have received your expected results. Amen.

TO PRAY FOR HEALING

Take a few days, preferably three to seven days, and fast. You may start your fast at 6:00 a.m. and end at 3:00 p.m. or 6:00 p.m. I recommend that those of you receiving treatment for chronic sicknesses check with your medical doctors before going into this fast. I recommend that you choose prayer topics from this book that correspond to your situation and pray aggressively during your fast. You will surely receive breakthrough, just like many hundreds of thousands of other people have received, in the name of Jesus Christ.

TO PRAY FOR DELIVERANCE

You may fast from seven to twenty-one days, depending on your medical condition and your ability to go through the fast. During this time, engage aggressively in the chosen prayer sections in this book. At the end, you will receive your victory.

4

Be Divinely Aligned with God

Part 1

WE MUST BE divinely aligned with God's will to see our destiny fulfilled. To align means to reposition yourself from being out of order to being in order with the will of God for your life. There are many factors that can displace you from His will: your character, your thought processes, your lifestyles, your habits, associations, or affiliations, addictions, speaking negative words or curses, and bad attitudes toward God. These and many other factors will displace you from your position with God. Satan knows this quite well and uses these situations to shorten our destinies by causing us to shift out of position with God.

In addition, involvement with witchcraft, the occult, deities, and secret societies will cause us to shift out of position with God. Being an atheist, agnostic, prideful, having a rebellious attitude, involvement in sexual perversion, lies, deceit, lack of faith in God, Satanism, and so forth will further displace us from God. God wants us to align with Him (John 15:5–8), to stay in the secret place with Him (Ps. 91:1), and to put our trust in Him and His word (Ps. 115:9). When we do this, we are guaranteed to be in His caring arms and protection. We must know that without Jesus Christ in our lives, we can do nothing.

These prayer points will align you with God and challenge satanic conspiracies and lies trying to displace you from God, restoring God's glory back upon your life.

SCRIPTURAL REFERENCES

Psalm 20:6 *Now I know that the Lord saves His anointed; He will answer him from His holy heaven With the saving strength of His right hand.*

John 15:5–8 *I am the vine, you are the branches. He who abides in Me, and I in him, bears much fruit; for without Me you can do nothing. If anyone does not abide in Me, he is cast out as a branch and is withered; and they gather them and throw them into the fire, and they are burned. If you abide in Me, and My words abide in you, you will ask what you desire, and it shall be done for you. By this My Father is glorified, that you bear much fruit; so you will be My disciples.*

1 Peter 5:6–10 *Therefore humble yourselves under the mighty hand of God, that He may exalt you in due time, casting all your care upon Him, for He cares for you. Be sober, be vigilant; because your adversary the devil walks about like a roaring lion, seeking whom he may devour. Resist him, steadfast in the faith, knowing that the same sufferings are experienced by your brotherhood in the world. But may the God of all grace, who called us to His eternal glory by Christ Jesus, after you have suffered a while, perfect, establish, strengthen, and settle you. To Him be the glory and the dominion forever and ever. Amen.*

1 Corinthians 1:9–14 *For this reason we also, since the day we heard it, do not cease to pray for you, and to ask that you may be filled with the knowledge of His will in all wisdom and spiritual understanding; that you may walk worthy of the Lord, fully pleasing Him, being fruitful in every good work and increasing in the knowledge of God; strengthened with all might, according to His glorious power, for all patience and longsuffering with joy; giving thanks to the Father who has qualified us to be partakers of the inheritance of the saints in the light. He has delivered us from the power of darkness and conveyed us into the kingdom of the Son of His love, in whom we have redemption through His blood, the forgiveness of sins.*

PRAYER POINTS

1) Start with praise and worship
2) Lord, thank you for Your redemptive power over me and my family today, in the mighty name of Jesus Christ.
3) Lord, thank you for Your grace and mercy upon my life and for what You did for me on the cross.
4) I ask You to forgive me of all my sins today and cleanse me with Your precious blood.
5) I confess that You are the Christ and the Son of God.
6) I confess that You were dead and buried, and on the third day You rose again from death.
7) I confess that You ascended into heaven and are seated on the right hand of the Father.
8) I ask You to come into my life and take possession of my body, soul, and spirit, in the mighty name of Jesus Christ.
9) Holy Spirit, thank you for being part of me and my destiny from this hour, in the mighty name of Jesus Christ.
10) I declare that from today, the Father, the Son, the Holy, and [your name] are one, in the mighty name of Jesus Christ.
11) I declare that I am aligned with the Father, the Son, and the Holy Spirit from today, in the mighty name of Jesus Christ.
12) Thank you, Lord, for Your divine alignment and for reordering my destiny to align with Your will for my life, in the mighty name of Jesus Christ.
13) Lord Jesus, purify my will with your precious blood today.
14) Forgive me for displacing myself out of Your will for my life in the past, in the mighty name of Jesus Christ.
15) Where is the Lord God of Elijah? Arise and change my identity to Your fire, in the mighty name of Jesus Christ.
16) Almighty God, ignite my will by your fire and let Your will become my will, in the mighty name of Jesus Christ.
17) Holy Ghost fire, Holy Ghost fire, fall upon me, fall upon me today and sanitize my blood from the top of my head to the soles of my feet, in the mighty name of Jesus Christ.

18) Almighty God, arise and change every satanic law that is written to displace me out of Your divine will for my life, for good, in the mighty name of Jesus Christ.
19) Almighty God, arise and erase every satanic law that is written to hinder my destiny by the blood of Jesus Christ, in the mighty name of Jesus Christ.
20) Almighty God, arise and fire the arrow of black out into the camp of my enemies today, in the mighty name of Jesus Christ.
21) I declare that the spirit of death and hell shall not overtake my life from this day forward, and forever and ever, in the mighty name of Jesus Christ.
22) I disobey every satanic law written against me this year, in the name of Jesus Christ.
23) O God, arise and align me to Your divine agenda for the remaining years of my life, in the mighty name of Jesus Christ.
24) O God, arise and put me into Your divine calendar for the rest of my life, in the mighty name of Jesus Christ.
25) My Father, let me work in Your divine timing for the remaining time of my life, in the mighty name of Jesus Christ.
26) I command my days to operate with God's will for my life this year, in the mighty name of Jesus Christ.
27) Satanic arrows shot into my position while I was in my mother's womb, I command you to be uprooted in the name of Jesus Christ.
28) Power of frustration assigned to pursue my destiny, die in the name of Jesus Christ.
29) Every evil wind blowing me out of my divine position, die in the name of Jesus Christ.
30) My Holy Spirit, arise and fight for me now, fight for me now, in the mighty name of Jesus Christ.
31) My Holy Spirit, arise and scatter my enemies into Your fire, in the mighty name of Jesus Christ.
32) Every power assigned to destroy my destiny, I say die, die, die, in the name of Jesus Christ.

33) Every enemy of my promotion and advancement affecting my life, I command you to scatter, scatter, and scatter in the name of Jesus Christ.
34) Every oppression of darkness in my life and my family line, die in the name of Jesus Christ.
35) You, satanic agent seated in my space, who authorized you? Clear out now by fire, clear out now by fire, in the name of Jesus Christ.
36) Multiple rivers of income and cash, I command you to locate me now, locate me now, in the name of Jesus Christ.
37) People and resources assigned to move me forward, appear to me this year, in the mighty name of Jesus Christ.
38) Power to excel in productivity, fall upon me now, in the mighty name of Jesus Christ.
39) Strange powers of my father's house, die by fire, in the name of Jesus Christ.
40) Anything in my body programmed against my destiny, scatter into the abyss, in the name of Jesus Christ.
41) Every power kicking against my glory, catch fire now, in the name of Jesus Christ.
42) Powers that are eating up my progress, die by fire right now, in the name of Jesus Christ.
43) Taproot of failure working against me, dry up in the name of Jesus Christ.
44) Every power spending the night to pull me down, be scattered into the abyss, in the mighty name of Jesus Christ.
45) Oh Lord, arise and give me my portion today, in the mighty name of Jesus Christ.
46) Oh Lord, arise and curse any power eating up my portion and my inheritance to die, in the name of Jesus Christ.
47) Every wicked power in the second heaven representing my family, die in the name of Jesus.
48) Every rod of affliction in the second heaven pursuing my happiness and peace, break, break and break, in the name of Jesus Christ.

49) Any problem and stubborn affliction that wants to kill me, die in the name of Jesus Christ.
50) Every mouth speaking against me with satanic anointing, oh Lord, transfer their arrows back to them, in the mighty name of Jesus Christ.
51) Every arrow of ancestral witchcraft hitting down my breakthrough, die in the name of Jesus Christ.
52) Every blessing stolen from my life by the powers of the night, I recover you now by fire, in the name of Jesus Christ.
53) Every household witchcraft pushing my destiny to stagnation, die by fire in the name of Jesus Christ.
54) Arrows of affliction flying after me in the day or by night, be crushed to ashes in the name of Jesus Christ.
55) I declare that all I lost over these years shall be returned back to me now, in the mighty name of Jesus Christ.
56) I declare that I shall recover and possess every good thing the enemy stole from me today, in the mighty name of Jesus Christ.
57) Destiny robbers, give back what you stole from me now, in the mighty name of Jesus Christ.
58) I repossess all my possessions from you, Satan, in the mighty name of Jesus Christ.
59) I declare that the angels of blessing must locate me now, in the mighty name of Jesus Christ.
60) I command that whatever the enemy is using to direct curses to me be cancelled and destroyed now, in the mighty name of Jesus Christ.
61) I command any family curse upon my life to break, break, and break, in the name of Jesus Christ.
62) O God, arise and use me to change my family history in the name of Jesus Christ.
63) I order divine alignment into my destiny today, in the mighty name of Jesus Christ.
64) I challenge my life to align with the will of God today, in the mighty name of Jesus Christ.

65) O God, reorder all my days to bring divine blessings into my life, in the mighty name of Jesus Christ.
66) Blood of Jesus, go behind me and sanitize every past generation in my family from generational curses, in the mighty name of Jesus Christ.
67) Blood of Jesus, go before me and sanitize every future generation in my family from generational curses, in the mighty name of Jesus Christ.
68) Dear Holy Spirit, be my friend today, in the mighty name of Jesus Christ.
69) Dear Holy Spirit, anoint me with Your fire, in the mighty name of Jesus Christ.
70) Dear Holy Spirit, send spiritual revival into my life today, in the mighty name of Jesus Christ.
71) Dear Holy Spirit, change my identity to Your fire, in Jesus's name.
72) Thank you, Lord, for answering all my prayers today, in the mighty name of Jesus Christ.

5

Be Divinely Alligned with God

Part 2

SCRIPTURAL READINGS

Psalm 119:1–8 Blessed are the undefiled in the way, Who walk in the law of the Lord! Blessed are those who keep His testimonies, Who seek Him with the whole heart! They also do no iniquity; They walk in His ways. you have commanded us To keep your precepts diligently. Oh, that my ways were directed To keep your statutes! Then I would not be ashamed, When I look into all your commandments. I will praise you with uprightness of heart, When I learn your righteous judgments. I will keep your statutes; Oh, do not forsake me utterly!

PRAYER POINTS

1) Start with praise and worship songs.
2) Every curse in my bloodline affecting my destiny now, die by the blood of Jesus Christ.
3) Witchcraft curses upon my family line, die by the blood of Jesus.
4) You, ancestral pharaohs pursuing my family, what are you pursuing my family for? I command you to turn back and destroy your senders by fire, in the name of Jesus Christ.

5) Satanic dedication of my family to evil deities and the occult, I command your covenants to break away from my family forever, in the name of Jesus Christ.
6) Any power that pursued my parents that is now pursuing me, I command you to die in the name Jesus Christ.
7) Anything buried by anybody that is dragging my family down, die in the Jesus Christ.
8) O Lord, send Your lifting power to lift me up now, in the mighty name of Jesus Christ.
9) O Lord, send Your anointing power to anoint me now, in the mighty name of Jesus Christ.
10) Collective captivity that is affecting my life, die in the name of Jesus Christ.
11) You, powers that have swallowed up my inheritance from me, I challenge you by fire to vomit my blessings today, in the mighty name of Jesus Christ.
12) Occult powers calling my name for evil, I command you to die in the name of Jesus Christ.
13) Every satanic coven entertaining my case, catch fire, in the mighty name of Jesus Christ.
14) Where is the Lord God of Elijah? Arise and kill every satanic prophet assigned to my life, in the mighty name of Jesus Christ.
15) Bondage of my father and mother's house, what are you waiting for? Die in the name of Jesus Christ.
16) Every satanic bondage in my neighborhood fighting against my family, die in the name of Jesus Christ.
17) Every satanic bondage in my place of birth oppressing my life, die in the name of Jesus Christ.
18) Every satanic bondage by unfriendly friends pushing my life to the dust, die in the mighty name of Jesus Christ.
19) Where is the Lord God of Elijah? Arise and increase my speed to prosperity and freedom, in the mighty name of Jesus Christ.
20) Any power that wants my family to suffer, you are a liar. Die in the name of Jesus.

21) Almighty God, send unto me the angels of power to fight for me, in the mighty name of Jesus Christ.
22) Inherited battles in my life, hear the word of the Lord. Die in the name of Jesus Christ.
23) Every law that needs to be suspended and cancelled for me to have my breakthrough, what are you waiting for? Be suspended and cancelled, in the name of Jesus Christ.
24) Every power that must die for me to have my breakthrough, what are you waiting for? Die in the name of Jesus Christ.
25) Every tongue that must be cut off for me to have my breakthrough, what is holding you back? Be cut off in the name of Jesus Christ.
26) Every battle refusing to be won for my sake, what are you waiting for? O God of David, arise and kill their soldiers and generals, in the mighty name of Jesus Christ.
27) Every battle refusing to be won for my sake, what are you waiting for? O God of David, arise and kill their Goliaths, in the mighty name of Jesus Christ.
28) O God that answers by fire, answer me now by fire, in the mighty name of Jesus Christ.
29) Almighty God, you are a consuming fire. Arise and consume all powers working against my happiness, working against my health, working against my promotion, working against my breakthrough, working against my life, and consume them all by your fire, consume them all by your fire, in the mighty name of Jesus Christ.
30) Almighty God, You are the Mighty Terrible One. Arise and terrorize every power working against my breakthrough, in the mighty name of Jesus Christ.
31) Almighty God, You are the God of thunder and fire. Arise and send your thunder and fire to destroy the enemies of my destiny today, in the mighty name of Jesus Christ.
32) Every satanic ice formed upon my destiny, melt by fire, in the mighty name of Jesus Christ.
33) Any satanic river incubating my blessings, dry up now, in the mighty name of Jesus Christ.

34) Any satanic valley in this city or somewhere else accumulating my blessings, vomit my blessings now, in the name of Jesus Christ.
35) Any satanic rock sitting on my destiny, be lifted off and be shattered by the rock of ages, in the mighty name of Jesus Christ.
36) Every satanic fence constructed around my blessings to put them in captivity, I command you to be uprooted, after the order of the walls of Jericho, in the mighty name of Jesus Christ.
37) Any satanic affliction glued to my life that has refused to let me go, be melted by the blood of Jesus Christ.
38) Any satanic signpost pointed to my destiny, be shattered in the name of Jesus Christ.
39) Any satanic roof covering my freedom, be brought down by the resurrection power of Jesus Christ.
40) Any satanic bird flying for my sake, be consumed by the fire of the Holy Ghost, in the mighty name of Jesus Christ.
41) Every satanic altar calling my name for evil in this city or elsewhere, be consumed by the fire of the Holy Ghost, in the mighty name of Jesus Christ.
42) Oh God, arise and crush every evil altar in this city harboring my blessings, in the mighty name of Jesus Christ.
43) Any demonic satellite transmitting signals to broadcast my blessings and inheritances to satanic networks, I challenge you by the fire of the Holy Ghost to burn down to ashes, in the mighty name of Jesus Christ.
44) Every satanic hole draining my blessings, I command you to be sealed by the blood of Jesus Christ.
45) Oh God, arise and release the anointing of wisdom of King Solomon upon my life today, in the mighty name of Jesus Christ.
46) Oh God that answers by fire, arise and melt all satanic freezers freezing my blessings, in the mighty name of Jesus Christ.
47) Oh cup of affliction, I will not drink from you. Begin to feed your owners with your affliction now, in the mighty name of Jesus Christ.

48) Every satanic dog barking for my sake, fall down and die, in the mighty name of Jesus Christ.
49) Any satanic insect and animal feeding on my destiny, be consumed by the fire of the Holy Ghost, in the mighty name of Jesus Christ.
50) Every spoken or written word in the past or present that has become a curse in my life, I command you to be nullified by the blood of Jesus Christ.
51) Oh Lord Jesus, go to the foundation of this city, and uproot all my buried blessings by your resurrection power, and bring them back to me, in the name of Jesus Christ.
52) Any satanic crucifixion of my destiny in this country, be consumed by the cross of Jesus Christ, in the mighty name of Jesus Christ.
53) Every satanic snake strangling my family blessings, be roasted by the fire of God, in the mighty name of Jesus Christ.
54) Every satanic snake swallowing my blessings, be swallowed after the order of the snake of Moses in Egypt, in the mighty name of Jesus Christ.
55) Oh Lord Jesus, anoint my life for greatness, in the mighty name of Jesus Christ.
56) Almighty God, pour your divine kerosene upon every cobra and serpent in my life, and destroy them today, in the mighty name of Jesus Christ.
57) My life, receive divine promotion now, in the mighty name of Jesus Christ.
58) You, foundational curses, I roast you by the fire of God, in the mighty name of Jesus Christ.
59) You, spirit of intimidation, I am not your candidate of shame. I overcome you by the blood of Jesus Christ.
60) I claim divine authority to keep my job and business successfully, in the mighty name of Jesus Christ.
61) I shall not be fired from my job because Jesus Christ is my boss, in the mighty name of Jesus Christ.

62) My boss and coworkers will celebrate my work because the Lord has anointed my hands with oil, in the mighty name of Jesus Christ.
63) You, evil raven in this city, you shall not eat up my blessings. I command you to be roasted by fire, in the mighty name of Jesus Christ.
64) You, evil graffiti on the freeways of this city written against my family, I cancel your afflictions and erase you by the blood of Jesus Christ, in the mighty name of Jesus Christ.
65) O Lord, forgive me for writing satanic graffiti on my neighborhood walls and public facilities, in the mighty name of Jesus Christ.
66) Almighty God, sanitize my body from all evil marks, graffiti, and tattoos by the blood of Jesus Christ, in Jesus's mighty name.
67) Lord Jesus, forgive me for bearing the mark of the devil on my body in the form of tattoos, in the mighty name of Jesus Christ.
68) O Lord, change me and make me a great leader in my community, in the mighty name of Jesus Christ.
69) Every evil camera taking my picture for witchcraft or occult circles, be roasted by the fire of God, in the mighty name of Jesus Christ.
70) I shall not die but live to declare the works of the Lord in my life, in the mighty name of Jesus Christ.
71) Lord Jesus, align my destiny with your divine destiny for me, in the mighty name of Jesus Christ.
72) I am blessed in the mighty name of Jesus Christ. Amen, amen, amen.

6

Closing Evil Portals from Your Destiny

EVIL PORTALS ARE common around us, and are positioned in our lives to help satanic agents, demonic neighbors, household strongmen, witches and wizards, familiar spirits, and unfriendly friends drain blessings away from our homes. These spiritual portals are not physically seen except by revelation of the Holy Spirit. These satanic and demonic messengers use these portals to bring abject poverty to your business, home, and bank account, and to cause confusion, complaints, and hardships for you in every area of your life. These prayer points will shut every evil portal from your life, from your home, and from your family, setting you up to receive divine healing and keep your blessings intact, in Jesus's mighty name.

SCRIPTURAL READING

Psalm 59:1–7 Deliver me from my enemies, O my God; Defend me from those who rise up against me. Deliver me from the workers of iniquity, And save me from bloodthirsty men. For look, they lie in wait for my life; The mighty gather against me, Not for my transgression nor for my sin, O Lord. They run and prepare themselves through no fault of mine. Awake to help me, and behold! you therefore, O Lord God of hosts, the God of Israel, Awake to punish all the nations; Do not be merciful to any wicked transgressors. Selah. At evening they return, They growl like a dog, And go all around the city. Indeed, they belch with their mouth; Swords are in their lips; For they say, "Who hears?"

1 Peter 5:8 *Be sober, be vigilant; because your adversary the devil walks about like a roaring lion, seeking whom he may devour.*

Esther 7:3-6 *Then Queen Esther answered and said, "If I have found favor in your sight, O king, and if it pleases the king, let my life be given me at my petition, and my people at my request. For we have been sold, my people and I, to be destroyed, to be killed, and to be annihilated. Had we been sold as male and female slaves, I would have held my tongue, although the enemy could never compensate for the king's loss." So King Ahasuerus answered and said to Queen Esther, "Who is he, and where is he, who would dare presume in his heart to do such a thing?" And Esther said, "The adversary and enemy is this wicked Haman!" So Haman was terrified before the king and queen.*

PRAYER POINTS

1) Start with praise and worship.
2) Lord Jesus, thank you for Your grace and mercy upon my life at this hour.
3) Forgive me of my sins and those of my family, and cleanse us with Your precious blood.
4) Give me victory today in this prayer session, and let my enemies be scattered.
5) I declare that any satanic portal transmitting evil signals into my life be sealed forever, in the mighty name of Jesus Christ.
6) Any satanic portal harboring my blessings, be consumed by the fire of the Holy Ghost, in the mighty name of Jesus Christ.
7) Any satanic agent opening demonic or satanic portals in my life, die in the name of Jesus Christ.
8) You, satanic agent hanging the keys of my destiny around your neck, I command you to release my keys to me now, in the mighty name of Jesus Christ.
9) You, cup of affliction against my life, be shattered, in the name of Jesus Christ.

10) Oh God, arise and seal every portal projecting sexual thoughts into my soul, in the mighty name of Jesus Christ.
11) You, satanic agents manipulating demonic men and women into my dreams to seduce and weaken my spirit, die by fire, die by fire, in the name of Jesus Christ.
12) Every witchcraft portal swallowing up my future, vomit it back by fire, in the mighty name of Jesus Christ.
13) Every witchcraft portal transmitting my soul to the wilderness, release me now and begin to transmit your owners into that wilderness, in the mighty name of Jesus Christ.
14) Any demonic transmission of my phone conversations to the demonic world, be terminated by the blood of Jesus Christ.
15) Any satanic manipulation using my pictures and information from any social medium against me, be roasted by fire, in the name of Jesus Christ.
16) Any satanic curse against my family because of social media, be reversed by the blood of Jesus Christ.
17) You, satanic priest calling my name for destruction using my information from social media, I command the thunder fire of God to strike you down, in the name of Jesus Christ.
18) I command every affliction against my life arising from social media to return to senders, in the mighty name of Jesus Christ.
19) I command every affliction against my children arising from social media to return to senders, in the name of Jesus Christ.
20) Any hole in my pocket, bank account, or wallet leaking out my finances, be sealed by the blood of Jesus Christ.
21) You, messenger of poverty living in my house, I issue a divine eviction against you today, in the name of Jesus Christ.
22) You, messenger of sickness living in my body, I command you to be cast into the abyss right now, in the name of Jesus Christ.
23) You, carrier of diseases assigned to my life, carry your load back to your sender, in the name of Jesus Christ.

24) I declare that I am full of good health and prosperity, in the name of Jesus Christ.
25) My destiny, I command you to prosper and be at peace, in the name of Jesus Christ.
26) You, spirit of gossip, my mouth has been washed by the blood of Jesus Christ. Therefore, I cast you out of my mouth in the name of Jesus Christ.
27) Any satanic bridge constructed against my destiny, be shattered to pieces, in the name of Jesus Christ.
28) Any satanic bridge conveying my blessings to the satanic world, be shattered by fire, in the name of Jesus Christ.
29) Any satanic bank accumulating my blessings, release my blessings now. Be uprooted and be destroyed by fire, in the name of Jesus Christ.
30) Every satanic bond connecting me to my place of birth in order to destroy my destiny, be broken to pieces, in the name of Jesus Christ.
31) Any satanic bond tying down my blessings, I command you to break to pieces and release my blessings back to me, in the mighty name of Jesus Christ.
32) Any satanic red light stopping my blessings, I command you to turn green for me to go, in the name of Jesus Christ.
33) Evil lights holding me down in one place, be consumed by the fire of God, in the name of Jesus Christ.
34) I destroy every stop sign keeping me stagnant in life, in the mighty name of Jesus Christ.
35) Almighty God, increase your power in my life, so I may excel from ordinary to extraordinary in the name of Jesus Christ.
36) You, stagnant water harboring my prosperity, I command you to dry up now, in the name of Jesus Christ.
37) You, satanic shelves holding my blessings, be scattered by fire, in the name of Jesus Christ.
38) You, witchcraft coven shelving my blessings, be consumed by fire, in the name of Jesus Christ.
39) You, satanic priest in charge of my destiny, die forever, in the name of Jesus Christ.

40) You, wicked mountain throwing down my blessings, be blown up by the fire of God, in the name of Jesus Christ.
41) Any satanic fruit given to me in my dream to eat, I flush you out of my body, by the blood of Jesus Christ.
42) You, satanic food administered to me in my dream, I flush you out of my body, in the name of Jesus Christ.
43) Any satanic water prepared for me to drink in my dream, I command you to turn to the blood of Jesus Christ in my body, in the name of Jesus Christ.
44) Any sickness in my body resulting from evil foods eaten in my dream, I command you to leave my body by fire, in the name of Jesus Christ.
45) My body, you are the temple of God. Receive divine cleansing now, by the blood of Jesus Christ.
46) My body, you are God's image in the earth. I declare that you shall not become an idol of worship, in the mighty name of Jesus Christ.
47) My body, you are God's instrument in the earth. I challenge you to prosper in good health, in the name of Jesus Christ.
48) Any evil wind blowing sickness into my body, I command you to return to your sender by fire, in the name of Jesus Christ.
49) Blood of Jesus, put out every satanic fire burning up my prosperity, in the name of Jesus Christ.
50) Every evil wind blowing confusion into my mind, I blow you back to your sender, in the name of Jesus Christ.
51) Almighty God, arise and shatter any satanic stop sign placed in the path of my destiny, in the mighty name of Jesus Christ.
52) Any evil access into my home, I command you to close forever, in the mighty name of Jesus Christ.
53) Any strange man or woman making your way into my marriage, I command you to return forever and ever, in the mighty name of Jesus Christ.
54) Any evil power opening satanic portals into my home to drain my blessings, be consumed by the fire of the Holy Ghost, in the mighty name of Jesus Christ.

55) You, power of failure planted in my home by powers of the night, be consumed by the fire of the Holy Ghost, in the mighty name of Jesus Christ.
56) Any satanic mirror placed in my home to monitor my destiny, I command you to shatter by the rock of ages, in the mighty name of Jesus Christ.
57) Any satanic neighbor gaining access to my home through an evil portal to cause harm to me and my family, I command you to be paralyzed and let your portal be shut off forever, in the mighty name of Jesus Christ.
58) Almighty God, position your angels around my home to watch over me and my family, in the mighty name of Jesus Christ.
59) Lord Jesus, promote me today from minimum to maximum, in your precious, mighty name.
60) Lord Jesus, increase me today from minimum to maximum, in your precious, mighty name.
61) Lord Jesus, expand my territory today after the order of Jabez, in your precious, mighty name.
62) Lord Jesus, make me the head over all my enemies and not the tail, in your precious, mighty name.
63) Lord Jesus, make me above all my enemies and not beneath them, in your precious, mighty name
64) My life, receive divine promotion now, in the mighty name of Jesus Christ.
65) My destiny, receive divine guidance today, in the mighty name of Jesus Christ.
66) I declare that I am the favored of the Lord, in the mighty name of Jesus Christ.
67) I declare that I am the healed of the Lord, in the mighty name of Jesus Christ.
68) I declare that I have the backing of heaven in my life, in the mighty name of Jesus Christ.
69) I declare that every satanic warehouse containing my blessings must release all my blessings today, and be permanently shut down forever, in the mighty name of Jesus.

70) I declare that every astral portal, all portals in the four winds, all portals through the ocean, all portals under the earth constructed or used for channeling my blessings away from my life, be destroyed today, be destroyed today, be destroyed today, in the mighty name of Jesus Christ.
71) I declare that I and my family are healed by the blood of Jesus Christ.
72) Any evil power using powers from the sun, the moon, the stars or crystals, stirring pots, voodoo dolls, graven images, evil dust or powder, private sanctums, pictures from social media, magic sticks, or evil animals and birds to cast spells and curses into my life, I command you to catch fire and burn to ashes, in the mighty name of Jesus Christ.
73) Thank you, Lord Jesus, for answering all my prayers today, in the mighty name of Jesus Christ. Amen, amen, amen.

7

Overcoming Pervasive Sexual Desires

SEXUAL SINS ARE a direct abomination before God. God created sex for mankind to reproduce itself, to unify opposite sexes in marriage and provide intimacy between man and wife. Sexual abuse was never part of God's plan for mankind. Sex was never to be abused as we see today in our homes, neighborhoods, and societies.

Almost everywhere, regardless of the society, social and income status, or neighborhood, many men and women are addicted to pornographic devices and sex paraphernalia. Some are involved in homosexual practices, incest, pedophilia, and rape, while a great majority are involved in fornication, adultery, prostitution, and sex slavery. Are these few minutes of insane pleasures and ungodly sexual behaviors worth spending eternity in hell? You still have the opportunity to repent for sexual immorality by asking Jesus Christ to forgive you and by pleading for His blood to sanitize your life right now. Who knows what's going to happen to you at this hour, this night, or tomorrow?

Leviticus 18:22 You shall not lie with a male as with a woman. It is an abomination.

Leviticus 20:13 If a man lies with a male as he lies with a woman, both of them have committed an abomination. They shall surely be put to death. Their blood shall be upon them.

Deuteronomy 23:17 There shall be no whore of the daughters of Israel, nor a sodomite of the sons of Israel.

1 Corinthians 6:9–11 *Do you not know that the unrighteous will not inherit the kingdom of God? Do not be deceived. Neither fornicators, nor idolaters, nor adulterers, nor homosexuals, nor sodomites, nor thieves, nor covetous, nor drunkards, nor revilers, nor extortioners will inherit the kingdom of God. And such were some of you. But you were washed, but you were sanctified, but you were justified in the name of the Lord Jesus and by the Spirit of our God.*

"A sodomite" here refers to a homosexual male who practices homosexuality, the perverted and unnatural vice for which the city of Sodom was known at that time. The term "sodomite," used above, does not refer to an inhabitant of Sodom or a descendant of an inhabitant, but to the whoring act of homosexuality that Sodom was known to practice. The whore and the sodomite are in the same category.

Genesis 19:4–8 *Now before they lay down, the men of the city, the men of Sodom, both old and young, all the people from every quarter, surrounded the house. And they called to Lot and said to him, "Where are the men who came to you tonight? Bring them out to us that we may know them carnally." So Lot went out to them through the doorway, shut the door behind him, and said, "Please, my brethren, do not do so wickedly! See now, I have two daughters who have not known a man; please, let me bring them out to you, and you may do to them as you wish; only do nothing to these men, since this is the reason they have come under the shadow of my roof."*

The Hebrew word for "know" in verse 5 is *yada*, a sexual term. It is used frequently to denote sexual intercourse (Genesis 4:1, 17, 25; Matthew 1:24, 25). The message in the context of Genesis 19 is clear. Lot pled with the men to "do not so wickedly." Homosexuality is wickedness and must be recognized as such, or else there is no hope for the homosexual who is asking for help to be extricated from his perverted way of life, according to God's Holy Spirit Bible site.

SCRIPTURAL READINGS

Romans 1:18-32

PRAYER POINTS

1) Start with praise and worship and give thanks to the Lord.
2) Lord Jesus, sanitize me and my family with your blood, the blood of Jesus Christ.
3) Lord Jesus, forgive me of my sins and the sins of my family, extending to the first generation.
4) Lord Jesus, remove every ancestral curse of sexual perversion from my life today, in the name of Jesus Christ.
5) Almighty God, lead me and my family in your righteousness, in the mighty name of Jesus Christ.
6) Dear Lord Jesus, give me the power to overcome my flesh and take my thoughts captive, in the mighty name of Jesus Christ.
7) Lord Jesus, I surrender all my will to you and receive your grace into my life this day, in the mighty name of Jesus Christ.
8) Lord Jesus, sanitize my thoughts by your fire and purify me from my head to my toes with your precious blood, in the mighty name of Jesus Christ.
9) You, spirit of homosexuality in my family, I uproot you by the resurrection power of Jesus Christ and cast you into the abyss forever, in the name of Jesus.
10) You, spirit of homosexuality in my life, I challenge you to melt by the fire of the Holy Ghost, in the mighty name of Jesus Christ.
11) You, blood of sexual perversion in my life, be washed away from my body with the blood of Jesus Christ, in the mighty name of Jesus.
12) You, spirit of homosexuality, I challenge your prophets to die by fire, in the name of Jesus Christ.
13) You, spirit of homosexuality, hear the word of the Lord. My body is not your home. I command you to come out of my life forever, in the name of Jesus Christ.
14) You, spirit of homosexuality, I denounce you today in my life, and I erase your mark from my head, by the blood of Jesus Christ.

15) You, spirit of homosexuality, I am the called of the Lord. I command you to let me go and live a normal life in Christ Jesus, in the name of Jesus Christ.
16) You, sexual Jericho in my life, I challenge you to fall down flat and become ashes, in the name of Jesus Christ.
17) You, spirit of sodomy, be consumed out of my life by fire after the order of Sodom and Gomorrah, in the name of Jesus Christ.
18) Almighty God, arise and challenge the spirit of homosexuality in my life to die by the fire of the Holy Ghost, in the name of Jesus Christ.
19) Almighty God, I am Your child. I repent of the sin of homosexuality in my life. Purge me by your fire, in the name of Jesus Christ.
20) Oh God, arise and terminate the urge for same-sex attraction in my flesh, in the mighty name of Jesus Christ.
21) Oh God, arise and sanitize my thoughts with the blood of Jesus Christ.
22) O Lord, arise and sanitize my soul with the blood of Jesus Christ.
23) O Lord, arise and cleanse me from sexual perversion and restore my sexual preference to conform to your will for my life, in the mighty name of Jesus Christ.
24) You, lustful spirits in my dream, I refuse to obey your advances for sexual intercourse from today, in the name of Jesus Christ.
25) You, prophets of pornography in my mind, I challenge you to die by the fire of the Holy Ghost, in the mighty name of Jesus Christ.
26) Oh God, arise and seal every portal projecting sexual thoughts into my soul, in the name of Jesus Christ.
27) Every demonic projection using the power of the full moon against my life, I command you to backfire in the name of Jesus Christ.
28) Every occult priest chanting incantations against my life using the power of the sun and the moon, die by fire in the name of Jesus Christ.

29) Every satanic altar preparing my spirit to fall into lust, I command you to catch fire, in the name of Jesus Christ.
30) Every satanic altar manipulating my destiny out of the will of God, roast by fire, in the name of Jesus Christ.
31) You, spirit of fear destabilizing my mind, I dethrone you from my life, in the name of Jesus Christ.
32) You, spirit of jealousy ruling over my marriage, I release the arrow of blackout against you, in the name of Jesus Christ.
33) You, spirit of insecurity troubling my marriage, I remove you from my marriage by fire, in the name of Jesus Christ.
34) Almighty God, empower me with self-control and a sound mind, in the mighty name of Jesus Christ.
35) Every power making me commit incest, be carried into the abyss by the east wind of God, in the mighty name of Jesus Christ.
36) You, spirit of fornication and lust controlling my mind and emotions, I challenge you by the Holy Ghost fire, in the name of Jesus Christ.
37) Every demonic spirit projecting sexual thoughts and lust for a strange partner in my marital life, be cut off by the sword of fire, in the name of Jesus Christ.
38) I bind the spirit of pedophilia in my life and cast it into the abyss forever, in the mighty name of Jesus Christ.
39) I issue a death sentence to every demon projecting pedophilic thoughts into my mind, in the name of Jesus Christ.
40) I challenge my thoughts with the fire of the Holy Spirit, and I command every generational curse of pedophilic involvement in my family to die forever, in the mighty name of Jesus Christ.
41) I sanitize my bloodline with the blood of Jesus Christ.
42) I denounce and reject the spirit of prostitution from my life today, in the mighty name of Jesus Christ.
43) Holy Spirit, set on your fire every spirit of sexual paraphernalia in my home, in the mighty name of Jesus Christ.
44) Holy Spirit, give me the willpower to cast out of my home every sex object leading me to commit sexual sins, in the mighty name of Jesus Christ.

45) I forever refuse to get involved in the sex trade, in the mighty name of Jesus Christ.
46) I refuse to become a pimp, and I challenge any power that tries to lure me into that trade by fire, in the mighty name of Jesus Christ.
47) I command the spirit of adultery in my life to be cast into the abyss, in the mighty name of Jesus Christ.
48) I arrest the prophets of adultery in my life and cast them into the abyss, in the mighty name of Jesus Christ.
49) Almighty God, empower me to resist any desire to commit adultery, in the mighty name of Jesus Christ.
50) Almighty God, arise and destroy the spirit of adultery and fornication in my life and in my family, in the mighty name of Jesus Christ.
51) I declare that I shall remain faithful to my husband or my wife, in the mighty name of Jesus Christ.
52) I declare that no weapon formed against my marriage shall prosper, in the mighty name of Jesus Christ.
53) I declare that any urge to sell my body for money must die by fire, in the mighty name of Jesus Christ.
54) I receive power to overcome incest and pornography in my life, in the mighty name of Jesus Christ.
55) Holy Spirit, arise and restore unto me power, love, and a sound mind today, in the mighty name of Jesus Christ.
56) I declare that my mind shall be fixed, trusting in the Lord Jesus Christ.
57) I command my eyes to be fixed on my Lord Jesus Christ and not on strange men or women, in the mighty name of Jesus Christ.
58) I declare that my children shall not be involved in any sexual sin, in the mighty name of Jesus Christ.
59) Almighty God, go before me and bind any sexual demon or spirit standing by to lead my children to commit sexual sins and cast the demon or spirit into the abyss, in the mighty name of Jesus Christ.

60) I declare that my children shall be the head and not the tail, in the mighty name of Jesus Christ.
61) I declare that my children shall live their lives by example and become role models for others to follow, in the mighty name of Jesus Christ.
62) I bind every spirit wife or husband meant to seduce me in my dreams, in the mighty name of Jesus Christ.
63) You, spirit wife tormenting my life and stopping me from getting married, I divorce you now and forever, in the name of Jesus Christ.
64) I remove your spiritual ring and return it to you, and I also include every other gift you might have given me in my dreams and in the spirit, knowingly and unknowingly, in the mighty name of Jesus Christ.
65) I declare that I am now married to Jesus Christ from this moment on and forever, in the mighty name of Jesus Christ.
66) I delete your spiritual last name from my name from today, and I declare that I will only answer to the name of Jesus Christ in my last name, in the mighty name of Jesus Christ.
67) Holy Spirit, send Your fire to burn and destroy every spiritual architect causing me to have wet dreams, in the mighty name of Jesus Christ.
68) I paralyze the effects of the spirit of perversion in my life from today, in the mighty name of Jesus Christ.
69) I command every witchcraft power manipulating sexual desires and thoughts into my life to die by fire, in the mighty name of Jesus Christ.
70) Lord Jesus, erase my name from every satanic altar programming my spirit to respond to illicit sexual habits and desires, in the mighty name of Jesus Christ.
71) I command the same sex spirit calling my name to commit homosexuality to collapse and melt by fire, in the mighty name of Jesus Christ.

72) Holy Spirit, pursue, overtake, and destroy every household strongman manipulating me into committing sexual sins, in the mighty name of Jesus Christ.
73) I declare that my body is the temple of God, and I must remain holy as the bride of Christ, in the mighty name of Jesus Christ.
74) Lord Jesus, remove all unholy thoughts from my mind today, in the mighty name of Jesus Christ.
75) Lord Jesus, sanitize my life by your precious blood and help me to remain faithful to you, in the mighty name of Jesus Christ.
76) Almighty God, remove and destroy every demon occupying my sexual life, in the mighty name of Jesus Christ.
77) I declare that I am blessed forever, in the mighty name of Jesus Christ.
78) I declare that my children and the subsequent generations are blessed forever, in the mighty name of Jesus Christ.
79) Lord Jesus, by your precious blood purify all blood contamination in my body as a result of sexual sins, in the mighty name of Jesus Christ.
80) Lord Jesus, forgive me for having sexual intercourse with someone in my bloodline, in the mighty name of Jesus Christ.
81) Lord Jesus, forgive any member of my family of any history of sexual perversion at this hour, in the mighty name of Jesus Christ.
82) Lord Jesus, forgive every ancestral or generational curse of sexual perversion in my family, in the mighty name of Jesus Christ.
83) Almighty God, forgive the sins of my father and mother and those of my forefathers and mothers to the first generation, in the name of Jesus.
84) Lord Jesus, forgive me for ever having sex with an animal or animals, in the mighty name of Jesus Christ.
85) Arise, O Lord, and put every demonic priest casting sexual spells upon me to shame, in the mighty name of Jesus Christ.

86) Lord Jesus, forgive me for taking pleasure in watching animals have sexual intercourse, in the name of Jesus Christ.
87) Lord Jesus, forgive me for ever performing oral or anal sex with anyone, in the mighty name of Jesus Christ.
88) Lord Jesus, please, please, please wash me and cleanse me with your precious blood today.
89) I declare that I am sanitized by Your precious blood today.
90) Forgive me, Lord, for ever having sex with an object that is designed as a male or a female organ, in the name of Jesus Christ.
91) Lord Jesus, deliver me from having anal intercourse with any human being, in the mighty name of Jesus Christ.
92) Lord Jesus, forgive me for using the money You have given me to purchase sexual paraphernalia, in the mighty name of Jesus Christ.
93) Lord Jesus, remove from us every curse that might have afflicted me and my household as a result of sexual sins today, in the mighty name of Jesus Christ.
94) Holy Spirit, I am sorry for ever offending You and causing you pain due to my past sexual preference and sins, in the mighty name of Jesus.
95) Holy Spirit, please be my friend and help me overcome sexual temptations, in the mighty name of Jesus Christ.
96) I declare that I am permanently healed and forgiven of my sexual sins and perversions, in the mighty name of Jesus Christ.
97) Thank you, Jesus, for forgiving all my sins today, in the name of Jesus Christ. Amen.

8

Receive Divine Protection Today Part 1

WE ARE COVERED by the blood of Jesus Christ and also receive divine protection through Jesus Christ. In His name, every knee shall bow. In His name, every tongue shall confess that He alone is Lord over all of heaven and the earth. As a sheep, you are guaranteed continuous protection by the Shepherd, our Lord Jesus Christ. No other god can give you such protection. In John, chapter 15, He wants us to abide in Him. As we stay connected with Christ, we receive His protection, His love, His nourishment, His guidance, and His counsel. As a child of God, you will take refuge under God's protection, guidance, and supervision. When the enemy comes against you as a flood, the Spirit of the Lord shall raise a standard against him. With Christ, you are never alone and will never be alone. Pray the following prayer points with all your heart, and you shall surely feel and receive God's protection.

SCRIPTURAL READING

Psalm 91:1–16

> He who dwells in the secret place of the Most High Shall abide under the shadow of the Almighty. I will say of the Lord, "He is my refuge and my fortress; My God, in Him I will trust." Surely He shall deliver you from the snare of the fowler And from the perilous

pestilence. *He shall cover you with His feathers, And under His wings you shall take refuge;*

His truth shall be your shield and buckler. You shall not be afraid of the terror by night, Nor of the arrow that flies by day, Nor of the pestilence that walks in darkness, Nor of the destruction that lays waste at noonday. A thousand may fall at your side, And ten thousand at your right hand; But it shall not come near you. Only with your eyes shall you look, And see the reward of the wicked. Because you have made the Lord, who is my refuge, Even the Most High, your dwelling place, No evil shall befall you, Nor shall any plague come near your dwelling; For He shall give His angels charge over you, To keep you in all your ways. In their hands they shall bear you up, Lest you dash your foot against a stone. You shall tread upon the lion and the cobra, The young lion and the serpent you shall trample underfoot. "Because he has set his love upon Me, therefore I will deliver him; I will set him on high, because he has known My name. He shall call upon Me, and I will answer him; I will be with him in trouble; I will deliver him and honor him. With long life I will satisfy him, And show him My salvation."

Isaiah 59:19 *So shall they fear The name of the Lord from the west, And His glory from the rising of the sun; When the enemy comes in like a flood, The Spirit of the Lord will lift up a standard against him.*

PRAYER POINTS

1) Almighty God, thank you for your continuous protection over me and my family, in the name of Jesus Christ.
2) Thank you for keeping me away from the destruction of the wicked one.
3) Thank you for your sustaining mercy and grace over my life.
4) Thank you for adopting me as your son/daughter through Christ Jesus.
5) You deserve the glory and the honor.
6) You are mighty and strong in battle.

7) May your name be praised forever, in the mighty name of Jesus Christ.
8) Almighty God, you are my rock and my salvation, and I shall not fear.
9) Arise and let the walls of Jericho in my life fall down after the order of Joshua, in the mighty name of Jesus Christ.
10) Arise and mount a wall of protection around me because of my enemies, and because I am helpless, in the mighty name of Jesus Christ.
11) Arise and pursue my enemies to the dust that I may receive freedom to live and worship you, in the mighty name of Jesus Christ.
12) Arise and destroy the enemies of my destiny by your battle-axe and cast them into the pit forever, in the mighty name of Jesus Christ.
13) Arise and silence every evil tongue decreeing curses over my life, in the mighty name of Jesus Christ.
14) Arise and stop every storm blowing over my peace in this world, in the mighty name of Jesus Christ.
15) Arise and challenge every stubborn situation in my life by your fire, in the mighty name of Jesus Christ.
16) Arise and calm every raging sea in my destiny today, in the mighty name of Jesus Christ.
17) Arise and calm down every hurricane uprooting and carrying my blessings away from me, in the mighty name of Jesus Christ.
18) Lord Jesus, let darkness disappear from my life and shine your light upon me, in the name of Jesus Christ.
19) Lord Jesus, remove every disappointment from my life by your fire, in the name of Jesus Christ.
20) Lord Jesus, deliver me from the spirit of failure to victory, in the name of Jesus Christ.
21) Lord Jesus, deliver me from the spirit of the tail to the head, in the mighty name of Jesus Christ.
22) Lord Jesus, remove every satanic device planted on the roof of my house to oppress and suppress me, and cast it into the sea of fire, in the name of Jesus Christ.

23) Lord Jesus, sanitize my garage with your precious blood and destroy all demons lodging in it, in the name of Jesus Christ.
24) Lord Jesus, release your fire to consume the spirit of perversion and seduction influencing my marriage and my marital bed, in Jesus's name.
25) Lord Jesus, challenge my room with your fire and melt every strange spirit meant to monitor my marital peace, in the name of Jesus Christ.
26) Lord Jesus, send your sword of fire to remove and destroy every strongman standing at the entrance of my house and stopping blessings from coming in, in the name of Jesus Christ.
27) Lord Jesus, destroy by your fire every spirit assigned to destroy my marriage, in the name of Jesus Christ.
28) Lord Jesus, arise and invade the kingdom of darkness holding my blessings, and return my stolen blessings back to me, in Jesus's name.
29) Every demonic pet and pest colonizing my habitation, I command you to be consumed by the fire of God, in the name of Jesus Christ.
30) Almighty God, arise and bless the work of my hands until the day of your return, in the mighty name of Jesus Christ.
31) Almighty God, I declare that my life shall continue to be in your hands. Place upon me and my family your umbrella of protection, in Jesus's name.
32) Dear Lord Jesus, help me to dwell under the shadow of the Almighty, in Jesus's name.
33) Dear Lord Jesus, I declare that you are my refuge and my fortress, and in you I will trust forever.
34) One thousand may fall on my side, and ten thousand at my right hand, but it shall not come near me and my family, in the mighty name of Jesus Christ.
35) I declare that no evil or sickness shall befall me and my family in all our days, in the mighty name of Jesus Christ.
36) Almighty God, I beseech you to set me on high and deliver me because I know your name, in the mighty name of Jesus Christ.

37) It is written, he who dwells in the secret place of the Most High shall abide under the shadow of the Almighty. O Lord, help me to continue to dwell in your presence and abide under your shadow forever.
38) O Lord, put an excellent spirit in my life after the order of Daniel, in the mighty name of Jesus Christ.
39) O God, arise and let my persecutors be scattered into the abyss, in the mighty name of Jesus Christ.
40) I am covered by the blood of Jesus Christ, in Jesus's name.
41) My children are covered by the blood of Jesus Christ, in the mighty name of Jesus Christ.
42) My family is covered by the blood of Jesus Christ, in Jesus's name.
43) My church is covered by the blood of Jesus Christ, in the mighty name of Jesus Christ.
44) I declare that I am protected by the fire of the Holy Spirit, in Jesus's name.
45) My bank account is covered by the blood of Jesus Christ, in the mighty name of Jesus Christ.
46) My conversations are covered by the blood of Jesus Christ, in the mighty name of Jesus Christ.
47) My footsteps are covered by the blood of Jesus Christ, in the mighty name of Jesus Christ.
48) O Lord, align me with your divine protection and don't let me fall out of it, in the mighty name of Jesus Christ.
49) I cover my feet with the blood of Jesus Christ, in the mighty name of Jesus Christ.
50) O Lord, prepare intercessors to pray for me always, in the mighty name of Jesus Christ.
51) O Lord, build a hedge of protection around me and my family, in the mighty name of Jesus Christ.
52) I declare that my labor shall not be in vain, in Jesus Christ.
53) I declare that I shall not sow and not reap, in Jesus Christ.
54) I declare that I shall not plant and not harvest, in Jesus Christ.
55) I declare that I am covered by the shadow of the Almighty God, in the name of Jesus Christ.

56) O Lord of host, You are one who touches the earth and it melts. Arise and touch my enemies to melt before me, in the name of Jesus Christ.
57) O Lord of host, I was nothing when You found me. Now that I am in Your hands, arise and establish me as a mighty pillar in the earth, in the name of Jesus Christ.
58) Dear Holy Spirit, show me a token for good and put an everlasting smile on my face, in the name of Jesus Christ.
59) O Lord of host, as the mountains surround Jerusalem, so surround me and my family with your heavenly protection, in the name of Jesus Christ.
60) O Lord of host, arise and lead me on the path of righteousness, help me to love you until we meet face-to-face, in the name of Jesus Christ.
61) I declare that the blessings of the Lord shall be upon my life and my family, and with favor the Lord will surround us as with a shield, in the mighty name of Jesus Christ.
62) O Lord, arise and chase out of my life every household wickedness holding me captive, in the mighty name of Jesus Christ.
63) O Lord, arise and uproot every root of failure planted around my life to keep me stagnant so I may not experience promotion, in Jesus's name.
64) Lord Jesus, I declare that I shall not die but live to declare your good works in my life, in the name of Jesus Christ. Amen.

9

Receive Divine Protection Today Part 2

SCRIPTURAL READING

Read Psalm 91:1–16.

PRAYER POINTS

1) Begin with aggressive praise and worship.
2) Lord, let all the glory come to You in this prayer session, in the name of Jesus Christ.
3) I declare that as I continue to sow my seed in the house of God, I shall reap a million-fold in return, in the mighty name of Jesus Christ.
4) I declare that as I plant my seed in the lives of people, I shall harvest a million-fold in return, in the mighty name of Jesus Christ.
5) I declare that I shall receive full retirement compensation from my job or business, and my life shall not be cut short by my enemies, in the mighty name of Jesus Christ.
6) I declare that all those who seek my downfall shall receive Christ, turn from their wicked ways, and begin to love me, in the mighty name of Jesus Christ.
7) I declare that my God shall supply all my needs according to His riches in glory by Christ Jesus.
8) I declare that whatever I did not achieve last year, I shall achieve this year, in the mighty name of Jesus Christ.

9) I declare that the enemy that pursued me yesterday must become my friend today, in the mighty name of Jesus Christ.
10) I command that the enemy that pursued my parents and is now pursuing me must die by fire, in the mighty name of Jesus Christ.
11) I declare that Jesus Christ is my refuge and my very present help in time of trouble.
12) I shall not die but live to declare the good works of the Lord in my life.
13) Holy Spirit, protect and guide me and my family from the powers of darkness, in the mighty name of Jesus Christ.
14) Holy Spirit, protect and cover me and my family from the powers of poverty, in the mighty name of Jesus Christ.
15) Holy Spirit, because you are for me, who can be against me? Arise and scatter my enemies into the abyss, in the mighty name of Jesus Christ.
16) Almighty God, arise and scatter every power pursuing me and my family, using the power of the sun, the moon, and the stars, into the abyss forever, in the mighty name of Jesus Christ.
17) Lord, do not let the enemy use me to destroy your church, in the mighty name of Jesus Christ.
18) Lord, do not let the enemy use any member of my family to destroy your church, in the mighty name of Jesus Christ.
19) Lord, do not let the enemy turn me or my family against your Kingdom, in the mighty name of Jesus Christ.
20) I bind the spirit of pride, rebellion, and fear in my life forever, in the mighty name of Jesus Christ.
21) I declare that what I could not achieve alone without Christ, I must achieve now with Jesus Christ.
22) Lord Jesus, uproot and destroy every satanic implant or device hidden from my eyes but present in my home, in the mighty name of Jesus Christ.
23) I command every satanic object buried under the foundation of my home in the past or present to be destroyed by the blood of Jesus Christ.

24) I declare that I shall not attract the spirit of poverty back to my home, in the mighty name of Jesus Christ.
25) I pursue and overtake all my blessings today, in the mighty name of Jesus Christ.
26) By the hand of the Almighty God, I recover all my blessings and bring them back into my life, in the mighty name of Jesus Christ.
27) I cover all my blessings now and in the future with the blood of Jesus Christ.
28) O God, arise and fix every defect in my destiny by your right hand, in the mighty name of Jesus Christ.
29) O God, arise and protect every blessing in my destiny from evil men and women, in the mighty name of Jesus Christ.
30) I resurrect my buried wealth and riches today by the resurrection power of Jesus Christ, in the mighty name of Jesus Christ.
31) I command the spirit of victory to come upon my life today, in the mighty name of Jesus Christ.
32) I command the spirit of success to come upon my life today, in the mighty name of Jesus Christ.
33) I command the spirit of peace to come upon my life today, in the mighty name of Jesus Christ.
34) I command the spirit of love to come upon my life today, in the mighty name of Jesus Christ.
35) I command the spirit of favor to come upon my life today, in the mighty name of Jesus Christ.
36) I command the spirit of failure to flee from my life today, in the mighty name of Jesus Christ.
37) I command the spirit of discouragement to flee from my life today, in the mighty name of Jesus Christ.
38) I command the spirit of fear to flee from my life today, in the mighty name of Jesus Christ.
39) I command the spirit of depression to flee from my life today, in the mighty name of Jesus Christ.
40) I command the spirit of anxiety to flee from my life today, in the mighty name of Jesus Christ.

41) I command the spirit of recklessness to flee from my life today, in the mighty name of Jesus Christ.
42) I command the spirit of waywardness to flee from my life today, in the mighty name of Jesus Christ.
43) I command the spirit of the vagabond to flee from my life today, in the mighty name of Jesus Christ.
44) I command the spirit of lust to flee from my life today, in the mighty name of Jesus Christ.
45) I command the spirit of the desert to flee from my life today, in the mighty name of Jesus Christ.
46) I command the spirit of sorrow and pain to flee from my life today, in the mighty name of Jesus Christ.
47) I command the spirit of loneliness to flee from my life today, in the mighty name of Jesus Christ.
48) I command the spirit of loss to flee from my life today, in the mighty name of Jesus Christ.
49) I command the spirit of devouring and plundering to flee from my life today, in the mighty name of Jesus Christ.
50) I challenge every demon breeding evil spirits into my life to die by fire, in the mighty name of Jesus Christ.
51) Lord Jesus, sanctify me with your precious blood today.
52) Lord Jesus, let Your precious blood wipe away every generational curse in my destiny, in the mighty name of Jesus Christ.
53) Lord Jesus, let Your precious blood wash away all garbage from my life, in the mighty name of Jesus Christ.
54) Lord Jesus, help me to see what You are seeing in me, in the mighty name of Jesus Christ.
55) Lord Jesus, help me to appreciate You the way you appreciate me, in the mighty name of Jesus Christ.
56) Lord Jesus, send down Your raindrops cover all my seeds today, in the mighty name of Jesus Christ.
57) I declare that my seed shall germinate and bear good fruits for me, in the mighty name of Jesus Christ.
58) Lord Jesus, build a hedge of protection over my seeds and harvests, in the mighty name of Jesus Christ.

59) Lord Jesus, remove spiritual termites from my harvest forever, in the mighty name of Jesus Christ.
60) Lord Jesus, destroy all evil money in my possession today, in the mighty name of Jesus Christ.
61) Lord Jesus, speak to every dry place in my life so that it can experience great rainfall, in the mighty name of Jesus Christ.
62) Holy Spirit, pursue every satanic raven out of my vineyard forever, in the mighty name of Jesus Christ.
63) Holy Spirit, arise and destroy every satanic dog leaking my sores spiritually, in the mighty name of Jesus Christ.
64) Holy Spirit, arise and heal all my spiritual sores and wounds today, in the mighty name of Jesus Christ.
65) Almighty God, arise and command victory for me today, in the mighty name of Jesus Christ.
66) Where is the Lord God of Moses? Arise and divide my Red Seas so I may cross over to victory, in the mighty name of Jesus Christ.
67) Where is the Lord God of Joshua? Arise and lead me into the promise land, in the mighty name of Jesus Christ.
68) Where is the Lord God of Abraham? Arise and multiply my future generations as the sand of the seashore, in the mighty name of Jesus Christ.
69) Where is the Lord God of Abraham? Arise and give me great wealth and riches beyond weight and measures, in the mighty name of Jesus Christ.
70) Almighty God, increase the days of my life and deliver me from the afflictions of sickness and diseases, in the mighty name of Jesus Christ.
71) I declare that I shall increase and prosper even as the stars of the heavens, in the mighty name of Jesus Christ.
72) Lord Jesus, arise and put a hedge of protection over me and my family.
73) Lord Jesus, lift me up from failure by your lifting power today.
74) Lord Jesus, arise and set all enemies of my destiny on fire.

75) I command my destiny to receive a divine solution today, in the name of Jesus Christ.
76) I command my life to align with the will of God for me today, in the name of Jesus Christ.
77) I command my life to receive divine breakthrough in every area of blessing, in the name of Jesus Christ.
78) I loose my life from all satanic chains and bondage now, in the name of Jesus Christ.
79) I loose my destiny from all satanic manipulation and lies, in the name of Jesus Christ.
80) Starting now, I loose my life from running around in satanic circles, in the name of Jesus Christ.
81) Almighty God, bless me and turn my life around for good, in the name of Jesus Christ.
82) Lord Jesus, thank you for answering all my prayers today, in Jesus's mighty name. Amen.

10

Take Control of Your Marriage

Part 1

MANY MARRIAGES FAIL because Christians are not praying for their spouses and their marriages. They are not taking time to cover their marriages in prayer and submitting their marriages to the lordship of Jesus Christ. Marriage is a spiritual union because it is divinely instituted. Due to the fact that marriage is not only a physical union but spiritual, it must be nurtured both physically and spiritually to ensure a lasting marriage relationship.

The greatest demand in any given marriage is emotional satisfaction. This must be cared for and treated as an egg so it does not fall to the ground and break. Paul compares our relationship with Christ to a marriage relationship between husband and wife. We enter marriage to love and meet the needs of our spouse, and for our spouse to meet our needs when there is a need. These needs could be listening to each other (communication), cooking for each other, running errands, romance, keeping each other company, sharing financial burdens, sharing emotional burdens, caring for each other, and consistently speaking each other's love language. When we are selfish and only desire our needs to be met and not the needs of our spouse, then the enemy is given an opportunity to feed that marriage with lies, and will ultimately destroy the marriage.

Marriage also requires us to overlook each other's faults and not keep inventory of our wrongs. The agape love of God plays an important role in this part of our marriage. It helps us overcome all the challenges we face with our spouse in the relationship and helps us bear each other's burdens with less weight. Any marriage relationship that combines physical affection with the Agape love of God will surely last a lifetime. Marriages fail due to the absence of God's Agape love in the relationship. Prayer is the oil that lubricates your marriage engine, keeping it running while you steer through the challenges. When the engine dries up because there is no oil, it will surely break down. This is why marriages fail. No prayer was given to lubricate the marriage to keep it going and healthy.

We must learn to apologize to our spouse when we wrong them. You may not have to be right to say you are sorry. If you know your spouse is hurting, you must make peace with him or her right away; otherwise, you too are not going to have peace. Simply saying "I am sorry" can take your marriage a long way in a positive direction. Investigate and know your spouse's love language and communicate the same to him or her all the time. If her love language is praise, then give her praise. If it is flowers, then give her flowers. If his love language is good food, then go into the kitchen and prepare him a sumptuous meal. It is said that the way to a man's heart is good food. You will keep him for a long time by giving him good food. On the other hand, you will keep her for a long time and enjoy your marriage by communicating her love language with her, and treating her like an egg.

As you pray the following prayer points with all your heart, the Lord will heal and restore your marriage for you.

SCRIPTURAL READINGS

Ephesians 5:22–33 Wives, submit to your own husbands, as to the L*ORD*. *For the husband is head of the wife, as also Christ is head of the church; and He is the Savior of the body. Therefore, just as the church is subject to Christ, so let the wives be to their own husbands in everything.*

Husbands, love your wives, just as Christ also loved the church and gave Himself for her, that He might sanctify and cleanse her with the washing of water by the word, that He might present her to Himself a glorious church, not having spot or wrinkle or any such thing, but that she should be holy and without blemish. So husbands ought to love their own wives as their own bodies; he who loves his wife loves himself. For no one ever hated his own flesh, but nourishes and cherishes it, just as the Lord does the church. For we are members of His body of His flesh and of His bones. "For this reason a man shall leave his father and mother and be joined to his wife, and the two shall become one flesh." This is a great mystery, but I speak concerning Christ and the church. Nevertheless let each one of you in particular so love his own wife as himself, and let the wife see that she respects her husband.

PRAYER POINTS

1) Lord Jesus, I thank You for blessing my marriage since its inception.
2) Thank You for blessing my family, my children, and my marriage by your precious name.
3) Thank You for God's sustaining grace upon my marriage and my family.
4) Lord, forgive us for our sins and for not putting you first in our marriage.
5) Dear Holy Spirit, shine Your light upon my family, in the mighty name of Jesus Christ.
6) Lord Jesus, I surrender my marriage and family into your holy hands for safekeeping and protection, in the mighty name of Jesus Christ.
7) My family is not for sale. I reject every satanic spirit trading my family blessings away, in the mighty name of Jesus Christ.
8) I cover my marriage and family with the precious blood of Jesus Christ.
9) Every satanic power sitting on my marriage and family blessings, be uprooted by fire, in the name of Jesus Christ.

10) Every household anti-marriage force sitting on my marriage, I command you to be removed and be cast into the pit, in the name of Jesus Christ.
11) O Lord, let your lifting power lift up my marriage from dust to glory, in the name of Jesus Christ.
12) O Lord, increase my love for my spouse daily and vice versa, in the name of Jesus Christ.
13) Lord Jesus, help us love you more and more, in Jesus's name.
14) Lord Jesus, help me love my husband more and more from today.
15) Lord Jesus, help me love my wife more and more from today.
16) Lord Jesus, let Your agape love be the engine of our marriage relationship starting now, in the name of Jesus Christ.
17) I bind every strange spirit unloading confusion into my marriage, in the name of Jesus Christ.
18) Holy Spirit, embrace my marriage now and nourish it forever, in Jesus's name.
19) Holy Spirit, breathe upon my marriage now and fill it with your Holy presence, in the name of Jesus Christ.
20) O Lord, let my marriage become the example that will encourage others to remain in their marriages, in the name of Jesus Christ.
21) Lord Jesus, perfuse your blood into my marriage today.
22) Every strange man acting against my marriage, catch fire in the name of Jesus Christ.
23) Every strange woman acting against my marriage, be consumed by the fire of the Holy Ghost, in the name of Jesus Christ.
24) You, strongman throwing stones of conflict into my marriage, be destroyed in the name of Jesus Christ.
25) You, strongwoman throwing stones of conflict into my marriage, be destroyed in the name of Jesus Christ.
26) I command the stones of strange men and women against my marriage to backfire, in the name of Jesus Christ.
27) Every evil curse working against my marriage and family, be reversed by the blood of Jesus Christ.

28) Every satanic curse upon my marriage, be cancelled in the name of Jesus Christ.
29) You, spirit of death assigned to my marriage and family, die by fire in the name of Jesus Christ.
30) Any ancestral curse pointing fingers at my marriage, be cut off in the name of Jesus Christ.
31) You, spirit of divorce attacking my marriage, be destroyed by fire, in the name of Jesus Christ.
32) Any satanic power that says that my marriage and my family shall not prosper, be consumed by fire, in the name of Jesus Christ.
33) I claim God's blessings for my family today, in Jesus's name.
34) I receive supernatural deliverance from our past lives in marriage, in the name of Jesus Christ.
35) I divorce every spirit husband today by fire, in Jesus's name.
36) I divorce every spirit wife today by fire, in the name of Jesus Christ.
37) You, demonic strongman assigned to destroy my destiny, be destroyed by the fire of God, in the name of Jesus Christ.
38) My family will not die, but live to fulfill the will of God in our lives, in the mighty name of Jesus Christ.
39) Holy Spirit, take over my family affairs and surround us by your fire.
40) My Lord Jesus Christ, thank you for your redemptive power in my marriage, which will never fail or diminish, in the name of Jesus Christ.
41) I ask You, Lord, to forgive all my sins, un-forgiveness, anger, and curse words that I have spoken over my marriage due to frustration, in the mighty name of Jesus Christ.
42) I release myself and my husband from every marital and ancestral curse from my family, in the name of Jesus.
43) I release myself and my wife from every marital and ancestral curse from my family, in the name of Jesus.
44) I renounce and break all evil curses and bewitchments put upon my marriage by any strongman or strongwoman, in the name of Jesus Christ.

45) I take authority and bind the strongman or strongwoman attached to the marriage department of my life, in the name of Jesus.
46) I command the fire of the Holy Ghost to consume any and all spells, curses, bewitchments, hexes, and covenants operating in my life, in the mighty name of Jesus Christ.
47) Lord Jesus, release my husband from the hand of a strange woman to come back to me, in your mighty name.
48) Lord Jesus, release my wife from the hand of a strange man to come back to me, in your mighty name.
49) I refuse to follow any evil pattern laid down or programmed by any of my ancestors in my family line, in the name of Jesus.
50) Anything present in my life that is antimarriage in nature must come out now and be destroyed, in the mighty name of Jesus.
51) I take authority in the name of Jesus and decree that my love for my husband shall be one hundredfold.
52) I take authority in the name of Jesus and decree that my love for my wife shall be one hundredfold.
53) I take authority and bind every spiritual deposit that could have been deposited in my wife's/husband's body to repel his/her love for me and cast it into the abyss forever, in the name of Jesus Christ.
54) Father Lord, whatever you did not plant in my husband/wife that is causing him/her to drift away from me, I ask you to please uproot it from her/his life in the mighty name of Jesus Christ.
55) I wash my marriage with the precious blood of Jesus Christ.
56) My marriage shall be a blessing to me and others, in Jesus's name.
57) My husband/wife and I will not have a divorce in this life. Now I declare that our marriage shall receive divine confirmation in heaven, in Jesus's name.
58) You, strongwoman, your days of bewitchment of my marriage are over. Today, I command you to receive divine

termination by the thunder fire of God, in the mighty name of Jesus Christ.

59) You, strongman, your days of bewitchment of my marriage are over. Today, I command you to receive divine termination by the thunder fire of God, in the mighty name of Jesus Christ.

60) I stand against any instituted and remotely programmed frustration in my marriage, and I command it to shatter into irreparable pieces, in the name of Jesus Christ.

61) Lord Jesus, restore happiness, smiling, and joy to my marriage again, in the mighty name of Jesus Christ.

62) Father Lord, I surrender my marriage into your mighty hands and ask that you return what is rightfully mine back to me, in Jesus's mighty name.

63) From this moment forward, I declare that my husband/wife shall remain faithful to me and I will remain faithful to him/her, in Jesus's name

64) Dear Lord Jesus, turn the heart of our children back to love and appreciate us again, in your mighty name.

65) I command every demonic voice causing my children to rebel against us to die by fire, in the name of Jesus Christ.

66) I release the peace of God over my children and no weapon formed against them shall prosper, in Jesus's mighty name.

67) I destroy all the effects and curses of multiple marriages in my life today, in the mighty name of Jesus Christ.

68) Lord, I repent of any blood covenant I might have entered into in my past relationships, in the mighty name of Jesus Christ.

69) Almighty God, release me from the bondage of any marine covenant, in the mighty name of Jesus Christ.

70) Almighty God, put a great smile in my household this year, in the mighty name of Jesus Christ.

71) Almighty God, save my marriage from physical and spiritual death, in the mighty name of Jesus Christ.

72) I set myself free from all evil powers of my father's house that may affect my marriage, in the mighty name of Jesus Christ.

73) I challenge all evil powers of my mother's family by the fire of the Holy Spirit, and I declare that I am free from such generational curses, in the mighty name of Jesus Christ.
74) I destroy all bewitchment of my marriage by witches and wizards in my family and in my neighborhoods, in the mighty name of Jesus Christ.
75) I challenge every strongman or strongwoman opposing my marriage by the fire of God to receive divine judgment, in the mighty name of Jesus Christ.
76) Lord, teach me the secret of keeping peace in my family now, in the name of Jesus Christ.
77) Lord, help me to know my wife's love language and to be able to speak it fluently, in the mighty name of Jesus Christ.
78) Lord, help me to know my husband's love language and to be able to speak it fluently, in the mighty name of Jesus Christ.
79) Lord, remove the spirit of pride and arrogance from my marriage so we can serve each other with humility and love, in the name of Jesus Christ.
80) Lord, arise and sit on the throne of our marriage today, in the name of Jesus Christ.
81) Lord, remove the spirit of offense and jealousy from my marriage today and cast it into the abyss, in the name of Jesus Christ.
82) Lord, help me to forgive my husband and forget all he's ever done to hurt me in our marriage, in the name of Jesus Christ.
83) Lord, help me to forgive my wife and forget all she's ever done to hurt me in our marriage, in the name of Jesus Christ.
84) Lord, give me a clean heart toward my spouse, in the name of Jesus Christ.
85) Lord, make me a woman of proverb 31 today, in Jesus's name.
86) Lord, make me a man after your own heart today, in Jesus's name.
87) Thank you, Lord, for answering all my prayers, in Jesus's mighty name. Amen.

11

Take Control of Your Marriage

Part 2

SCRIPTURAL READINGS

Psalm 91, Psalm 51

PRAYER POINTS

1) Lord Jesus, erase every generational effect of divorce in my family against my marriage today, in the mighty name of Jesus Christ.
2) Lord Jesus, I repent for ever tattooing the image of my past relationship on my body, which may be affecting me and my marriage today, in the mighty name of Jesus Christ.
3) Lord Jesus, erase every tattoo on my body that could have been a covenant from my past relationships, in the mighty name of Jesus Christ.
4) I declare that I am sanitized by the blood of Jesus Christ, in the mighty name of Jesus Christ.
5) Lord Jesus, I repent for having an affair with a married spouse in my past, in the mighty name of Jesus Christ.
6) Lord Jesus, I repent for committing adultery in my marriage, and I ask you to minister to my husband/wife to forgive me, in the mighty name of Jesus Christ.

7) Lord Jesus, I now dedicate my sex life to you, and I ask you to bless our marriage with a fulfilled sex life, in the mighty name of Jesus Christ.
8) Lord Jesus, help me to love my wife more and more, in the mighty name of Jesus Christ.
9) Lord Jesus, give me the strength to satisfy my spouse sexually, in the name of Jesus Christ.
10) Almighty God, help me to please my spouse sexually, in the mighty name of Jesus Christ.
11) Almighty God, do not let me desire another while still being married to my spouse, in the mighty name of Jesus Christ.
12) Lord Jesus, let me be satisfied with the partner you have given me, in the name of Jesus Christ.
13) Lord Jesus, help me to love my husband more and more, in the mighty name of Jesus Christ.
14) Lord Jesus, give me the strength to forgive my husband/wife for cheating on me, in the mighty name of Jesus Christ.
15) I declare that I shall love my husband/wife more than myself, in the mighty name of Jesus Christ.
16) Holy Spirit, increase your love for us today, in the mighty name of Jesus Christ.
17) Holy Spirit, teach me how to love my spouse more from today, in the mighty name of Jesus Christ.
18) Holy Spirit, give and restore to me the love I never received as a child from my parents, in the mighty name of Jesus Christ.
19) Holy Spirit, direct me to see all the good things in my husband/wife from today, in the mighty name of Jesus Christ.
20) Holy Spirit, help me to see more beauty in my wife from this day on, in the mighty name of Jesus Christ.
21) Lord Jesus, help me to see my husband better than I saw him when we first met, in the mighty name of Jesus Christ.
22) Almighty God, help me to pray daily for my marriage and my family, in the mighty name of Jesus Christ.
23) Almighty God, do not let me go through a divorce just like my parents did, in the mighty name of Jesus Christ.

24) I refuse to settle for a divorce in my marriage, in the mighty name of Jesus Christ.
25) Lord Jesus, choose the right man/woman for me to marry when I am ready to be married, in the mighty name of Jesus Christ.
26) Lord Jesus, do not let me marry out of infatuation and frustration, in the mighty name of Jesus Christ.
27) Lord Jesus, let me seek Your will for my marriage and connect to it, in the mighty name of Jesus Christ.
28) I declare that my marriage and my family shall be blessed forever, in the mighty name of Jesus Christ.
29) Lord, make me a virtuous woman for my husband, in the mighty name of Jesus Christ.
30) Lord, make me a godly man for my wife, in the mighty name of Jesus Christ.
31) Lord, do not let me listen to gossip that may destroy my marriage, in the mighty name of Jesus Christ.
32) Holy Spirit, arise and remove the tongue of condemnation against my marriage and family, in the mighty name of Jesus Christ.
33) Almighty God, please fix Your eyes on my marriage for me, in the mighty name of Jesus Christ.
34) I declare that I am a winner and not a loser in this marriage, in Jesus's name.
35) Lord Jesus, let me enjoy the pleasure of sex with my husband always, in the mighty name of Jesus Christ.
36) Lord Jesus, help me enjoy the pleasure of sex with my wife always, in the mighty name of Jesus Christ.
37) Lord Jesus, let me have ultimate sexual satisfaction from my husband/wife from today, in the mighty name of Jesus Christ.
38) Lord Jesus, do not let me admire anyone else sexually but my husband/wife, in the mighty name of Jesus Christ.
39) O God, remove any sexual urge outside of my marriage from me, in the mighty name of Jesus Christ.

40) Almighty God, restore my wife's/husband's libido so we can enjoy sexual intercourse together according to your will for us, in the mighty name of Jesus Christ.
41) Lord Jesus, do not let me or my spouse depend on any sexual object or pornographic material in order to gain sexual satisfaction, in the mighty name of Jesus Christ.
42) O Lord Jesus, help me to achieve maximal sexual pleasure while making love to my husband/wife, in the mighty name of Jesus Christ.
43) Dear Holy Spirit, make me and my spouse see ourselves as one and love each other as such, in the mighty name of Jesus Christ.
44) I declare that from today, I shall have a fulfilled marriage relationship with my husband/wife, in the mighty name of Jesus Christ.
45) I declare that from today, my body belongs to Jesus Christ and my spouse only, in the mighty name of Jesus Christ.
46) I challenge my body with the fire of the Holy Spirit and cancel any sexual thoughts and lust outside of my marriage, in Jesus's name.
47) O Lord, correct any sexual organ deformity and dysfunction in me and my spouse, and restore new functional sexual organs in us, in Jesus's name.
48) O Lord, remove every unfriendly friend from my life that may introduce me to sexual sin, in the mighty name of Jesus Christ.
49) I declare that my body is the temple of God, and I shall keep it holy because He is holy, in the mighty name of Jesus Christ.
50) I declare that my marriage shall be meaningful and provide a reason to live and last through our lifetime, in the mighty name of Jesus Christ.
51) I declare that every bit of evil handwriting against my marriage is now reversed by the blood of Jesus Christ.
52) I erase every contamination of my marriage by strange spirits with the blood of Jesus Christ.

53) I refuse to give up my marriage to a strange man/woman, in the mighty name of Jesus Christ.
54) O Lord, do not let the enemy use my children to destroy my marriage, in the mighty name of Jesus Christ.
55) Almighty God, do not let the enemy use me or my spouse to destroy our marriage, in the mighty name of Jesus Christ.
56) I declare that I am healed from all the abuse of my former marriage, in the name of Jesus Christ.
57) Lord Jesus, arise and cleanse all scars and rejections from my previous marriage so I can remarry and enjoy my new marriage, in Jesus's name.
58) O Lord of host, help me to forgive my former husband/wife for all the abuse and injustice done to me, in the name of Jesus Christ.
59) Lord Jesus, do not let me judge my new marriage after the standards of my old marriage, in the name of Jesus Christ.
60) O Lord, break every curse of poverty inherited from my former marriage, in the name of Jesus Christ.
61) Lord, erase every case of rape and abuse inflicted against me by my former husband, from my mind, soul, and spirit, in the name of Jesus Christ.
62) Lord, help me be able to love again and even more, in Jesus's name.
63) Lord Jesus, let your joy be my strength from now on, in Jesus's name.
64) Lord, forgive me for the part I played toward the failure of my first marriage, in the name of Jesus Christ.
65) Lord, I cannot do without my first husband/wife. As he/she has not remarried, please put us back together and make us love ourselves more than in the past, in the name of Jesus Christ.
66) Lord, let all my expectations of my spouse be conformed to your will so I may not drive him/her away, in the name of Jesus Christ.
67) Lord, teach me how to give unconditional love to my husband, in the name of Jesus Christ.

68) Lord, teach me how to give unconditional love to my wife, in the name of Jesus Christ.
69) Lord, give me the strength to be open to my wife about everything in my life, in the name of Jesus Christ.
70) Lord, give me the strength to be open to my husband about everything in my life, in the name of Jesus Christ.
71) Lord, do not let my husband/wife use my honesty and openness toward him/her as a weapon to abuse me physically, verbally, and emotionally, in the name of Jesus Christ.
72) Lord, help me to trust my husband/wife with my secrets, in the name of Jesus Christ.
73) Lord, bind us together with your holiness, in the mighty name of Jesus Christ.
74) Lord, do not let me use the standards of my previous marriage in my new marriage, in the name of Jesus Christ.
75) Father, help me to forget about my past hurts and embrace my future with renewed hope and faith, in the name of Jesus Christ.
76) Lord, do not send me a man or woman that will exploit me out of the blessings you have given me through marriage, in the name of Jesus Christ.
77) Lord, send me my soul mate so I can enjoy the material blessings you have given me with him/her without sorrow, in the name of Jesus Christ.
78) I come against any premeditated marriage with the intention to defraud me of my inheritance, in the name of Jesus Christ.
79) O Lord, expose any defrauding intention of any man or woman intending to marry me for material gains, right before I say yes at the altar, in the mighty name of Jesus Christ.
80) Lord, do not let me use or exploit my spouse to gain ill-gotten wealth, in the name of Jesus Christ.
81) Lord, do not let my spouse use me or exploit our marriage to gain ill-gotten wealth, in the name of Jesus Christ.

82) O Lord, let me marry for love and still be very financially comfortable with my husband/wife, in the name of Jesus Christ.
83) Lord, blind the eyes of demonic in-laws from seeing and contending against progress in our marriage, in the name of Jesus Christ.
84) Lord, set a watchman over our walls and don't let him sleep until you have established our marriage and made it a praise in the earth, in the name of Jesus Christ.
85) My marriage receives divine favor from God today, in Jesus's name.
86) My marriage receives divine mercy from God today, in Jesus's name.
87) My marriage receives divine promotion from God today, in Jesus's name.
88) My marriage receives divine breakthrough from God today, in Jesus's name.
89) My marriage receives divine peace from God today, in Jesus's name.
90) My marriage receives divine material blessings from God today, in Jesus's name.
91) My marriage receives divine longevity from God today, in Jesus's name.
92) My marriage receives divine cleansing from God today, in Jesus's name.
93) My marriage receives divine freedom from God today, in Jesus's name.
94) Thank you, Lord, for answering all my prayers and our prayers today, in the name of Jesus Christ. Amen.

12

Claim Back Your Financial Potential

Part 1

MANY OF US were destined to be millionaires but have failed because of evil powers of our fathers' houses pulling and dragging us down. Other factors responsible for our failures and inabilities to experience godly financial promotions are lack of sowing in the house of God, not blessing the poor, not blessing the widow and the fatherless, our lifestyles, past involvement with the occult, household strongholds, and curses of poverty, bribery, cheating, and corruption.

There are three levels of blessings in our lives.

    a) **Wealth and Riches:** A person can be wealthy and rich but devoid of God's glory and grace because he does not have Christ in his life. Wealth and riches without Christ lead to a life of emptiness and frustration. Despite so much wealth, the individual in this category is typically unfulfilled spiritually and uncertain of the future without his wealth and riches. People in this category usually resort to drugs, alcohol abuse, sexual sins, and unruly lifestyles. They may think they are gods to those who look up to them. They treat their subjects with disdain and hate correction, advice, and confrontation. Pride and arrogance may become their shield to hide their fears of the unknown. They are never satisfied, as satisfaction only comes from receiving Christ into our lives. Some in this category depend on those who look up to them for strength, and once the fans disapprove of them because of bad publicity, their strength fails and they resort to depression and emotional roller coasters.

b) **Prosperity**: Prosperous people may not have a lot of wealth and riches, but they have Christ in their lives, among other things. A life with Christ is one of peace and blessings with a future full of hope, not threatened by uncertainty. Prosperous people understand hope and faith in God, and look up to God and not man for satisfaction and comfort. Most Christians are in this category. God is viewed and regarded as the source for all wealth and riches; therefore, glory and thanksgiving are given to Him. A prosperous person takes everything into account and gives thanks to God for all. People in this category are usually satisfied with the little or more at their disposal. Prosperity is all around, including in marriage, good health, and sound minds. They may go through storms, but they have Christ as their undertaker, deliverer, and shepherd. Many prosperous people are extremely wealthy, and this puts them in the next blessing category below.

c) **Minister of Finance**: This level is only achieved through the trust God has for us. A giving and generous Christian will one day find himself in this category because God can trust him. To become a minister of finance, one must be willing to give all or whatever God commands him to give either to another, a group, a church, an orphanage, a non-profit foundation, etc. The goal is typically to build and expand the kingdom of God, to feed and help the poor, the widowed, the fatherless, the stranger, victims of disaster, and above all, to win souls for Christ. God uses the minister of finance as a conduit to channel His resources to the poor and those He wants to bless. Ministers of Finance never lack resources to give, and God never stops them from blessing themselves and their families except when there is an abuse, as in the wealth and riches category.

SCRIPTURAL REFERENCES

Malachi 3:10–12 *"Bring all the tithes into the storehouse, That there may be food in My house, And try Me now in this," Says the* Lord *of hosts, "If I will not open for you the windows of heaven And pour out for you such blessing That there will not be room enough to receive it. And I will rebuke the devourer for your sakes, So that he will not destroy the fruit of your ground, Nor shall the vine fail to bear fruit for you in the field," Says the* Lord *of hosts; "And all nations will call you blessed, For you will be a delightful land," Says the* Lord *of hosts.*

Genesis 41:49 *Joseph gathered very much grain, as the sand of the sea, until he stopped counting, for it was immeasurable.*

2 Corinthians 9:6–8 *But this I say: He who sows sparingly will also reap sparingly, and he who sows bountifully will also reap bountifully. So let each one give as he purposes in his heart, not grudgingly or of necessity; for God loves a cheerful giver. And God is able to make all grace abound toward you, that you, always having all sufficiency in all things, may have an abundance for every good work.*

PRAYER POINTS

1) Begin Your prayer session with praise and worship.
2) Dear Lord Jesus, thank You for making me a channel of blessings for your Kingdom.
3) Forgive me of my sins in the past and present, in the mighty name of Jesus Christ.
4) I acknowledge You as the ultimate supplier of good gifts to your people.
5) Thank You for this prayer session, and I ask for your supernatural blessings to come upon me and my family now, in the mighty name of Jesus Christ.

6) Lord Jesus, restore with all my blessings the years that the swarming locust, the crawling locust, the chewing locust, and the consuming locust have eaten from me, in the mighty name of Jesus Christ.

7) Lord Jesus, my blessings are in your hands. Destroy every ancestral power contending for my blessings and successes, in Jesus's name.

8) O Lord, let me and my family eat and be satisfied in your goodness toward us, in the mighty name of Jesus Christ.

9) Almighty God, you are my God, let me never be put to shame, in the mighty name of Jesus Christ.

10) Anointing to prosper, fall upon my hands today, in Jesus's name.

11) O Lord, deliver and set my hands free from all satanic bondage tying down my financial blessings, in the mighty name of Jesus Christ.

12) I shall keep and multiply every financial blessing that God has blessed me with, in the mighty name of Jesus Christ.

13) I command the fire of God to consume and destroy every financial robber assigned to devour blessings in my life, in the mighty name of Jesus Christ.

14) Almighty God, make prosperous the work of my hands beyond my wildest imagination, in the mighty name of Jesus Christ.

15) I shall prosper and be in good health even as my soul prospers, in the mighty name of Jesus Christ.

16) I reject and denounce every leaking hole in the pocket of my life, in the mighty name of Jesus Christ.

17) By the arrows of fire, I challenge every strongman of poverty assigned to monitor and destroy my destiny, in the mighty name of Jesus Christ.

18) Every strongman projecting losses into my life, I challenge you to die by fire, in the mighty name of Jesus Christ.

19) Almighty God, I reject every financial burial in my life by fire and by thunder, in the mighty name of Jesus Christ.

20) All satanic money in my possession, I release you out of my hands into the fire of the Holy Ghost, in the mighty name of Jesus Christ.
21) Lord Jesus, rescue my finances from satanic wells and storage banks, in the mighty name of Jesus Christ.
22) Lord Jesus, cleanse my hands from every financial failure with your blood, in the mighty name of Jesus Christ.
23) Every stronghold of loss in my life, be scattered by fire, in Jesus's name.
24) Almighty God, release my promotion for me today, in Jesus's name.
25) My blessing shall be as the sand of the sea, until I am unable to count, for it shall be immeasurable, in the name of Jesus Christ.
26) O Lord, let these coming years of my life bring abundant blessings to me and my family, in the name of Jesus Christ.
27) O Lord, make me fruitful in the land you have given me, in Jesus's name.
28) O Lord, make me forget the pain of the past and release harvests into my future, in the name of Jesus Christ.
29) I command the spirit of success to come upon me that I may prosper as Joseph prospered in the house of Potiphar the Egyptian, in the name of Jesus Christ (Gen. 39:1–6).
30) O Lord, make me become successful and command all that I do to prosper after the order of Joseph in Egypt, in the name of Jesus Christ.
31) O Lord, bless me and command all that I sow in your house to return a million fold back to me this year, in the name of Jesus Christ (Gen 26:12–13).
32) O Lord, make me begin to prosper and continue to prosper until I become abundantly prosperous, in the name of Jesus Christ.
33) O Lord, increase my financial capacity and let me become mightier than my enemies, in the name of Jesus Christ.
34) O Lord, bless me and multiply my descendants, for I am your servant, in the name of Jesus Christ.

35) O Lord, let my enemies know that you are with me and that I am the blessed of the Lord, in the name of Jesus Christ.
36) O Lord, let rivers of living water come out of the wells of my life, in the name of Jesus Christ.
37) O Lord, send multiple rivers of income to flow into my life, in the mighty name of Jesus.
38) Almighty God, as Abraham could not count the stars of heaven, so shall I not be able to count my blessings, for they shall be innumerable, in the mighty name of Jesus Christ.
39) I declare that I am a blessing to many in the earth, in the name of Jesus Christ.
40) I challenge every dry area of my life to receive divine healing and now begin to produce floods of blessings, in the name of Jesus Christ.
41) May God bless me with the dew of heaven, with the fatness of the earth, and with plenty of grain and wine, in the name of Jesus Christ (Gen. 27:28).
42) O Lord, bless everyone who blesses me, in the name of Jesus Christ.
43) O Lord, let the nations of the earth call me blessed, in the name of Jesus Christ.
44) O Lord, lead me to where my blessings are located, in the name of Jesus Christ.
45) O Lord, let my blessings refuse to locate my enemies but locate me always, in the name of Jesus Christ.
46) I shall have good health and enjoy the fullness of God's blessings in my life, in the name of Jesus Christ.
47) O Lord, as I seek you, let me be found by you, in Jesus's mighty name (1 Chron. 28:9).
48) Almighty God, bless me and do not let my hands be weak in serving you, in the name of Jesus Christ (2 Chron. 15:7).
49) As you promised, reward the work of my hands, in the name of Jesus Christ.
50) O Lord Jesus, let me find rest in you all year round (2 Chron. 15:15).

51) I shall be established because I believe in the Lord my God, in the name of Jesus Christ (2Chron. 20:20).
52) O Lord, arise and fight for me now, for I have positioned myself and stand still before you.
53) I challenge and cancel the spirit of frustration from my life so I may serve my God without regrets, in the name of Jesus Christ.
54) O Lord, help me to collect my spoils in abundance until my storage capacity is filled, in the name of Jesus Christ.
55) O Lord, this is my turn-around time. Turn things around for me today, in the name of Jesus Christ.
56) O Lord, clean and purify everything the enemy has defiled in my life with the blood of Jesus Christ.
57) O Lord, prepare my territory for victory and blessings and chase away my enemies into the abyss, in the name of Jesus Christ.
58) O Lord, bring your full and abundant provision into my life and manifest your total presence in every situation that I face, in Jesus's name
59) Almighty God, expose my enemies to me so I may know and be watchful.
60) I will enter my inheritance and restoration this season and also the next season, in the name of Jesus Christ.
61) My blessings will not pass me by in this season, in the name of Jesus Christ.
62) Lord Jesus, position me to receive promotion in this season, in the name of Jesus Christ.
63) I reject and cancel the spirit of displacement from my destiny, in the name of Jesus Christ.
64) Dear Lord, uproot and destroy the spirit of poverty and lack from my life, in the name of Jesus Christ.
65) Every generational curse found in my destiny, be consumed by fire, in the name of Jesus Christ.
66) I receive healing and deliverance for my finances today, in the name of Jesus Christ.
67) Every power tampering with my destiny, die by fire, in the name of Jesus Christ.

68) Every power tampering with my promotion, die by fire, in the name of Jesus Christ.
69) Every power tampering with my victory, die by fire, in the name of Jesus Christ.
70) Every power tampering with my prosperity, die by fire, in the name of Jesus Christ.
71) Every power tampering with my happiness, die by fire, in the name of Jesus Christ.
72) Every power tampering with my money, die by fire, in the name of Jesus Christ.
73) Every power tampering with my safe deposits, die by fire, in the name of Jesus Christ.
74) Every power tampering with my life, die by fire, in the name of Jesus Christ.
75) Every power tampering with my children, die by fire, in the name of Jesus Christ.
76) Every power tampering with my success, die by fire, in the name of Jesus Christ.
77) Lord Jesus, I thank you for answering all my prayers at this hour, in the name of Jesus Christ. Amen.

13

Claim Back Your Financial Potential

Part 2

SCRIPTURAL REFERENCES

Psalm 112:1–10 *Praise the Lord! Blessed is the man who fears the Lord, Who delights greatly in His commandments. His descendants will be mighty on earth; The generation of the upright will be blessed. Wealth and riches will be in his house, And his righteousness endures forever. Unto the upright there arises light in the darkness; He is gracious, and full of compassion, and righteous. A good man deals graciously and lends; He will guide his affairs with discretion. Surely he will never be shaken; The righteous will be in everlasting remembrance. He will not be afraid of evil tidings; His heart is steadfast, trusting in the Lord. His heart is established; He will not be afraid, Until he sees his desire upon his enemies. He has dispersed abroad, He has given to the poor; His righteousness endures forever; His horn will be exalted with honor. The wicked will see it and be grieved; He will gnash his teeth and melt away; The desire of the wicked shall perish*

Psalm 4:1–3 *Blessed is he who considers the poor; The Lord will deliver him in time of trouble. The Lord will preserve him and keep him alive, And he will be blessed on the earth; you will not deliver him to the will of his enemies. The Lord will strengthen him on his bed of illness; you will sustain him on his sickbed.*

PRAYER POINTS

1) Almighty God, increase your grace upon my life to receive promotion today, in the mighty name of Jesus Christ.
2) Almighty God, I challenge my bank account by your generous power to become healthy and prosperous, in the mighty name of Jesus Christ.
3) Almighty God, I refuse to labor in vain but must reap the fruit of my labor, in the mighty name of Jesus Christ.
4) Almighty God, illuminate my path to success, in the mighty name of Jesus Christ.
5) Lord Jesus, I reject and refuse to entertain failure in my life, in the mighty name of Jesus Christ.
6) Lord Jesus, pour down your blessings upon my family today, in the mighty name of Jesus Christ.
7) I receive divine power to prosper from above, in the name of Jesus Christ.
8) I cancel every satanic conspiracy against my finances today, in the mighty name of Jesus Christ.
9) Every satanic robber positioned at my business, work, or home to steal my blessings away, be consumed by fire, in the mighty name of Jesus Christ.
10) Every demonic opposition to my financial breakthrough, be scattered by the rock of ages, in the mighty name of Jesus Christ.
11) I command every demonic seizure of my destiny to be restored to me by fire, in the mighty name of Jesus Christ.
12) Lord Jesus, let my breakthrough become my family's breakthrough, in the mighty name of Jesus Christ.
13) I receive my breakthrough now; therefore I have become prosperous, in the mighty name of Jesus Christ.
14) I command every power sitting on my breakthrough to be destroyed by the thunder and fire of God, in the mighty name of Jesus Christ.
15) I am victorious against any financial failure in my life, in the mighty name of Jesus Christ.

16) Power to increase in prosperity, come upon me now, in the mighty name of Jesus Christ.
17) Lord Jesus, I thank you for blessing me beyond my wildest dreams, in the mighty name of Jesus Christ.
18) Lord Jesus, I thank you for blessing every member of my household with supernatural finances, in the mighty name of Jesus Christ.
19) I shall prosper even as my soul prospers, in Jesus's dear name.
20) O Lord, send your lifting power to lift me up financially from the stronghold of poverty, in the mighty name of Jesus Christ.
21) I must increase in wealth and riches until the sun and moon are no more, in the mighty name of Jesus Christ.
22) Lord Jesus, speak to my wilderness and cause it to become irrigated by the Holy Spirit, in the mighty name of Jesus Christ.
23) Lord Jesus, send divine rain to fall upon every dry area of my life, in the mighty name of Jesus Christ.
24) I receive divine moisturizer for divine growth and expansion today, in the mighty name of Jesus Christ.
25) Every evil curse spoken into my money and my bank account, I command you to melt away by the blood of Jesus Christ.
26) Every power draining my finances from my purse and handbag, be consumed by fire, in the mighty name of Jesus Christ.
27) Every power directing drowning debts into my household, be consumed by the fire of the Holy Ghost, in the mighty name of Jesus Christ.
28) Every power producing multiple debts through unnecessary credit card approvals to my name, I launch you into the abyss forever, in the mighty name of Jesus Christ.
29) Every power using credit cards to keep me in perpetual debt, I destroy you by the rock of ages, in the mighty name of Jesus Christ.
30) Almighty God, deliver me from continuing to put myself in debt through excessive and unnecessary purchases and expenses, in the mighty name of Jesus Christ.

31) I bind every spirit of obsession for buying what I do not need, in the mighty name of Jesus Christ.
32) I destroy every waster spirit in my life, in the mighty name of Jesus Christ.
33) I plead the blood of Jesus Christ over my spending habits and command every addiction to wasteful spending to die by fire, in the mighty name of Jesus Christ.
34) Holy Spirit, empower me to overcome the prodigal spirit in my life and set your fire to consume it to ashes, in the mighty name of Jesus Christ.
35) O Lord Jesus, enlarge my territory and financial capacity today, in the mighty name of Jesus Christ.
36) O Lord Jesus, help me to give willingly and generously to the building of God's house and kingdom, in the mighty name of Jesus Christ.
37) I declare that I shall have peace and joy when giving to the house of God, in the mighty name of Jesus Christ.
38) I declare that every evil spirit fighting against my generosity and willingness to give to the house of God be shattered by the rock of ages, in the mighty name of Jesus Christ.
39) I declare that as God blessed Joseph in Egypt, so shall I be blessed in this city, in the mighty name of Jesus Christ.
40) I declare that as God blessed Solomon with wisdom and riches, so shall I be blessed in my life, in the mighty name of Jesus Christ.
41) I declare that my blessings shall never pass me by, in Jesus's name.
42) Every satanic agent assigned to direct blessings away from my destiny, die by fire, die by fire, in the mighty name of Jesus Christ.
43) I claim divine financial acceleration into my life today, in Jesus's name.
44) I claim double times double blessings into my life today, in Jesus's mighty name.
45) I declare that my double times double blessings must shine forth today, in the mighty name of Jesus Christ.

46) Every satanic stone sitting down on my blessings, I command you to roll over onto your owner's blessings, in the mighty name of Jesus Christ.
47) Every satanic string tying down by expansion, be broken into pieces forever, in the mighty name of Jesus Christ.
48) Every arrow of affliction shot into my position to displace me from prosperity, be shattered to pieces, in the mighty name of Jesus Christ.
49) Every evil bird eating up my progress and promotion, die by fire, in the mighty name of Jesus Christ.
50) Every satanic agent burying my financial potential anywhere, die in the mighty name of Jesus Christ.
51) Evil altars calling my name to tag poverty spirits in the second heaven, I command you to crash from your foundations, in the mighty name of Jesus Christ.
52) I sanitize with the blood of Jesus Christ all evil monies that have gotten into my hands through normal business transactions, in the mighty name of Jesus Christ.
53) Every satanic pen used in signing evil checks to me during the normal course of my business transactions, which are now fighting against my financial freedom, I command you to dry up and become dust in the mighty name of Jesus Christ.
54) I recall all my blessings traded away by satanic merchants from the north, south, east, and west, in the mighty name of Jesus Christ.
55) I declare that I am blessed beyond any explanation, in Jesus's name.
56) I declare that my family is free from the curse of poverty today, in the mighty name of Jesus Christ.
57) Lord, send my angels to go into every corner of the earth to search and bring back my blessings to me, in the mighty name of Jesus Christ.
58) Lord, let all your angels carrying my blessings locate me with them today, in the mighty name of Jesus Christ.
59) Lord, silence every evil tongue declaring curses upon my prosperity, in the mighty name of Jesus Christ.

60) Lord, do unto my stubborn enemies what you did to Pharaoh and his troops in the Red Sea, in the mighty name of Jesus Christ.
61) Every stubborn spirit of poverty that has refused to let me go, be drowned in the Red Sea, in the name of Jesus Christ.
62) Every stubborn spirit of poverty that has refused to let me go, be drowned by the east wind that plagued Egypt, in the name of Jesus Christ.
63) Every stubborn spirit of poverty that has refused to let me go, be drowned in the pit of fire, in the name of Jesus Christ.
64) Every stubborn spirit of poverty that has refused to let me go, be consumed to pieces by the Lion of the tribe of Judah, in the name of Jesus Christ.
65) Every stubborn spirit of poverty that has refused to let me go, become pillars of salt with your senders, after the order of Lot's wife, in the name of Jesus Christ.
66) I am free in the mighty name of Jesus Christ.
67) Thank You, Lord, for answering all my prayers, in the mighty name of Jesus Christ. Amen.

14

O Lord, Send Your Revival Now

Part 1

A CHURCH THAT does not pray is spiritually cold and quiet as a cemetery. We can simply conclude that such a church is a lukewarm church. A Christian that doesn't pray or read the word of God is equally lukewarm and requires spiritual revival or awakening. It is hard to maintain a spirit-filled church without prayers and fasting. Some churches pray quite often while some don't. If your church is not a praying church or does not pray for you or your fellow members, then such a church organization does not deserve your membership. You must realize that your church at this point is only a social gathering, as far as it is spiritually concerned.

When your love for God has waxed cold, one of the physical symptoms that manifests is a prayerless lifestyle. You will not feel the excitement and motivation to attend consistent and further prayer meetings, Bible studies, or regular Sunday services, due to discouragement and spiritual complacency. Once you have withdrawn, the enemy comes into your life and plants afflictions, lies, deception, offenses, betrayal, and hatred. Ultimately, the enemy will kill and destroy your faith, as well as your mortal body, unless God intervenes by His grace and mercy.

You are to pray unceasingly. That means you must seize every opportunity to communicate with God through prayers and to read His word. This is what will set you on fire for God and spiritually revive you from your lukewarm position. We must be flaming Christians willing to do His work with authority and power. This will put us in the position to demonstrate His signs and wonders to unbelievers, so they may believe and give glory to God. Remember, you are to keep the fire burning through prayers and reading His word.

SCRIPTURAL REFERENCES

Revelation 2:4–5 Nevertheless I have this against you, that you have left your first love. Remember therefore from where you have fallen; repent and do the first works, or else I will come to you quickly and remove your lamp stand from its place—unless you repent.

Revelations 3:14 And to the angel of the church of the Laodiceans write, "These things says the Amen, the Faithful and True Witness, the Beginning of the creation of God: 'I know your works, that you are neither cold nor hot. I could wish you were cold or hot. So then, because you are lukewarm, and neither cold nor hot, I will vomit you out of My mouth. Because you say, "I am rich, have become wealthy, and have need of nothing"—and do not know that you are wretched, miserable, poor, blind, and naked.'"

2 Chronicles 6:12–42,
2 Chronicles 20:1–30

PRAYER FOR CHURCH REVIVAL

PRAYER POINTS

1) Almighty Father, thank you for giving us your church to worship and glorify your Holy name, in the name of Jesus Christ.
2) Thank you for allowing us to proclaim the name of Jesus Christ in our midst.
3) Thank you for the leading of the Holy Spirit in our meetings.
4) Thank you for continued mercy and grace upon us despite our lukewarm attitudes toward you.
5) Forgive us for being complacent and taking your work casually, in the name of Jesus Christ.

6) Forgive us for backsliding and turning away from your call in our lives, in the mighty name of Jesus Christ.
7) Forgive our leaders for not showing good leadership to shepherd your sheep.
8) Send your fire to burn in us again and set us apart for you and your Kingdom, in the name of Jesus Christ.
9) Anoint us with your Holy Spirit today and establish your holy presence with us, in the mighty name of Jesus Christ.
10) Cleanse, purify, and sanctify us with the blood of Jesus Christ.
11) As we confess our sins to you, O Lord, let it be known that we have repented, and accept our supplications to you, in the name of Jesus Christ.

12) Almighty God, arise, O Lord, to your resting place. Arise to [name of church], you and the power of your word, in the mighty name of Jesus Christ.
13) Lord Jesus, arise to this house, arise to [name of church], and establish your permanent presence forever with us until Jesus Christ returns, in Jesus's mighty name. Amen.
14) Almighty God, establish your salvation in this house. Let everyone who comes to this house unsaved, by your grace, receive salvation, in the name of Jesus Christ.
15) Almighty God, establish your great mercy in [name of the church] and have mercy on us leaders and on all our members, in the mighty name of Jesus Christ.
16) Almighty God, establish your Shekinah glory upon [name of church]. Arise and dwell in [name of church], your tabernacle, and let your glory shine forth, in the name of Jesus Christ.
17) Almighty God, place [name of church] in your perfect will for this generation on earth, in the name of Jesus Christ.
18) Almighty God, place [name of church] under the shadow of your wings, in the name of Jesus Christ.
19) Almighty God, assign your ministering angels permanently to [name of church] so as to minister day and night before your people, in the name of Jesus Christ.

20) Almighty God, lead us into your presence at all times through our praise and worship, in the name of Jesus Christ.
21) Almighty God, we call forth for your revival to now fall upon [name of church], in the name of Jesus Christ.
22) Almighty God, place [name of church] in the right position with your will at all times, in the name of Jesus Christ.
23) O Lord God, let your priests be clothed with salvation. Let our pastors, our ministers, our leaders, our praise team, our staff, and all churches that will originate from [name of church] or partner with us be clothed with your glory and salvation, in the name of Jesus Christ.
24) Let every member of this ministry, here and abroad, from all four corners of the earth, and all nations that you are about to give us, be clothed with your salvation and glory, in the mighty name of Jesus Christ.
25) Let the city of (____), the land that you swore to give us as our inheritance, be open to [name of church].
26) Let the gates of our inheritance be declared open to [name of church].
27) We, your chosen people, shall possess all your blessings in the city of ____, in the mighty name of Jesus Christ.
28) O Lord, let your saints rejoice in your goodness because of [name of church] in [city].
29) As you promised us according to your finished work on the Cross of Calvary, let everyone who comes here with an infirmity, sickness, cancer, or any physical ailment receive total healing, in the name of Jesus Christ.
30) As you promised us according to your finished work, let everyone who calls in for prayers or contacts us through our I-Church, website, Internet, radio, television, or by telephone with an infirmity, sickness, cancer, or any physical ailment receive total healing and deliverance, in the name of Jesus Christ.
31) Almighty God, as you also promised according to your finished work, arise today. Deliver and set every captive who

comes into [name of church] free from satanic bondage, in the name of Jesus Christ.

32) Lord Jesus, according to your finished work on the cross, arise and make the blind to see, the dead to rise, the crippled and the lame to walk, when they come into [name of church], in the name of Jesus Christ.

33) Lord Jesus, according to your finished work on the cross, increase your anointing in [name of church] and let your presence be seen in every area, in the mighty name of Jesus Christ.

34) O Lord Jesus, forgive our sins when we ask for forgiveness, and cleanse all who call for your mercy with your precious blood.

35) O Lord Jesus, you are not man that should lie, nor the son of man that should repent. According to your finished work, release your financial blessings upon this house, so that your kingdom will be expanded beyond our boundaries and borders, in the name of Jesus Christ.

36) Lord Jesus, according to your finished work on the cross, open now the storehouse in heaven and begin the supernatural transfer of your wealth to us from today, so that we may bless your Kingdom to prosper according to your will, in the name of Jesus Christ.

37) It is written, "Whatever we declare shall be established." Let all we have declared today be established, in the mighty name of Jesus Christ.

38) It is written, "Whatever we bind on earth shall be bound in heaven, and whatever we loose on earth shall be loosed in heaven." Let all we bind in this ministry remain bound and what we loose in church remain loosed, in the mighty name of Jesus Christ.

39) I declare that the power of holiness shall come upon [name of church] today, in the name of Jesus Christ.

40) I declare that the power of inspiration shall come upon [name of church] today, in the name of Jesus Christ.

41) I declare that the power of healing and miracles shall come upon [name of church] today, in the name of Jesus Christ.
42) I declare that the power of revival shall come upon [name of church] today, in the name of Jesus Christ.
43) I declare that the power of increased vision shall come upon [name of church] today, in the name of Jesus Christ.
44) I declare that the power of restoration shall come upon [name of church] today, in the name of Jesus Christ.
45) I declare that the power of success shall come upon [name of church] today, in the name of Jesus Christ.
46) I declare that the power of righteousness shall come upon [name of church] today, in the name of Jesus Christ.
47) I declare that the power of wisdom and knowledge shall come upon [name of church] today, in the name of Jesus Christ.
48) I declare that the power of advancement shall come upon [name of church] today, in the name of Jesus Christ.
49) I declare that the power of benefits and promotion shall come upon [name of church] today, in the name of Jesus Christ.
50) I declare that the power of territorial expansion shall come upon [name of church] today, in the name of Jesus Christ.
51) I declare that the power of understanding and problem-solving ideas shall come upon [name of church] today, in the name of Jesus Christ.
52) I declare that the power of winning souls for Christ shall come upon [name of church] today, in the name of Jesus Christ.
53) I declare that the power of greatness shall come upon [name of church] today, in the name of Jesus Christ.
54) I declare that the power of unity shall come upon [name of church] today, in the name of Jesus Christ.
55) I declare that the power of loyalty to Christ shall come upon [name of church] today, in the name of Jesus Christ.
56) I declare that the power of deliverance shall come upon [name of church] today, in the name of Jesus Christ.

57) I declare that the power of divine health shall come upon [name of church] today, in the name of Jesus Christ.
58) I declare that the power of the divine network shall come upon [name of church] today, in the name of Jesus Christ.
59) I declare that the power of divine connection shall come upon [name of church] today, in the name of Jesus Christ.
60) I declare that the power of strategic position shall come upon [name of church] today, in the name of Jesus Christ.
61) I declare that the power of supernatural increase shall come upon [name of church] today, in the name of Jesus Christ.
62) I declare that the power of the fivefold office shall come upon [name of church] today, in the name of Jesus Christ.
63) I declare that the power of the manifestations of the gifts of the spirit shall come upon [name of church] today, in the name of Jesus Christ.
64) I declare that the power of the fruits of the spirit shall come upon [name of church] today, in the name of Jesus Christ.
65) I declare that the power of the gift of love shall come upon [name of church] today, in the name of Jesus Christ.
66) I declare that the power of the gift of compassion shall come upon [name of church] today, in the name of Jesus Christ.
67) I declare that the power of truth shall come upon [name of church] today, in the name of Jesus Christ.
68) I declare that the power of mercy shall come upon [name of church] today, in the name of Jesus Christ.
69) I declare that the dunamis power of God shall come upon [name of church] today, in the name of Jesus Christ.
70) I declare that the power of excellence shall come upon [name of church] today, in the name of Jesus Christ.
71) I declare that the power of divine victory shall come upon [name of church] today, in the name of Jesus Christ.
72) I declare that the power of divine truth shall come upon [name of church] today, in the name of Jesus Christ.
73) I declare that the power of goodness shall come upon [name of church] today, in the name of Jesus Christ.

74) I declare that the power of justice shall come upon [name of church] today, in the name of Jesus Christ.
75) I declare that the power of the agape love shall come upon [name of church] today, in the name of Jesus Christ.
76) I declare that the power of signs and wonders shall come upon [name of church] today, in the name of Jesus Christ.
77) I declare that the power of overcoming shall come upon [name of church] today, in the name of Jesus Christ.
78) I declare that the power of divine favor shall come upon [name of church] today, in the name of Jesus Christ.
79) I declare that the power of evangelism shall come upon [name of church] today, in the name of Jesus Christ.
80) I declare that the power to shepherd God's flock shall come upon [name of church] today, in the name of Jesus Christ.
81) I declare that the power to bind and loose shall come upon [name of church] today, in the name of Jesus Christ.
82) I declare that the power to set the captive free shall come upon [name of church] today, in the name of Jesus Christ.
83) I declare that the power to baptize by fire shall come upon [name of church] today, in the name of Jesus Christ.
84) I declare that the power of salvation shall come upon [name of church] today, in the name of Jesus Christ.
85) I declare that the power to walk in abundant grace shall come upon [name of church] today, in the name of Jesus Christ.
86) I declare that the power to live in your freedom shall come upon [name of church] today, in the name of Jesus Christ.
87) I declare that the power of multiplication shall come upon [name of church] today, in the name of Jesus Christ.
88) I declare that the power to reject condemnation shall come upon [name of church] today, in the name of Jesus Christ.
89) I declare that the power to withstand trials shall come upon [name of church] today, in the name of Jesus Christ.
90) I declare that the power to preach the word of God shall come upon [name of church] today, in the name of Jesus Christ.

91) I declare that the power to be filled with the word of God shall come upon [name of church] today, in the name of Jesus Christ.
92) I declare that the power of teaching the word of God shall come upon [name of church] today, in the name of Jesus Christ.
93) I declare that the power to resist the devil shall come upon [name of church] today, in the name of Jesus Christ.
94) I declare that the power to believe the word of God shall come upon [name of church] today, in the name of Jesus Christ.
95) I declare that the power of unity shall come upon [name of church] today, in the name of Jesus Christ.
96) I declare that the power to receive supernatural power and authority from God shall come upon [name of church] today, in the name of Jesus Christ.
97) I declare that the power of friendship with God shall come upon [name of church] today, in the name of Jesus Christ.
98) I declare that the power to live a sinless life shall come upon [name of church] today, in the name of Jesus Christ.
99) I declare that the power of prayer shall come upon [name of church] today, in the name of Jesus Christ.
100) I declare that the power of faith shall come upon [name of church] today, in the name of Jesus Christ.
101) I declare that the power of supernatural encounters shall come upon [name of church] today, in the name of Jesus Christ.
102) I declare that the power of spiritual advancement shall come upon [name of church] today, in the name of Jesus Christ.
103) I declare that the power of physical advancement shall come upon [name of church] today, in the name of Jesus Christ.
104) I declare that the power of fruitfulness shall come upon [name of church] today, in the name of Jesus Christ.
105) Almighty God, arise and destroy every satanic power that stands against the expansion of [name of church], in the name of Jesus Christ.

106) Almighty God, arise and destroy by fire every satanic prophet assigned to prophesy against [name of church], in the name of Jesus Christ.
107) Almighty God, arise and destroy by fire every religious strongman assigned to speak curses against [name of church], in the mighty name of Jesus Christ
108) You, evil powers of [city], hear the word of the Lord: we command you to take your hands off our destinies today, in the name of Jesus Christ.
109) You, powers of the north, south, east, and west of [city] binding the church of God in chains, we command your chains to break off and shatter by fire, in the name of Jesus Christ.
110) Every religious and satanic strongman prophesying death against [name of church], against our families, against our lives, we command you to roast by fire, in the name of Jesus Christ.
111) Almighty God, from this day, let your healing power fall upon [name of church], in the name of Jesus Christ.
112) Almighty God, from today, let your peace fall upon [name of church], in the name of Jesus Christ.
113) Almighty God, from today, let your prosperity fall upon [name of church].
114) Almighty God, from today, let your kingdom be expanded in [name of church] in the name of Jesus Christ.
115) [Name of church] shall not fail (repeat three times), and what we have declared shall be established. As we enter this covenant with you, O Lord on earth, so shall it be in your heaven today, in the mighty name of Jesus Christ. Amen, amen, amen.

15

O Lord, Send Your Revival Now

Part 2

SCRIPTURAL REFERENCES

Exodus 15:23–26 *Now when they came to Marah, they could not drink the waters of Marah, for they were bitter. Therefore the name of it was called Marah. And the people complained against Moses, saying, "What shall we drink?" So he cried out to the* Lord, *and the* Lord *showed him a tree. When he cast it into the waters, the waters were made sweet. There He made a statute and an ordinance for them, and there He tested them, and said, "If you diligently heed the voice of the* Lord *your God and do what is right in His sight, give ear to His commandments and keep all His statutes, I will put none of the diseases on you which I have brought on the Egyptians. For I am the* Lord *who heals you."*

PRAYER POINTS

1) Start with praise and worship and give thanks to God.
2) Lord Jesus, strengthen our faith to believe in your salvation, and in the work you have called us to do in [name of church].
3) Lord Jesus, do not let Your church become a house of bitterness as the waters of Marah, in the name of Jesus Christ.

4) Lord Jesus, heal [name of church] and release a sweet spirit upon us, in the mighty name of Jesus Christ.
5) Holy Spirit, you are the spirit of truth. Release your truth and righteousness into [name of church], in the name of Jesus Christ.
6) [Name of church] shall be above only and not beneath, in the name of Jesus Christ.
7) [Name of church] shall give to many nations and shall borrow from none, in the name of Jesus Christ.
8) Lord Jesus, let boldness and the power of God come upon [name of church] today, in the name of Jesus Christ.
9) [Name of church] shall not miss the mark but shall fulfill God's destiny for us, in the mighty name of Jesus Christ.
10) In the name of Jesus Christ, a multitude of people shall go to heaven because of [name of church].
11) In the name of Jesus Christ, a multitude of people shall receive salvation because of [name of church].
12) In the name of Jesus Christ, a multitude of people shall reach their destinies in life because of [name of church].
13) In the name of Jesus Christ, a multitude of people shall receive financial prosperity because of giving to your work in [name of church].
14) In the name of Jesus Christ, a multitude of people shall come through the doors of [name of church] and serve God with all their hearts.
15) I command the anointing of excellence to fall upon [name of church], in the mighty name of Jesus Christ.
16) Lord, send your fresh fire and fresh anointing to fall upon [name of church], in the name of Jesus Christ.
17) O God, arise and let every enemy of [name of church] be scattered, in the name of Jesus Christ.
18) Holy fire of revival, fall upon [name of church], in the name of Jesus Christ.
19) Holy Spirit, do not let [name of church] engage in rebellion against you, in the name of Jesus Christ.

20) Almighty God, I rebuke every spirit of dispute and opposition in [name of church], in the mighty name of Jesus Christ.
21) We command the spirit of loyalty to come upon [name of church] members today, in the mighty name of Jesus Christ.
22) Lord, we command heaven to open and release prosperity upon [name of church], in the name of Jesus Christ.
23) We take authority and bind all principalities and powers operating against [name of church], in the name of Jesus Christ.
24) We break every inherited covenant against [name of church], in the name of Jesus Christ.
25) Every evil power that attacks a new church that is now attacking [name of church], we command you to be roasted by fire in the name of Jesus Christ.
26) Every chain of inherited witchcraft that attacks a new church that is now attacking [name of church], we break you into pieces in the name of Jesus Christ.
27) Every chain of territorial power that attacks a new church in [city] that is now attacking [name of church], be destroyed in the name of Jesus Christ.
28) Every altar speaking against a new church that is now speaking against [name of church], we silence you forever in the name of Jesus Christ.
29) Holy Spirit, breathe on [name of church] today, in the name of Jesus Christ.
30) Holy Spirit, heal every hurt and offense inside [name of church], in the mighty name of Jesus Christ.
31) Almighty God, bless every member of the [name of church] family, in the name of Jesus Christ.
32) Lord, we call the spirit of love to come into [name of church] and remain here forever, in the name of Jesus Christ.
33) Holy Ghost fire, ignite and burn in [name of church] and bring revival to the glory of God, in the name of Jesus Christ.
34) We command every form of rebellion in our leadership to flee, in the name of Jesus Christ.

35) Lord Jesus, break every yoke of backwardness against [name of church], in your mighty, precious name.
36) Holy Spirit, ignite your apostolic mantle in [name of church] by your fire, in the name of Jesus Christ.
37) Holy Spirit, ignite your prophetic mantle in [name of church] by your fire, in the name of Jesus Christ.
38) Holy Spirit, ignite your evangelical mantle in [name of church] by your fire, in the name of Jesus Christ.
39) Holy Spirit, ignite your pastoral mantle in [name of church] by your fire, in the name of Jesus Christ.
40) Holy Spirit, ignite your teaching mantle in [name of church] by your fire, in the name of Jesus Christ.
41) Lord Jesus, expand [name of church] beyond and across the seas, in the name of Jesus Christ.
42) Lord Jesus, let all your promises for [name of church] be fulfilled in this city, in the name of Jesus Christ.
43) Lord Jesus, establish the foundation of [name of church] on a solid rock, in the name of Jesus Christ.
44) Holy Spirit, have your way in every department of [name of church], in the mighty name of Jesus Christ.
45) Almighty God, let every spiritual contamination in [name of church] receive divine cleansing by the blood of Jesus Christ.
46) We command every evil conspiracy and accusation against [name of church] to shatter into pieces, in the mighty name of Jesus Christ.
47) We silence every evil tongue speaking against [name of church] in the name of Jesus Christ.
48) We dismantle every manipulation of [name of church] by a religious strongman in the name of Jesus Christ.
49) We challenge every wicked tongue speaking death upon [name of church] by fire, in the mighty name of Jesus Christ.
50) We call forth the divine favor of God in heaven to come down upon [name of church], in the mighty name of Jesus Christ.
51) Holy Spirit, fill [name of church] with all your spiritual gifts and double anointing, in the mighty name of Jesus Christ.

52) Holy Spirit, let all who come to [name of church] never leave the same way as they came, but be transformed by your glory and the renewing of their minds, in the mighty name of Jesus Christ.
53) Holy Spirit, do not let members of [name of church] be tired of doing God's work, in the mighty name of Jesus Christ.
54) Lord Jesus, bestow prosperity and blessings upon (name of church) today, in the name of Jesus Christ.
55) Almighty, be our undertaker as we move by faith to do your work, in the name of Jesus Christ.
56) Almighty God, show us your glory in this ministry, in the name of Jesus Christ.
57) I command the gates of bondage in our ministry to fall down after the order of the walls of Jericho, in the name of Jesus Christ.
58) Thank you, Lord, for answering all our prayers, in the name of Jesus Christ. Amen.

16

Reversing Evil Covenants in Your Destiny

Part 1

EVIL COVENANTS RESULT in curses inherited directly or indirectly by involvement or exposure to the occult, witchcraft, deities, or psychics, or from our generational bloodline. Evil covenants can be caused by people directly or indirectly, or be entered into either directly or indirectly. Evil covenants are destructive and can become a big problem in the lives of people and in their families, cities, countries, or nations for many generations. God's children must be set free and released from these covenants; otherwise, they will remain impoverished and afflicted throughout their lives. Many destinies have been lost and destroyed because of evil covenants.

When people enter relationships with other gods and worship them through the occult, witchcraft, and so on, they are eternally bound in covenants with such gods. They are also forever in conflict and in rebellion against the Almighty God, the creator of heaven and earth. Unless they repent for their sins and receive Jesus Christ as their Lord and Savior, such people or nations will remain under the curses of these evil covenants for generations. The following prayer points are designed to break evil covenants spiritually and set you free from their curses.

SCRIPUTRAL REFERENCES

Colossians 2:13–15 *And you, being dead in your trespasses and the uncircumcision of your flesh, He has made alive together with Him, having forgiven you all trespasses, having wiped out the handwriting of requirements that was against us, which was contrary to us. And He has taken it out of the way, having nailed it to the cross. Having disarmed principalities and powers, He made a public spectacle of them, triumphing over them in it.*

Galatians 3:12–14 *Yet the law is not of faith, but "the man who does them shall live by them." Christ has redeemed us from the curse of the law, having become a curse for us (for it is written, "Cursed is everyone who hangs on a tree"), that the blessing of Abraham might come upon the Gentiles in Christ Jesus, that we might receive the promise of the Spirit through faith.*

PRAYER POINTS

1) Start this prayer session with praise and worship and give thanks to God for your life.
2) I thank you, Lord, for your mercy, grace, and favor in my life, and for listening to my prayers at this hour, in the name of Jesus Christ.
3) Almighty God, forgive me for my sins and for any association with the occult and witchcraft. Cleanse me with the blood of Jesus Christ
4) Almighty God, uproot every curse that the enemy has planted in my life, in the name of Jesus Christ.
5) Almighty God, arise and let your fire fall upon every spirit of destruction in my life, in the name of Jesus Christ.
6) O Lord, turn every bad situation in my life for good, in Jesus's name.
7) O Lord, turn all impossibilities in my life to possibilities, in Jesus's name.
8) My life, I challenge you to receive divine promotion now, in Jesus's name.

9) My destiny, reject every curse upon you today, in Jesus's name.
10) My body, reject every affliction done to you, in the name of Jesus Christ.
11) Every spirit commanding death into any area of my life, receive paralysis by thunder and by fire, in the name of Jesus Christ.
12) Every evil parental association in my life, I command you to be cut off by the sword of fire, in the name of Jesus Christ.
13) Almighty God, I electrify myself today by fire from the top of my head to the soles of my feet. Let every family curse upon my life be removed forever, in the name of Jesus Christ.
14) I wash every curse of poverty from my life by the blood of Jesus Christ.
15) I wash every curse of failure from my life by the blood of Jesus Christ.
16) I declare that I am released from the curse of mental and physical sickness brought against me by evil powers of my father's house, in the name of Jesus Christ.
17) I challenge every curse of schizoaffective disorder in my family, by the fire of the Holy Spirit.
18) I command the curse of premature death in my life to receive divine termination and death, in the name of Jesus Christ.
19) I declare that I am free from the curse of oppression and generational stagnation, in the name of Jesus Christ.
20) I denounce any involvement with the occult and witchcraft from today, and I release myself from their curses by the blood of Jesus Christ.
21) I command every witch doctor casting spells and curses into my life to receive divine judgment by fire, in the name of Jesus Christ.
22) I declare that every curse of premature termination of marriage or divorce in my life is hereby nullified, in the name of Jesus Christ.
23) I challenge the prophets of doom in my life to shatter to pieces by fire, in the name of Jesus Christ.

24) I reverse every curse of bad reputation in my life forever by fire, in the name of Jesus Christ.
25) I reverse every curse of profitless hard work in my life by the blood of Jesus, in the name of Jesus Christ.
26) I reverse every curse of laziness in my life by the blood of Jesus Christ, in the name of Jesus Christ.
27) I denounce by fire every association with marine spirits from today, in the name of Jesus Christ.
28) I challenge all marine spirit prophets working against my life to catch fire and die, in the name of Jesus Christ.
29) I counter every curse decreed against my life in satanic altars by the blood of Jesus Christ, and I cover myself totally with the precious blood of Christ, in the name of Jesus Christ.
30) I release myself and my family from self-destruction and suicides, in the name of Jesus Christ.
31) I release myself from any association with my family deities, in the name of Jesus Christ.
32) I command every family deity in my life to burn down to ashes by the fire of the Holy Ghost, in the name of Jesus Christ.
33) O Lord, let me become a miracle and a testimony for all in your kingdom, in the name of Jesus Christ.
34) From today, my life shall experience divine blessings and promotion, in the name of Jesus Christ.
35) From today, my destiny shall only increase and not decrease as in the past, in the name of Jesus Christ.
36) I release myself from the curse of the law of death, in the name of Jesus Christ.
37) Holy Spirit, uproot me from the bondage and from the root of satanic stagnation and put me on the platform of wealth and prosperity, in the name of Jesus Christ.
38) I release myself from the bondage of evil altars, in the name of Jesus Christ.
39) I have overcome the powers of marine altars by the power of Jesus Christ, in the name of Jesus Christ.
40) I cancel the curse of chronic sickness from my life and family, in the mighty name of Jesus Christ.

41) I rebuke every witchcraft power manipulating my destiny to failure, in the mighty name of Jesus Christ.
42) Almighty God, arise and deliver me from evil powers and their oppression, in the name of Jesus Christ.
43) I declare that every curse of strife in my family will not prosper, in the name of Jesus Christ.
44) I command the chain and curse of disunity in my family to break and shatter to pieces, in the name of Jesus Christ.
45) I command every reproductive organ taken from my body and placed in occult banks to return to me now, in the name of Jesus Christ.
46) Lord Jesus, remove and return to me all personal items belonging to me that are placed in satanic banks and storage, in the name of Jesus Christ.
47) Lord Jesus, remove and return to me all personal items belonging to me that are placed in witches' covens, in the name of Jesus Christ.
48) Lord Jesus, remove and return to me all personal items belonging to me that are placed in witch doctors' shrines, in the name of Jesus Christ.
49) Lord Jesus, remove and return to me all personal items belonging to me that are buried in the earth, in the seas, hung in the heavens, buried in the forest, placed in occult temples, or placed before deities, in the name of Jesus Christ.
50) Lord Jesus, arise and release me from every padlock used in locking and casting away my destiny to the sea, the forest, witches' covens, deities, marine temples, or shrines, in the mighty name of Jesus Christ.
51) Lord Jesus, thank you for healing and delivering me today from evil covenants, in Jesus's mighty name. Amen.

17

Reversing Evil Covenants in Your Destiny

Part 2

SCRIPTURAL REFERENCES

Psalm 51:1–19

PRAYER POINTS

1) Start with praise and worship.
2) Every satanic curse that attacked my parents that is now attacking me, be removed from my life forever, in the name of Jesus Christ.
3) I am set free from the law of sin and death through Christ Jesus.
4) Every curse of infirmity attacking my body, be dried up by fire, in the name of Jesus Christ.
5) Almighty God, destroy the hands of witch doctors working against me, in the name of Jesus Christ.
6) O Lord Jesus, send your fire to destroy every witchcraft gathering against my life, in the name of Jesus Christ.
7) O Lord Jesus, let your thunder fire strike and destroy every witchcraft altar calling my name for evil, in the name of Jesus Christ.

8) In the name of Jesus Christ, let every family witchcraft practice in my life die by fire.
9) In the name of Jesus, all demonic agents attached to my destiny must surrender and be cut off forever.
10) In the name of Jesus Christ, I will not die but live to declare God's glory in my life.
11) Every astral projection against me and my family, be arrested by fire, in the name of Jesus Christ.
12) Every satanic power calling my name in the second heaven, be silenced forever in the name of Jesus Christ.
13) Every astral altar chanting incantations against me, be brought down by thunder and by fire, in the name of Jesus Christ.
14) I reject any transfer of evil spirits into my life by ancestors, parents, family, or friends, in the name of Jesus Christ.
15) Every stubborn curse that has refused to let me go, hear the word of the Lord: shatter, shatter, shatter, in the name of Jesus Christ.
16) I plead for the blood of Jesus over me to scatter every spirit that has refused to let me go, in the name of Jesus Christ.
17) Every witchcraft spirit attempting to build a wall or prison against my destiny, fall down and die, in the name of Jesus Christ.
18) Almighty God, destroy every spiritual parasite in my body, in the name of Jesus Christ.
19) O Lord, send your axe of fire to my foundation and uproot every evil implantation attacking my destiny and success.
20) Let the resurrection power of Jesus Christ uproot and destroy every stubborn problem in my life today, in the mighty name of Jesus Christ.
21) Lord Jesus, break every generational connection to any satanic covenant in my family, in the mighty name of Jesus Christ.
22) Every curse that is now affecting me because of an evil contract with my career, I command you to catch fire, in the name of Jesus Christ.
23) Every curse placed upon me in my career's path, to become famous against my salvation, I declare you null and void, in the name of Jesus Christ.

24) I terminate every association with satanic covenants in my career's path today, in the name of Jesus Christ.
25) I cover myself and my family with the blood of Jesus, and I declare that no weapon formed against me shall prosper, in the mighty name of Jesus Christ.
26) I break by the sword of fire every curse of corruption placed upon my head through bad business deals, in the name of Jesus Christ.
27) I reverse every generational curse in my family by the blood of Jesus Christ, in the name of our Lord and Savior, Jesus Christ.
28) Every evil poison I might have swallowed in my past that is now affecting my life, be neutralized by the blood of Jesus Christ.
29) Every effect of satanic food and sacrifices affecting me now from my past, I cancel you forever in the name of Jesus Christ.
30) I nullify every curse in my life arising from placental dedication to a deity, cult, or witchcraft, in the name of Jesus Christ.
31) Almighty God, from this day forward, there shall be no more sickness and disease affecting me and my family as a result of evil curses, in the name of Jesus Christ.
32) I vomit every satanic poison I have swallowed and I declare that they will not have any effect on me, in the name of Jesus Christ.
33) I break all evil authority over my life, in the name of Jesus Christ.
34) I release myself from the bondage of evil altars forever and ever, in the name of Jesus Christ.
35) From today, I am released and freed from all curses that affected my life, in the name of Jesus Christ.
36) From today, my family is released and freed from all curses that affected us, in the name of Jesus Christ. Amen.

18

Destroy Territorial Powers and Claim Back Your Blessings

JUST LIKE YOU may have a satellite transmission station in your neighborhood or a satellite dish over your roof to bring signals to your television to see what is happening around you and around the world, so does the devil have tracking tools to monitor your movements and progress wherever you are in the world. The aim is to manipulate and deter your blessings, to stop your progress and render you fruitless, useless, and unproductive.

Also, just as we are vessels of Christ, your neighbors, friends, family members, or even coworkers could be satanic vessels used by the devil to cast afflictions, curses, and spells on you. These witch doctors, cultists, satanic prophets, sorcerers, diviners, psychics, and common household agents may use satellites, crystals, mirrors, circles, mediums, animals, birds, plants, and different portals to monitor and track your progress all day long.

God has given us power and authority to overcome them all through effective and fervent prayers. Since the devil does not understand terms like *love, goodness, kindness, blessings, peaceful negotiation*, and *harmony*, you cannot afford to pray modestly when battling your enemy for freedom. Most times, the enemy will not give up and will bewitch your family beyond your lifetime. You must take your God-given authority and destroy their networks and their wicked powers against you and your family. Victory is assured when your enemy is taken out or defeated, in this case by aggressive, fiery prayers.

SCRIPTURAL REFERENCES

1 Chronicle 4:9–10 *Now Jabez was more honorable than his brothers, and his mother called his name Jabez, saying, "Because I bore him in pain." And Jabez called on the God of Israel saying, "Oh, that you would bless me indeed, and enlarge my territory, that your hand would be with me, and that you would keep me from evil, that I may not cause pain!" So God granted him what he requested.*

2 Samuel 6:11 *The ark of the L*ORD *remained in the house of Obed-Edom the Gittite three months. And the L*ORD *blessed Obed-Edom and all his household. Now it was told King David, saying, "The L*ORD *has blessed the house of Obed-Edom and all that belongs to him, because of the ark of God." So David went and brought up the ark of God from the house of Obed-Edom to the City of David with gladness. And so it was, when those bearing the ark of the L*ORD *had gone six paces, that he sacrificed oxen and fatted sheep. Then David danced before the L*ORD *with all his might; and David was wearing a linen ephod. So David and all the house of Israel brought up the ark of the L*ORD *with shouting and with the sound of the trumpet.*

1 Chronicles 13:14 *The ark of God remained with the family of Obed-Edom in his house three months. And the L*ORD *blessed the house of Obed-Edom and all that he had.*

Mark 3:27 *No one can enter a strongman's house and plunder his goods, unless he first binds the strongman. And then he will plunder his house.*

Matthew 12:28–30 *But if I cast out demons by the Spirit of God, surely the kingdom of God has come upon you. Or how can one enter a strongman's house and plunder his goods, unless he first binds the strongman? And then he will plunder his house. He who is not with Me is against Me, and he who does not gather with Me scatters abroad.*

PRAYER POINTS

1) Lord, thank you for this hour of prayer, and I declare that victory is already mine, in Jesus's mighty name.
2) Forgive me of my sins and cleanse me with the precious blood of Jesus Christ, in the name of Jesus.
3) Forgive us of the sins we have committed—my house, my family, and my neighborhood—in the name of Jesus Christ.
4) Forgive me for knowingly and unknowingly involving myself in sinful acts in my neighborhood, in the name of Jesus Christ.
5) Almighty God, enlarge my territory in this city today, in the mighty name of Jesus Christ.
6) O Lord Jesus, bless me indeed in this city today, in the mighty name of Jesus Christ.
7) O Lord Jesus, let your hand bring blessings upon me today in this city, in the mighty name of Jesus Christ.
8) O Lord Jesus, from this day forward, keep me from all evils in this city, in the mighty name of Jesus Christ.
9) Almighty God, do not allow me to cause pain to another from today, in the mighty name of Jesus Christ.
10) Almighty God, destroy every witchcraft altar erected against me in my neighborhood, in the name of Jesus Christ.
11) Almighty God, send down your fire and consume every satanic altar built in my neighborhood against my family, in the name of Jesus Christ.
12) Almighty God, let your lightning fire strike and destroy every false god that is tormenting my household and my neighborhood, in Jesus's name.
13) Fire of God, burn down all evil hands projecting destruction into my home and my neighborhood, in the name of Jesus Christ
14) Almighty God, set your fire on the citadel of poverty erected against my family and in my neighborhood, in the name of Jesus Christ.

15) O Lord, arise and destroy by your fire every satanic prophet casting spells and curses on my family and in my neighborhood, in the name of Jesus Christ.
16) Let every evil mansion built upon my house and occupied by satanic prophets catch fire, in the name of Jesus Christ.
17) O Lord, arise and let all my Herods receive spiritual decay, in the name of Jesus Christ.
18) O Lord, arise and let all my Goliaths receive spiritual meltdown, in the name of Jesus Christ.
19) O Lord, arise and let my Red Seas divide after the order of Moses.
20) O Lord, arise and destroy the principalities of my neighborhood contending against my destiny, in the name of Jesus Christ.
21) Almighty God, release your arrows against the powers that have refused to let me go and be at peace, in the name of Jesus Christ.
22) You, power of addiction holding my family captive, become ashes today, in the name of Jesus Christ.
23) [Name of city] stronghold, hear the word of the Lord. Release my blessings now, in the name of Jesus Christ.
24) [Name of city] stronghold retaining my blessings, it is written: you are beneath me. I command you to die by fire, in the name of Jesus Christ.
25) [Name of city] stronghold oppressing me and my children, we are ambassadors for Christ. We are immunized by heaven against all your afflictions. Set us free now, in the name of Jesus Christ.
26) [Name of city] stronghold afflicting my health, release me now or be consumed by fire, in the name of Jesus Christ.
27) [Name of city] stronghold controlling my destiny, break into pieces, in the name of Jesus Christ.
28) [Name of city] stronghold calling my name out for evil, begin to fight against yourself now, in the name of Jesus Christ.

29) [Name of city] stronghold stealing my blessings, I command you to return my blessings a millionfold, in the name of Jesus Christ.
30) You, evil powers of [city] throwing parties for my downfall, be cast into the abyss forever, in the name of Jesus Christ.
31) You, evil powers of [city] binding me and my family in bondage, loose your hold now. Loose your hold on me and my family, in the name of Jesus Christ.
32) You, evil powers of [city] displacing me from my home, [city] is my inheritance. I command you to leave town now, in the name of Jesus Christ.
33) Every witchcraft power forcing me to foreclose on my home, be evicted from my neighborhood now by fire, in the name of Jesus Christ.
34) Every poverty-projecting spirit in my neighborhood forcing me to foreclose on my home, I displace you into the abyss today, in the name of Jesus Christ.
35) You, household wickedness fighting against my breakthrough, what are you waiting for? Die in the name of Jesus Christ.
36) You, evil power that wants me dead, who gave you such authority over me? Die in the name of Jesus Christ.
37) O Lord, uproot every monitoring device used against my life in my house and neighborhood, and cast them into the abyss, in the name of Jesus Christ.
38) I challenge by fire every prophet of Baal standing against my life, in the name of Jesus Christ.
39) Every satanic agent representing me and my family in this city, I command you to die, in the name of Jesus Christ.
40) Holy Spirit, arise and fight for me now, fight for me now, in the mighty name of Jesus Christ.
41) I declare that I shall prosper above all my enemies in this neighborhood, in the name of Jesus Christ.
42) I declare that I shall live in peace and harmony in this neighborhood, in the name of Jesus Christ.

43) O Lord, let every human agent used by the devil to project evil against me repent and receive your salvation, in the name of Jesus Christ.
44) O Lord, arise and reveal yourself to all my household strongmen and strongwomen acting as satanic agents against me, in the name of Jesus Christ.
45) O Lord, shatter and destroy every monitoring satellite, crystal, or mirror used against me and my family, in the name of Jesus Christ.
46) O Lord, arise and destroy every satanic animal or bird used to bewitch me and my family, in the name of Jesus Christ.
47) Lord Jesus, let every evil bird flying for my sake fall down and die, in the name of Jesus Christ.
48) Lord Jesus, let every serpent and scorpion used against my life turn against their senders, in the mighty name of Jesus Christ.
49) I receive my full blessings from heaven today, in the name of Jesus Christ.
50) I claim my maximum benefits from heaven today, in the name of Jesus Christ.
51) Father, pursue, overtake, and recover all my blessings from the enemy for me, in the name of Jesus Christ.
52) I declare that my business shall continue to prosper after the order of Isaac, in the name of Jesus Christ.
53) I claim divine blessings for all my children today, in the name of Jesus Christ.
54) Holy Spirit, lift me up by your lifting power and launch me into your accelerated promotion, in the name of Jesus Christ.
55) Lord Jesus, drain all evil powers from my enemies and render them powerless and useless, in the name of Jesus Christ.
56) Lord Jesus, uproot every satanic gate erected against me in my neighborhood and cast them into the abyss, in the name of Jesus Christ.
57) Lord Jesus, release multiple streams of income into my home, in the name of Jesus Christ.

58) Lord Jesus, pursue my enemies out of this neighborhood forever, in the name of Jesus Christ.
59) When you bless a man, no man can curse him, Lord Jesus, as my enemies curse me. I declare that you bless me more and more, in the name of Jesus Christ.
60) Almighty God, arise and smash into pieces every satanic satellite network pitched against me in my neighborhood, in the mighty name of Jesus Christ.
61) I command all satanic pictures, graffiti, images, cast images, symbols, signboards, and molten images positioned in my neighborhood as instruments of spells, curses, and torture against God's people to melt by fire and be carried away forever, in the mighty name of Jesus Christ.
62) I declare that the peace of God shall take over my neighborhood, in the mighty name of Jesus Christ.
63) I declare that the mercy of God shall take over my neighborhood, in the mighty name of Jesus Christ.
64) I declare that the glory of God shall take over my neighborhood, in the mighty name of Jesus Christ.
65) I declare that the blessings of the Lord shall take over my neighborhood, in the mighty name of Jesus Christ.
66) I declare that my neighborhood shall not become a slum, in the mighty name of Jesus Christ.
67) I declare that all strongmen and strongwomen in my neighborhood be moved out or face instant and eternal divine judgment.
68) I declare that every young man in my neighborhood must prosper and live to fulfill his destiny according to God's purpose for his life.
69) I declare that every young woman in my neighborhood must prosper and live to fulfill her destiny according to God's purpose for her life.
70) I declare that every power that says we shall not live to the full length of our days must die by fire, in the name of Jesus Christ.

71) I declare that every power that says we shall not succeed and prosper in my neighborhood must die by fire, in the name of Jesus Christ.
72) I command every wicked power cutting short destinies in my neighborhood to die by fire and by thunder, in the mighty name of Jesus Christ.
73) Thank you, Holy Spirit, for winning this battle for me today, in the name of Jesus Christ.

19

This Is My Time to Shine

OUR FATHER IN heaven has given us freedom to choose and embrace light (righteousness, salvation, and eternal life) or embrace darkness (sin, judgment, and death). We as Christians are children of light and should reflect the light of God. Once you are in Christ Jesus, righteousness, salvation, and eternal life with God are automatically yours. Christ rose from death and ruled over us with His precious, marvelous light, and called us out of darkness into His light. You are to arise and shine forth and glow with the glory of God. The world has to see you differently and want what you have. Let your light so shine before your family, your friends, your co-workers, and all who come to you. Shine forth and be happy and good to all. You are a chosen generation, a royal priesthood, a holy nation, a peculiar people called out of darkness into that marvelous, precious light in Christ Jesus. You are chosen, set apart, and given the power and authority to declare and receive as a prince or princess, as a priest, the blessings of God because of His abounding mercy and grace.

The following prayer points will bring restoration to you, remove fear, remove discouragement, empower you, and give you confidence to take authority and receive blessing into every area of your life. Amen.

SCRIPTURAL REFERENCES

1 Peter 2:9–10 But you are a chosen generation, a royal priesthood, a holy nation, His own special people, that you may proclaim the praises of Him who called you out of darkness into His marvelous light; who once were not a people but are now the people of God, who had not obtained mercy but now have obtained mercy.

Matthew 5:14–18 *"You are the light of the world. A city that is set on a hill cannot be hidden. Nor do they light a lamp and put it under a basket, but on a lamp stand, and it gives light to all who are in the house. Let your light so shine before men, that they may see your good works and glorify your Father in heaven.*

Isaiah 60:1–5 *Arise, shine; For your light has come! And the glory of the LORD is risen upon you. For behold, the darkness shall cover the earth, And deep darkness the people; But the LORD will arise over you, And His glory will be seen upon you. The Gentiles shall come to your light, And kings to the brightness of your rising. Lift up your eyes all around, and see: They all gather together, they come to you; your sons shall come from afar, And your daughters shall be nursed at your side. Then you shall see and become radiant, And your heart shall swell with joy; Because the abundance of the sea shall be turned to you, The wealth of the Gentiles shall come to you.*

Isaiah 60:19–22 *The sun shall no longer be your light by day, Nor for brightness shall the moon give light to you; But the LORD will be to you an everlasting light, And your God your glory. Your sun shall no longer go down, Nor shall your moon withdraw itself; For the LORD will be your everlasting light, And the days of your mourning shall be ended. Also your people shall all be righteous; They shall inherit the land forever, The branch of My planting, The work of My hands, That I may be glorified. A little one shall become a thousand, And a small one a strong nation. I, the LORD, will hasten it in its time.*

PRAYER POINTS

1) Lord Jesus, thank You for the gospel, and thank you for what you did on the cross for me.
2) Forgive me of my sins and cleanse me by Your precious blood
3) I declare that You are the Christ and I receive You into my life today.
4) Lord Jesus, I declare that this is the day that you have made, and I shall rejoice and be glad in it.

5) I declare that You are my light and my salvation, and I shall not fear.
6) I declare that, though war may rise against me, I shall be confident of your protection.
7) I receive your light and glory today upon my life and family, in Jesus's name.
8) Lord, arise and let Your light shine upon me and let Your glory be risen upon me, in Jesus's mighty name.
9) Let men and women run to me because of your glorious radiance around me and receive your salvation unto eternity.
10) Lord, use me and let me be Your light to this generation.
11) I declare that that sun shall not smite me this day and the moon shall not smite me this night.
12) I declare that I shall be a light to the blind, and I shall lead many to Christ.
13) I declare that I am blessed beyond human comprehension, and all nations shall be blessed through me.
14) I declare that I shall continue to be illuminated in God's radiance and glory because of Christ Jesus in my life.
15) I declare that no evil power shall stand against me all the days of my life, in the mighty name of Jesus Christ.
16) I declare that I shall be filled with God's wisdom and become a mentor to many in the kingdom of God.
17) I declare that my life shall become an encouragement and a celebration to those who are discouraged, in the mighty name of Jesus Christ.
18) I challenge the spirit of discouragement to come out of my life now, in the mighty name of Jesus Christ.
19) Holy Spirit, make me a blessing to someone always, in the mighty name of Jesus Christ.
20) Lord, show me your glory and let your kingdom come into my life, in Jesus's mighty name.
21) Holy Spirit, give me my portion today, in the mighty name of Jesus Christ.

22) Holy Spirit, touch me with your anointing today, in the mighty name of Jesus Christ.
23) Holy Spirit, fill me with your power to excel in praise and worship of the Almighty, in the mighty name of Jesus Christ.
24) Lord Jesus, let me shine under the shadows of your wings forever.
25) Lord Jesus, show me a token for good and let all who hate me be ashamed.
26) Lord Jesus, smile upon me today and put a big smile upon my face for you.
27) Lord Jesus, open the windows of heaven and let your blessings pour upon me.
28) Lord Jesus, restore to me the blessings that were stolen from me from the time I was born, in the mighty name of Jesus Christ.
29) Lord Jesus, restore my beauty to what it was with you before creation, in the mighty name of Jesus Christ.
30) Holy Spirit, anoint my head with your oil and make my cup run over, in the mighty name of Jesus Christ.
31) Lord, I declare that your goodness and mercy shall follow and overtake me all the days of my life.
32) Holy Spirit, cancel all my appointments with poverty and death from my schedules, in the mighty name of Jesus Christ.
33) Holy Spirit, schedule my appointments with victory, promotion, increase, financial prosperity, and wealth, and position me to keep these appointments with them unfailingly, in the mighty name of Jesus Christ.
34) Blood of Jesus, erase my name from any family bondage contending against my freedom, in the name of Jesus Christ.
35) Almighty God, nullify my connection to any generational curse in my family by the blood of Jesus Christ, in the mighty name of Jesus Christ.
36) Almighty God, by your right hand seal every hole in my life leaking away my blessings, in the mighty name of Jesus Christ.

37) Lord Jesus, by your right hand remove every evil pocket in my life emptying my blessings into satanic storage, in the mighty name of Jesus Christ.
38) Lord Jesus, sow back into my life every pocket carrying my blessings outside of my life, in the name of Jesus.
39) O Lord Jesus, cover the roof of my life with your glory so I may continue to shine forth forever, in the mighty name of Jesus Christ.
40) Lord Jesus, do not let the rain of agony and frustration leak upon me through the roof of my life, in the name of Jesus Christ.
41) Lord Jesus, channel both earthly and heavenly blessings into my life and help me build the kingdom of God on earth, in the name of Jesus Christ.
42) Witchcraft portals directing my blessings away in my neighborhood, be sealed by the blood of Jesus Christ.
43) Every satanic portal transporting money away from my house into any satanic bank, catch fire, in the name of Jesus Christ.
44) Almighty God, arise and shut every spiritual portal devouring my blessings, in the name of Jesus Christ.
45) O God, arise and plunder all who plunder my life, in the name of Jesus Christ.
46) You, satanic neighbors chanting incantations against my destiny, I command you to be evicted as my neighbor by fire, in the name of Jesus Christ.
47) In the name of Jesus Christ, I declare that I shall possess my blessings and possessions, and no weapon formed against me shall prosper.
48) In the name of Jesus Christ, I declare that I shall possess my thousands and millions, and no devouring spirit shall devour me again.
49) In the name of Jesus Christ, I declare that I am the possessor of heaven and earth after the order of Abraham.
50) In the name of Jesus Christ, I declare that I shall dwell and prosper in this city in peace.

51) In the name of Jesus Christ, I declare that I shall flourish in abundant provision, give to the poor, and build the house of God.
52) In the name of Jesus Christ, I declare that I shall give in excess to the house of God.
53) In the name of Jesus Christ, I declare that I shall have all godly friends.
54) In the name of Jesus Christ, I declare that my life shall become a blessing to others.
55) In the name of Jesus Christ, I declare that I shall live a sickness- and disease-free life, and prosper in health.
56) In the name of Jesus Christ, I declare that no evil eye shall monitor me and my family.
57) Almighty God, do not reveal my premature testimonies to my enemies, and if they know of them, arise and destroy the powers fighting to stop my testimonies from coming to pass, in the name of Jesus Christ.
58) Almighty God, blind the eyes of the enemy from monitoring my destiny and cover my destiny with the precious blood of Jesus Christ, in the name of Jesus Christ.
59) O Lord Jesus, remove and destroy evil powers keeping inventory of your blessings in my life, in the name of Jesus Christ.
60) In the name of Jesus Christ, I declare that I shall live an accident-free life.
61) In the name of Jesus Christ, I declare that my human enemies shall become born again and love me with God's agape love.
62) In the name of Jesus Christ, I declare that every dry area in my life shall be saturated by God's divine moisturizer forever.
63) In the name of Jesus Christ, I declare that I shall not live in bondage but shall live in God's glorious freedom.
64) In the name of Jesus Christ, I declare that I shall not die but live to declare the good works of the Lord in my life.
65) In the name of Jesus Christ, I declare that I shall be above only and not beneath.

66) In the name of Jesus Christ, I declare that my children shall be a blessing to me and others.
67) In the name of Jesus Christ, I declare that I shall be a blessing to my children and others.
68) In the name of Jesus Christ, I declare that I shall have a safe and secure marriage.
69) In the name of Jesus Christ, I declare that I shall live in victory and not in fear.
70) Holy Spirit, terminate any appointment with fear in my life, in the mighty name of Jesus Christ.
71) In the name of Jesus Christ, I declare that my name shall be written in the Lamb's book of life.
72) Almighty God, remember the good works of my hands and bless me, in the mighty name of Jesus Christ.
73) I declare that I shall increase while my enemies decrease, in the mighty name of Jesus Christ.
74) Lord Jesus, extend your staff of authority over me and empower me to subdue my enemies to the dust, in the mighty name of Jesus Christ.
75) Almighty God, give me power to trample worldly oppression and affliction against my life, in the mighty name of Jesus Christ.
76) Almighty God, take away the cup of pain and suffering from my life, in the mighty name of Jesus Christ.
77) Almighty God, do not consider my afflictions small before you, but be my undertaker, in the mighty name of Jesus Christ.
78) I declare that I shall dwell in peace and freedom in this city.
79) I declare that every household wickedness contending against my breakthrough in life must die by fire, in the mighty name of Jesus Christ.
80) I declare that the glory of the Lord shall rest upon me as in the days of Solomon the king.
81) Holy Spirit, shut every door against contentions and agitations in my life, in the mighty name of Jesus Christ.
82) I receive spiritual revival in my life today from you, Lord, in the mighty name of Jesus Christ.

83) I receive power today from you, Lord, to overcome my weaknesses, in the mighty name of Jesus Christ.
84) Today my victories are guaranteed by you, Lord, in the mighty name of Jesus Christ.
85) In the name of Jesus Christ, I declare that my God shall supply all my needs according to His riches in glory by Christ Jesus. Amen, amen, amen.

20

Victory over Satanic Conflict in Your Home

IT IS IMPORTANT for God's children to dwell together in peace and harmony. The enemy always wants to bring conflict and disunity to Christian homes in order to destabilize them. To overcome this, couples must walk and work together and agree to maintain stability in all areas of their lives to reduce or avoid conflict. It is common for the enemy to use unfriendly friends to gossip about your family members or judge or conspire against a spouse at the detriment or expense of the other spouse, so as to separate or break them up. This is why it is important for spouses to be transparent and not keep secrets from each other.

You will be asked not to tell your husband or your wife the secret that has just been exposed to you. You will be forced to cross your fingers or swear to maintain the secrecy of information that is already a lie, just so it can be used against your spouse and destroy your home. As Christians, we must take our problems to God and not man. We must avoid gossip, slander, conspiracy, lies, and the fabrication of untruthful stories against others. The story you hear may sound true, but is it really true? Your husband or your wife may have been accused of adultery, but is it really true? If it is true that adultery has been committed, have you taken time to ask God to remove the spirit of adultery from him/her and restore your spouse to you before deciding to pack out of the house or throw him/her out of the house?

Couples must learn to forgive each other, agree with each other, share with each other, sacrifice for each other, and enjoy each other. If you are married or going to be married, your goal should be to carry the burden of that relationship by prayer to God and call down blessings, peace, and unity upon it. It is advisable to speak to your pastor and have him counsel your family as your spiritual father in Christ, should any situation arise out of your control. If children are involved, make sure you both speak one voice while disciplining them. Do not have split opinions on how your child or children should be disciplined and to what measure in front of that child or children. Wait until you are both alone.

Learning how to manage your finances and letting your spouse get involved in the process is necessary to avoid financial conflict, overspending, or stinginess. You may be a conserver and your spouse may be a spender. You must look for that threshold that will create a balance in your relationship. To do this, you must learn to understand each other, walk together, work together, be in the house of God as a family, and most especially, pray together. God will bless your marriage and your home and drive away conflict as you take your matters to Him and Him alone, in Jesus's mighty name. Amen.

SCRIPTURAL REFERENCES

Amos 3:3 *You only have I known of all the families of the earth; Therefore I will punish you for all your iniquities. Can two walk together, unless they are agreed?*

Isaiah 59:19 *So shall they fear The name of the Lord from the west, And His glory from the rising of the sun; When the enemy comes in like a flood, The Spirit of the Lord will lift up a standard against him.*

Ephesians 4:26 *Be angry, and do not sin: do not let the sun go down on your wrath.*

Psalm 103:8 *The Lord is merciful and gracious, Slow to anger, and abounding in mercy. He will not always strive with us, Nor will He keep His anger forever. He has not dealt with us according to our sins, Nor punished us according to our iniquities. For as the heavens are high above the earth, So great is His mercy toward those who fear Him; As* *far as the east is from the west, So far has He removed our transgressions from us. As a father pities his children, So the* Lord *pities those who fear Him. For He knows our frame; He remembers that we are dust.*

PRAYER POINTS

1) This is the time to sing praise and worship to the Lord.
2) Begin to thank God for His grace and mercy toward you and your family.
3) Begin to confess your sins to God and ask Him for forgiveness.
4) Lord Jesus, forgive me and my family of every conflict in the past, in the name of Jesus Christ.
5) Lord Jesus, forgive us of our inability to live in peace in our home without conflict, in the name of Jesus Christ.
6) Lord Jesus, forgive us of the spirit of unforgiveness in our home, in the name of Jesus Christ.
7) Almighty God, let your peace and joy reign in my home from today, in the name of Jesus Christ.
8) Lord Jesus, send your peace and freedom to my life and marriage today, in the name of Jesus Christ.
9) I destroy every architect of conflict in my life and in my home, in the name of Jesus Christ.
10) I paralyze and destroy every agent of conflict in my family, in the name of Jesus Christ.
11) Every satanic conflict working against my marriage, be destroyed, in the name of Jesus Christ.
12) All territorial powers working against my happiness, be destroyed, in the name of Jesus Christ.
13) Every satanic altar erected against my happiness, be uprooted by fire, in the name of Jesus Christ.
14) Every satanic altar erected against my marriage, be uprooted by fire, in the name of Jesus Christ.
15) Every satanic strongman chanting incantations against my home, against my family, be consumed by fire, in the name of Jesus Christ.

16) Every bit of marine witchcraft contending against my marriage, be consumed to ashes, in the name of Jesus Christ.
17) Every conflict instigator assigned to instigate problems and conflict in my home, return to your senders and begin to plunder them, in the name of Jesus Christ.
18) Every curse of marital trouble affecting my marriage, be destroyed, in the name of Jesus Christ.
19) I command every spirit of rebellion and strife put upon my home by evil powers of my father's house to die by fire, in the name of Jesus Christ.
20) I plead for the blood of Jesus Christ to flush my home and purify it forever, in the name of Jesus Christ.
21) I command all activities of strange men or women fueling problems in my home to die by fire, in the name of Jesus Christ.
22) I command all enemies of peace in my home to be paralyzed and flushed out forever, in the name of Jesus Christ.
23) I bind the spirit of jealousy and hatred in my home and cast it into fire, in the name of Jesus Christ.
24) I bind the spirit of conflict among my children and cast it into the abyss, in the name of Jesus Christ.
25) I silence every tongue casting spells on my home, in the name of Jesus Christ.
26) I return every satanic storm blowing into my home to its sender, in the name of Jesus Christ.
27) Holy Spirit, shine your light upon my family and magnify us in your glory, in the name of Jesus Christ.
28) I cover my family with the blood of Jesus Christ, in the name of Jesus Christ.
29) Almighty God, heal all marital wounds in my home and give us your peace, in the name of Jesus Christ.
30) Almighty God, sanitize my spouse and myself with the blood of Jesus Christ, in the name of Jesus Christ.
31) Almighty God, sanitize my children with the blood of Jesus Christ, in the mighty name of Jesus Christ.

32) Almighty God, cancel every problem arising in my home because of my in-laws, in the name of Jesus Christ.
33) Lord Jesus, send every affliction in my life and home due to demonic in-laws back to its sender, in the name of Jesus Christ.
34) Lord Jesus, remove every affliction from my home arising from my previous marriage, in the name of Jesus Christ.
35) I terminate every evil link to my former marriage that is causing affliction in my home, in the name of Jesus Christ.
36) I destroy every Goliath of marriage contending against the peace of God in my home, in the name of Jesus Christ.
37) I nullify every known and unknown blood covenant affecting my marriage today by the blood of Jesus Christ, in the name of Jesus Christ.
38) I terminate and cancel every known and unknown association with marine witchcraft by the blood of Jesus Christ, in the name of Jesus Christ.
39) From today, I divorce every spirit husband by the fire of the Holy Ghost and nullify every spiritual covenant that existed between us forever by the blood of Jesus Christ, in the name of Jesus Christ.
40) From today, I divorce every spirit wife by the fire of the Holy Ghost and nullify every spiritual covenant that existed between us forever by the blood of Jesus Christ, in the name of Jesus Christ.
41) I remove from my finger every spiritual wedding ring and return it to the owner, in the name of Jesus Christ.
42) I remove any spiritual wedding gown or tuxedo in my possession and return it to the owner, in the name of Jesus Christ.
43) I declare that I am free to marry my earthly and God-given husband without any intervention or opposition by a spirit husband, in Jesus's name.
44) I declare that I am free to marry my earthly and God-given wife without any intervention or opposition by a spirit wife, in Jesus's name.

45) I declare that I shall have a divorce-free marriage and I shall live in peace with my spouse for all my days on earth, in the name of Jesus Christ.
46) Thank you, Lord, for answering my prayers, in the name of Jesus Christ.

21

Power to Change Spiritual Lanes in Your Life

Part 1

LIFE ITSELF IS a path that everyone must walk carefully in order to successfully make it to the end. Your destiny has its place in this path, and many people by wrong association have been displaced from their positions in the path of life. As a result, they fall short in reaching great destinies and end up in great failures.

Many destinies have been shattered by our choices, lifestyles, degrees of passion, and willingness to succeed while going along this path. Many who are willing sometimes do not have the necessary support to sail through the storms of life, which could be moral, ethical, financial, physical, spiritual, emotional, psychological, or environmental. These are obstacles in life's spiritual lanes that hinder God's children from entering their destinies except by prayer and God's intervention. Some have been able to overcome these storms or obstacles through proper parental support and guidance, association with a church, societal support, and resource availability. On the other hand, many have encountered failures in reaching their destinies due to lack of exposure to these available resources.

On the spiritual side, the evil powers of your father's house or generational curses are serious obstacles to reaching your destiny. These are known to place massive limitations on our paths and hinder every effort that would lead to successful accomplishments in life. In addition, involvement with the occult, witchcraft, worship of deities, sin, rebellion, and disobedience against God will further complicate a smooth transition to a successful destiny in the path of life. We need God's intervention and deliverance to overcome these hurdles in our spiritual lanes so we can successfully enter our destinies. The following prayer points will help you get back in position, if or when you are displaced from the path of life.

SCRIPTURAL REFERENCES

John 14:6 Jesus said to him, "I am the way, the truth, and the life. No one comes to the Father except through Me."
Zech. 2:5 Jerusalem shall be inhabited as towns without walls, because of the multitude of men and livestock in it. "For I," says the L<small>ORD</small>, *"will be a wall of fire all around her, and I will be the glory in her midst."*
*Also read **Isaiah 62:1–9.***

PRAYER POINTS

1) O Lord, I thank you for this prayer program, and I declare that I will be restored to the path of my destiny today, in the mighty name of Jesus Christ.
2) O Lord, forgive me for displacing myself from your will for my life, in the name of Jesus Christ.
3) Lord, forgive my sins, the sins of my father's house, the sins of my city, the sins of my country, and the sins of this land, and flush them out with the blood of Jesus Christ.
4) I ask for your divine purpose and direction to manifest during this prayer program in my life, in the mighty name of Jesus Christ.
5) O Lord, let me travel in the path you have chosen for me, and lead me forward and not backward, in the mighty name of Jesus Christ.
6) Almighty God, send your angel to be my spiritual road map to success, in the mighty name of Jesus Christ.

7) I declare that I shall travel in the lane and speed you have chosen for me so I may arrive safely in your time for my life, in the mighty name of Jesus Christ.
8) My life, hear the word of the Lord. You shall not yield to any evil sign on the way to your destiny, in the mighty name of Jesus Christ.
9) Any satanic power directing me away from my divine destiny, be consumed by fire, in the mighty name of Jesus Christ.
10) Any family deity manipulating my life to change spiritual lanes so as to lead me to failure, I command you to die, in the mighty name of Jesus Christ.
11) Every ancestral curse forcing me out of God's will for my life, catch fire, in the mighty name of Jesus Christ.
12) Any enchantment or divination directed at my destiny to fail, backfire, backfire, in the mighty name of Jesus Christ.
13) I command all evil powers of my father's house fighting against my victory to die, in the mighty name of Jesus Christ.
14) All evil powers from my place of birth affecting my destiny, I command you to die, in the mighty name of Jesus Christ.
15) Holy Spirit, arise and terrorize all satanic agents mounting spiritual roadblocks against my prosperity, in the mighty name of Jesus Christ.
16) Holy Spirit, arise and seal every spiritual pit excavated to house my blessings, in the mighty name of Jesus Christ.
17) I command any satanic strongman assigned to cause confusion in my life to die by fire, die by fire, in the mighty name of Jesus Christ.
18) I declare that wealth and riches shall be in my house forever and ever, in the mighty name of Jesus Christ.
19) I decree that my life shall not rotate around setbacks, in the mighty name of Jesus Christ.
20) I decree that my life shall not rotate in circles, in the mighty name of Jesus Christ.
21) I decree that I shall not keep obstructing myself from one day to another, in the mighty name of Jesus Christ.

22) Almighty God, establish me and move my life from failure into a great testimony, in the mighty name of Jesus Christ.
23) Almighty God, establish me and move my life from failure into victory, in the mighty name of Jesus Christ.
24) Almighty God, remove me from every ungodly spiritual lane and place me in the path of righteousness for your name's sake, in the mighty name of Jesus Christ.
25) Almighty God, remove and cast out every unfriendly friend assigned to bring confusion and manipulation into my life and to misdirect me from my destiny, in the mighty name of Jesus Christ.
26) Almighty God, shut down every satanic highway constructed to bring destruction into my life, in the mighty name of Jesus Christ.
27) You, carriers of evil loads in my divine path, I evict you from my path by thunder and by fire, in the mighty name of Jesus Christ.
28) You, planters of evil trees in my divine path, I command you to uproot your trees and carry them with you, in the mighty name of Jesus Christ.
29) O Lord, flood my spiritual highway with supernatural wealth and blessings, in the mighty name of Jesus Christ.
30) O Lord, illuminate my path and let your glory be seen upon me and my family, in the mighty name of Jesus Christ.
31) I command the favor of God to pursue and overtake me all the days of my life, in the mighty name of Jesus Christ.
32) O Lord Jesus, do not let me go alone. Travel with me on the highway to my destiny, in the mighty name of Jesus Christ.
33) O Lord Jesus, position your angels to mount roadblocks against any satanic agent trespassing on my spiritual highway, in the mighty name of Jesus Christ.
34) I command every satanic rain pouring evil afflictions into my divine path to terminate now, in the mighty name of Jesus Christ.
35) O Lord Jesus, reveal all secret enemies travelling with me on my path to success and flush them out by your precious blood, in the mighty name of Jesus Christ.

36) I command all satanic messengers in my life to roast by fire, roast by fire, roast by fire, roast by fire, in the mighty name of Jesus Christ.
37) Every satanic restaurant in my dreams feeding me with satanic food to spiritually slumber, roast by fire, roast by fire, roast by fire, in the mighty name of Jesus Christ. [Repeat three times.]
38) Where is the Lord God of Elijah? Arise and consume all satanic money in my possession by your fire, in the mighty name of Jesus Christ.
39) Where is the Lord God of Elijah? Arise and consume every dream stealer in my life by fire, in the mighty name of Jesus Christ.
40) O God, arise and lead me in a smooth path, that I may tread peacefully to my destiny, in the mighty name of Jesus Christ.
41) Almighty God, arise and remove every obstacle that may force me out of your presence and divine destiny, in the mighty name of Jesus Christ.
42) Almighty God, arise and cause evil arrows shot into my divine destiny to backfire, in the mighty name of Jesus Christ.
43) Almighty God, arise and send your angels to repair and clean every damage done to my spiritual highway, in the mighty name of Jesus Christ.
44) Almighty God, arise and use the blood of Jesus Christ to purify my destiny, in the mighty name of Jesus Christ.
45) Almighty God, arise and set a watchman over my divine path, in the mighty name of Jesus Christ.
46) Lord Jesus, arise and destroy all evil construction workers assigned to work against my destiny.
47) Lord Jesus, blow up and break to pieces by your spiritual dynamite every evil bridge transporting confusion to my destiny, in the name of Jesus Christ.
48) Arise, O Lord, and set my destiny on your fire for good, in the name of Jesus Christ.
49) Let my life and destiny become a celebration to you, in the mighty name of Jesus Christ.

50) Let the blood of Jesus Christ clean up every satanic spillage in my destiny, in the mighty name of Jesus Christ.
51) I shall remain the head and not the tail, in the mighty name of Jesus Christ.
52) Lord, make me be the first in my family to fulfill your divine destiny if none has done so in the past.
53) Almighty God, correct all failures in my family and let them be fulfilled in me as victories.
54) I shall possess my possessions this day in the name of Jesus Christ.
55) I shall receive promotion in every opportunity for promotion in my life, in the mighty name of Jesus Christ.
56) I declare that every good thing my father or mother could not achieve, I shall achieve in the name of Jesus Christ.
57) I declare that my health shall not be a hindrance to my destiny, in the mighty name of Jesus Christ.
58) I declare that I shall be in good health and prosper all the days of my life, in the mighty name of Jesus Christ.
59) Lord, thank you for your loving kindness and tender mercy toward me and my family today, in the mighty name of Jesus Christ.
60) Thank you, Lord, for answering all my prayers, in Jesus's name. Amen.

22

Power to Change Spiritual Lanes in Your Life

Part 2

PRAYER POINTS

1) Start with praise and worship
2) O God, arise and order my footsteps to walk in the path you have chosen for me, in the mighty name of Jesus Christ.
3) My destiny shall not catch satanic fire, in the mighty name of Jesus Christ.
4) O Lord, let your trumpet of peace blow into my life forever, in the mighty name of Jesus Christ.
5) Every evil eye spying on my destiny, become blinded forever, in the mighty name of Jesus Christ.
6) Every evil camera planted on my spiritual lanes to monitor my progress in life, be shattered into pieces, in the mighty name of Jesus Christ.
7) Every satanic device monitoring my progress from my place of birth, be roasted by the fire of God, in the mighty name of Jesus Christ.
8) Every remote control used to program my life for failure, catch fire, catch fire, catch fire, in the mighty name of Jesus Christ.
9) O Lord Jesus, sanitize my destiny's lanes and footsteps with your precious blood, in the mighty name of Jesus Christ.

10) I clean my spiritual paths with the blood of Jesus Christ.
11) I order divine purification of my destiny with the blood of Jesus Christ.
12) My life, receive divine provision and abundant prosperity until the moon is no more, in the mighty name of Jesus Christ.
13) O God, arise and destroy every destiny destroyer in my family, in the mighty name of Jesus Christ.
14) O God, arise and consume by your fire every demonic vehicle carrying my blessings away to destruction, in the mighty name of Jesus Christ.
15) O God, arise and destroy every satanic driver transporting my blessings to satanic warehouses, in the mighty name of Jesus Christ.
16) O God, arise and cut off every evil tongue that has risen up against me in judgment, in the mighty name of Jesus Christ.
17) O God, arise and cut off every evil tongue that will rise up against me in judgment, in the mighty name of Jesus Christ.
18) Every satanic agent staying up at night to frustrate my destiny, I command you to sleep, sleep, and sleep and do not wake up, do not wake up, in the mighty name of Jesus Christ.
19) I command every crystal monitoring my life to shatter into pieces, in the mighty name of Jesus Christ.
20) Every satanic pot stirring and cooking my blessings, be shattered into pieces, in the mighty name of Jesus Christ.
21) I command every evil power from satanic altars monitoring my life to fall down and die, in the mighty name of Jesus Christ.
22) I bind all bewitchments of my destiny and blessings, past, present, and future, and cast them all into the abyss, in the mighty name of Jesus Christ.
23) I silence every tongue of affliction projecting satanic arrows into my life, and I shut them up forever and ever, in the mighty name of Jesus Christ.

24) I reverse and remove every satanic curse placed upon my life and destiny, past, present, and future, by the blood of Jesus Christ.
25) I reverse and erase by the blood of Jesus Christ every bit of satanic handwriting expressed in my DNA against my destiny, in the mighty name of Jesus Christ
26) I challenge my DNA by the fire of the Holy Ghost to decode every generational curse working against me in my family, in the mighty name of Jesus Christ.
27) I command every bit of ancestral handwriting of incest and sexual perversion in my DNA to melt by fire, in the mighty name of Jesus Christ.
28) I command the curse of poverty expressed in my DNA to melt by fire, melt by fire, melt by fire, in the mighty name of Jesus Christ.
29) I bind every satanic spirit transferring curses into my family from generation to generation and cast them into the everlasting pit, in the mighty name of Jesus Christ.
30) Holy Ghost fire, consume and destroy every point of connection responsible for generational curses in my life, in the mighty name of Jesus Christ.
31) Any spiritual bridge supporting the transport of generational curses into my life and destiny, be shattered into pieces, in the mighty name of Jesus Christ.
32) I command every satanic agent directing the traffic of generational curses in my life and family to die by fire, die by fire, die by fire, in the mighty name of Jesus Christ.
33) Every evil wind carrying generational curses into my life, dry up now and forever, in the mighty name of Jesus Christ.
34) Every evil water keeping generational curses in my life alive, dry up forever, in the mighty name of Jesus Christ.
35) O God, arise and expand the lanes of success and prosperity in my life, in the mighty name of Jesus Christ.
36) O God, position men to bless me wherever I find myself in my spiritual highway, in the name of Jesus Christ.

61) I uproot every satanic arrow shut into my position while in my mother's womb, in the name of Jesus Christ.
37) O God, arise and furnish the highway of my destiny with divine gold, in the mighty name of Jesus Christ.
38) I erase all evil marks on my forehead, turning my blessings away by the blood of Jesus Christ.
39) I roast every evil hand that has touched me in order to dry up my blessings, by fire, in the name of Jesus Christ.
40) You, destiny robbers in my family, be consumed by the fire of God, in the name of Jesus Christ.
41) You, secret agent of darkness in my family pretending to be my friend but bewitching my destiny, die today by fire, in the mighty name of Jesus Christ.
42) I declare that I shall not sigh anymore, but I shall sing songs of joy to my Jesus Christ forever and ever, in the name of Jesus Christ.
43) I declare that I shall not travel on my spiritual highway as an amateur anymore, but I shall travel as a champion for Christ, in the name of Jesus Christ.
44) I declare that I shall ascend the ladder of success in my life from today, and shall not descend forever, in the name of Jesus Christ.
45) O Lord, turn my life today from nothing to something, in the name of Jesus Christ.
46) O Lord, turn me today from a slave to a princess, in the name of Jesus Christ.
47) O Lord, turn me today from a slave to a prince, in the name of Jesus Christ.
48) O Lord, change my status today from a servant to a son, because I am in Christ Jesus, in the name of Jesus Christ.
49) O Lord, change my status today from a servant to a daughter, because I am in Christ Jesus, in the name of Jesus Christ.
50) O Lord Jesus, promote me today from a servant to a lord over all my enemies, in the name of Jesus Christ.

51) O Lord Jesus, I declare that I am worth something now. Do something outstanding with me, in the name of Jesus Christ.
52) O Lord Jesus, I declare that this remnant is still worth something, so do anything you wish with my life, in the name of Jesus Christ.
53) Dear Lord Jesus, I surrender to your will for my life this day, in the name of Jesus Christ.
54) I declare that I shall soar like the eagle in the heavens, for the rest of my life, in the name of Jesus Christ.
55) Holy Spirit, please remove every stumbling stone from my path and cast them into the pit, in the name of Jesus Christ.
56) Holy Spirit, show me your glory today and let me dwell in your presence forever, in the name of Jesus Christ.
57) Holy Spirit, reverse every bitter word against my destiny toward their senders, in the name of Jesus Christ.
58) Holy Spirit, arise and challenge by your fire the spirit of witchcraft fighting against my destiny, in the name of Jesus Christ.
59) Holy Spirit, make me your friend forever, in the name of Jesus Christ.
60) Holy Spirit, put the love of God in my heart for people and convince them to receive Jesus Christ as Lord and Savior when I speak about Him, in the name of Jesus Christ.
61) Holy Spirit, change me for good and baptize me by your fire, in the name of Jesus Christ.
62) Holy Spirit, do not transfer your anointing away from my life but transform it to your glory, in the name of Jesus Christ.
63) Holy Spirit, establish and make me a praise in the earth, in the name of Jesus Christ.
64) Holy Spirit, let my enemies bless me after the order of Balaam, in the mighty name of Jesus Christ.
65) I shall live to declare the good works of the Lord in my life, in the mighty name of Jesus Christ.
66) I declare that from this day, my destiny has turned around for good, in the mighty name of Jesus Christ.

67) As you blessed Joseph in Egypt, O Lord Jesus, arise and bless me today.
68) I declare that I shall stand still and see the salvation of the Lord in my life, in the mighty name of Jesus Christ.
69) I declare that the enemy I have seen today, I shall see no more forever, in the mighty name of Jesus Christ.
70) I declare that the Lord shall fight all my battles on time for me, in the mighty name of Jesus.
71) Thank you, Lord, for restoring my spiritual lane for my destiny.
72) Thank you, Lord, for answering all my prayers, in the name of Jesus Christ. Amen.

23

Receive Breakthrough in Your Storm

GOD HAS GIVEN you the power and authority to speak to your storm and be calmed. No storm is greater than the power of God in you. You must learn to confront your storm head-on through prayer and fasting and the word of God, and watch it dissipate away. Every storm in your life is a test of your faith, and when your faith prevails, your promotion also prevails.

In Mark 4:35–41, we see that the disciples were fearful and had no faith. They even questioned Jesus's loyalty by asking if He cared that they were perishing. We as Christians are still doing this today. When we don't see our petition come when we want and how we want it, we begin to blame God. We ask questions like, "God, why did you let this happen to me?" or, "Why haven't you healed me?" or, "Why didn't God heal my husband/wife/child/etc.?" When we do this, we are questioning God's loyalty to us. The disciples questioned His loyalty because of fear and lack of faith in Him. They focused on the storm instead of Christ. Today, we look at our situations instead of looking up to God. By looking at the situation, we are still in control and in charge. When we decide to look up to God, we give up control over our situations to Him. Then our fears disappear so that we are empowered to face the storm head-on and break through it.

The following prayer points will empower you to face your storms head-on and receive victory in the name of Jesus Christ.

SCRIPTURAL REFERENCES

Mark 4:35–41 *On the same day, when evening had come, He said to them, "Let us cross over to the other side." Now when they had left the multitude, they took Him along in the boat as He was. And other little boats were also with Him. And a great windstorm arose, and the waves beat into the boat, so that it was already filling. But He was in the stern, asleep on a pillow. And they awoke Him and said to Him, "Teacher, do you not care that we are perishing?"*

Then He arose and rebuked the wind, and said to the sea, "Peace, be still!" And the wind ceased and there was a great calm. But He said to them, "Why are you so fearful? How is it that you have no faith?" And they feared exceedingly, and said to one another, "Who can this be, that even the wind and the sea obey Him!"

PRAYER POINTS

1) O Lord, I thank you for this prayer program, in the mighty name of Jesus Christ.
2) Lord, I also thank you in advance for answering all my prayers today, in the mighty name of Jesus Christ.
3) Almighty God, I ask you for an open heaven and divine protection during this prayer session, in the mighty name of Jesus Christ.
4) I cast out every authority against this prayer session in the mighty name of Jesus Christ.
5) Lord, I challenge this environment and territory by your fire and I ask for your divine presence now, in the name of Jesus Christ.
6) I cast out every territorial power standing as an obstacle to my breakthrough, in the mighty name of Jesus Christ.
7) I cover my household with the precious blood of Jesus Christ.
8) Let my church become a citadel of blessings, in the name of Jesus Christ.

9) O Lord, increase our numbers in this city so that your glory may be seen in us, in the mighty name of Jesus Christ.
10) O Lord, build a wall and be the wall of fire around us today, in the mighty name of Jesus Christ.
11) Almighty God, be the glory in our midst today, in the mighty name of Jesus Christ.
12) Almighty God, I am the apple of your eye. Let those who rise against me be shaken off by your holy hand, in the mighty name of Jesus Christ.
13) Almighty God, I am your inheritance. Take possession of me and my family in the mighty name of Jesus Christ.
14) O Lord, arise from your holy habitation and choose me as your inheritance, in the mighty name of Jesus Christ.
15) O Lord, you have chosen me to prosper in this city. Rebuke the spirit of poverty in my life, in the mighty name of Jesus Christ.
16) O Lord, take away my filthy garments and clothe me with your rich robes, in the mighty name of Jesus Christ.
17) O Lord, sanitize my hand with the blood of Jesus Christ, in the mighty name of Jesus Christ.
18) O Lord, open a new fountain of prosperity to channel your blessings into my life, in the mighty name of Jesus Christ.
19) O Lord, rebuke every evil power that stands at your right hand to oppose your blessings for me and my family, in the mighty name of Jesus Christ (Zech. 3:2).
20) Almighty God, put a clean turban on my head so that my head shall be lifted up above all my enemies, in the mighty name of Jesus Christ.
21) O Lord, let the angels of promotion carrying my blessings locate me now, in the mighty name of Jesus Christ.
22) O Lord Jesus, devour my devourers by your fire and burn them to ashes, in the mighty name of Jesus Christ.
23) O Lord Jesus, arrest all spiritual robbers of my financial blessings and put them in everlasting chains, in the mighty name of Jesus Christ.

24) O Lord Jesus, make me a wondrous sign in this city, in the mighty name of Jesus Christ.
25) O Lord Jesus, show me a sign for God, in the mighty name of Jesus.
26) O Lord, make me a wondrous miracle to glorify your name, in the mighty name of Jesus Christ.
27) Almighty God, make me a branch that bears righteous fruits to your glory, in the mighty name of Jesus Christ.
28) Almighty God, let me bear the fruit of Holiness before you, in the mighty name of Jesus Christ.
29) Almighty God, I command the seed of growth and prosperity to be planted in my life from today, in the mighty name of Jesus Christ.
30) Almighty God, let the root of growth and prosperity become deeply rooted in my life, in the name of Jesus Christ.
31) Almighty God, arise and decree that I shall be the head and not the tail in the earth, in the mighty name of Jesus Christ.
32) Almighty God, I decree that I shall be above only and shall not be beneath, in the mighty name of Jesus Christ.
33) O Lord, arise and shatter every door that is shut against my victory, in the mighty name of Jesus Christ.
34) Holy Spirit, let me have victory in every storm I face in my life, in the mighty name of Jesus Christ.
35) I declare that I am already a winner and not a loser, in the mighty name of Jesus Christ.
36) Every storm of failure in my life, I rebuke you to be still and be at peace after the order of Jesus Christ, in the mighty name of Jesus Christ.
37) Every storm of mental disorder in my life, I rebuke you to be still and be at peace after the order of Jesus Christ, in the mighty name of Jesus Christ.
38) Every storm of generational curse in my life, I rebuke you to be still and be at peace after the order of Jesus Christ, in the mighty name of Jesus Christ.

39) Every storm of satanic oppression in my life, I rebuke you to be still and be at peace after the order of Jesus Christ, in the mighty name of Jesus Christ.
40) Every storm of cancer in my life, I rebuke you to be still and be at peace after the order of Jesus Christ, in the mighty name of Jesus Christ.
41) Every storm of miscarriage in my life, I rebuke you to be still and be at peace after the order of Jesus Christ, in the mighty name of Jesus Christ.
42) Every storm of obsessive-compulsive disorder in my life, I rebuke you to be still and be at peace after the order of Jesus Christ, in the mighty name of Jesus Christ.
43) Every storm of depression in my life, I rebuke you to be still and be at peace after the order of Jesus Christ, in the mighty name of Jesus Christ.
44) Every storm of wet dream in my life, I rebuke you to be still and be at peace after the order of Jesus Christ, in the mighty name of Jesus Christ.
45) Every storm of nightmare in my life, I rebuke you to be still and be at peace after the order of Jesus Christ, in the mighty name of Jesus Christ.
46) Every storm of poverty in my life, I rebuke you to be still and be at peace after the order of Jesus Christ, in the mighty name of Jesus Christ.
47) Every storm of household wickedness in my life, I rebuke you to be still and be at peace after the order of Jesus Christ, in the mighty name of Jesus Christ.
48) Every storm of childlessness in my life, I rebuke you to be still and be at peace after the order of Jesus Christ, in the mighty name of Jesus Christ.
49) Every storm of drug and alcohol addiction in my life, I rebuke you to be still and be at peace after the order of Jesus Christ, in Jesus's name.
50) Every storm of obesity in my life, I rebuke you to be still and be at peace after the order of Jesus Christ, in the mighty name of Jesus Christ.

51) Every storm of backwardness and stagnation in my life, I rebuke you to be still and be at peace after the order of Jesus Christ, in the mighty name of Jesus Christ.
52) Every storm of unemployment in my life, I rebuke you to be still and be at peace after the order of Jesus Christ, in Jesus's name.
53) Every storm of lust and unfaithfulness in my life, I rebuke you to be still and be at peace after the order of Jesus Christ, in Jesus's name.
54) Every storm of hatred against my life, I rebuke you to be still and be at peace after the order of Jesus Christ, in the mighty name of Jesus Christ.
55) Every storm of loneliness in my life, I rebuke you to be still and be at peace after the order of Jesus Christ, in the mighty name of Jesus Christ.
56) Every storm of lies and gossip against my life, I rebuke you to be still and be at peace after the order of Jesus Christ, in Jesus's name.
57) Every storm of bewitchment in my life, I rebuke you to be still and be at peace after the order of Jesus Christ, in the mighty name of Jesus Christ.
58) Every storm of masturbation in my life, I rebuke you to be still and be at peace after the order of Jesus Christ, in the mighty name of Jesus Christ.
59) Every storm of misfortune in my life, I command you to be still and be at peace after the order of Jesus Christ, in Jesus's name.
60) Every storm of spells against my life, I command you to be still and be at peace after the order of Jesus Christ, in the mighty name of Jesus Christ.
61) Every storm of marine witchcraft against my life, I command you to be still and be at peace after the order of Jesus Christ, in Jesus's name.
62) Every storm of postpartum depression in my life, I command you to be still and be at peace after the order of Jesus Christ, in the mighty name of Jesus Christ.

63) Every storm of HIV/AIDS in my life, I command you to be still and be at peace after the order of Jesus Christ, in the mighty name of Jesus Christ.
64) Every storm of homosexual behavior in my life, I command you to be still and be at peace after the order of Jesus Christ, in Jesus's name.
65) Every storm in entertainment career fighting against my carrier, I command you to be still and be at peace after the order of Jesus Christ, in Jesus's name.
66) Every storm of sickness and disease in my life, I command you to be still and be at peace after the order of Jesus Christ, in the mighty name of Jesus Christ.
67) Every storm of stroke in my life, I command you to be still and be at peace after the order of Jesus Christ, in the mighty name of Jesus Christ.
68) Every storm of liver and kidney disease in my life, I command you to be still and be at peace after the order of Jesus Christ, in the mighty name of Jesus Christ.
69) Every storm of heart failure in my life, I command you to be still and be at peace after the order of Jesus Christ, in the mighty name of Jesus Christ.
70) Every storm of prostitution in my life, I command you to be still and be at peace after the order of Jesus Christ, in the mighty name of Jesus Christ.
71) Every storm of the Antichrist in my life, I command you to be still and be at peace after the order of Jesus Christ, in the mighty name of Jesus Christ.
72) Every storm of tumors in my body, I command you to be still and be at peace after the order of Jesus Christ, in the mighty name of Jesus Christ.
73) Every storm of evil power from my mother's family in my life, I command you to be still and be at peace after the order of Jesus Christ, in the mighty name of Jesus Christ.
74) Every storm of fear and anxiety in my life, I command you to be still and be at peace after the order of Jesus Christ, in Jesus's name.

75) Every storm of traffic tickets in my life, I command you to be still and be at peace after the order of Jesus Christ, in the mighty name of Jesus Christ.
76) Every storm of legal problems in my life, I command you to be still and be at peace after the order of Jesus Christ, in the mighty name of Jesus Christ.
77) Every storm of failing examinations in my life, I command you to be still and be at peace after the order of Jesus Christ, in the mighty name of Jesus Christ.
78) Every storm of doubt and unbelief in my life, I command you to be still and be at peace after the order of Jesus Christ, in the mighty name of Jesus Christ.
79) O Lord, remove every other storm from my life today and forever, in the name of Jesus Christ.
80) Thank you, Lord, for answering all my prayers today, in the name of Jesus Christ. Amen.

24

My Darkness and Storms Are Over

REGARDLESS OF WHO you are, you will most likely face some storms in your life. God uses the beginning parts of our lives to train and educate us about the world He created, with assistance from our parents, guardians, churches, and our society up to about the age of thirty years. During these youthful years, many feel that they know it all and cannot be advised or corrected. Many run away from God, while many also run to God with the support of godly parents and their guidance. All these are preparations we need in order to go into the next phase, which is likely to last another thirty years. This is the phase of storms, the phase we must climb up and descend, the phase of mountains and troughs, the phase in which many crash away and die or crash and survive. In this phase you will have to deal with marriage, money, children, business, jobs, investments, church, other religious or ungodly affiliations, temptations, hardship, failures, prosperity, sickness, lifestyles, adventures of life, discoveries, and so on.

Your success in the second phase depends on your foundation and the preparation received from the first phase. Making God your number one and placing Him at the center of it all already makes you a candidate for success. Some call it a midlife crisis, but I call it attending the University of the Holy Spirit (John 16:13). Whether you were naturally educated in the first part of your life will not prevent you from attending the University of the Holy Spirit. Because it is a spiritual school for you to develop your faith in God, to test your heart and love for God, to align your destiny with the will of God, and to prepare you to become a mentor for His kingdom, everyone—I mean everyone—has to attend. That's why a midlife crisis is very intense for some of us.

The test is different for everyone, depending on your purpose and destiny. No one can go through it for you except you. You may have parental support, family support, or support from friends, work, etc. However, you are still responsible to weather the storms of life. Your wealth and riches may not help you while going through it. If they do, they will certainly not stop the process of the storm. In this phase, we face the worst years of our lives as we rise and fall and rise again. This phase is characterized by tests and temptations. For most people, divorce is strong during this period, as well as financial battles and loss of income, court battles, complicated health issues, family problems, addictions, suffering, rebellion, and disobedience against God. It doesn't matter whether you are rich or poor, a Christian or non-Christian, black or white; you must surely go through this training. While some people turn to psychics, the occult, witchcraft, and Satanism for answers, many others still hold on to their strong faith in God to see them through. In all of these storms, Jesus Christ is the answer, and we must hold on to Him for our victory.

The last phase of the storm starts after the second phase. This is the phase of wisdom—a phase in which you become a mentor, a teacher of wisdom, and an adviser to others based on your experiences in life. Many people still carry over some lessons from the previous phase into this phase. Some have used their experiences to write books, tell stories, and counsel others. Many have also accepted defeats from the storms of life and given up on themselves, their families, and God.

Jesus Christ has the power and authority to speak to your storms so they may cease, regardless of what phase you find yourself in the storm. All He has to say is, "Be still," and your storm shall obey. Life is a storm that comes and goes. No rain ever falls forever. With Jesus

Christ on your side, you shall weather through your storm with authority, power, and the peace of Christ in you. If you are going through a storm now, the following prayer points will help you get through it to the end with peace. Amen.

SCRIPTURAL REFERENCES

Mark 4:35–41 *On the same day, when evening had come, He said to them, "Let us cross over to the other side." Now when they had left the multitude, they took Him along in the boat as He was. And other little boats were also with Him. And a great windstorm arose, and the waves beat into the boat, so that it was already filling. But He was in the stern, asleep on a pillow. And they awoke Him and said to Him, "Teacher, do you not care that we are perishing?"*

Then He arose and rebuked the wind, and said to the sea, "Peace, be still!" And the wind ceased and there was a great calm. But He said to them, "Why are you so fearful? How is it that you have no faith?" And they feared exceedingly, and said to one another, "Who can this be, that even the wind and the sea obey Him!"

PRAYER POINTS

1) Lord, thank you for shining your light upon my darkness today.
2) Thank you for blowing away the storms of my life and giving me peace.
3) Thank you for illuminating my destiny with your glory today.
4) Thank you for being the joy of my life and giving me victory in every battle.
5) O God, arise and unlock my destiny today, in Jesus's name.
6) O God, arise and shine your light more into my life today, in the mighty name of Jesus Christ.
7) O God, arise and increase my territory and boundary today, in the mighty name of Jesus Christ.
8) O God, arise and let all my disappointments become my testimonies, in the name of Jesus Christ.

9) O God, arise and recharge the power base of my destiny today, in the name of Jesus Christ.
10) O God, let my joy and peace overflow today, in Jesus's name.
11) From today, I declare that I shall cease to be a burden to anyone, in the mighty name of Jesus Christ.
12) I declare that all my burdens shall be lifted off my shoulders, by the lifting power of the Holy Ghost, in the mighty name of Jesus Christ.
13) I declare that every yoke upon my neck shall be removed from me today, in the mighty name of Jesus Christ.
14) O Lord, erase by the blood of Jesus Christ every mark of hardship and suffering from my hands today, in the mighty name of Jesus Christ.
15) O Lord, erase every satanic mark from my hands today by the blood of Jesus Christ, in the mighty name of Jesus Christ.
16) I command every evil mark tattooed on my body to be erased by the blood of Jesus Christ.
17) Every spiritual mark placed in my body to cause me pain and losses, be erased by the blood of Jesus Christ.
18) Let no evil trouble me, for I bear in my body the mark of Jesus Christ, in the mighty name of Jesus Christ.

19) Because I bear the mark of Jesus Christ, every other mark on my body, whether physical or spiritual, must be erased by the blood of Jesus Christ.
20) I declare that my life shall know supernatural peace from today, in the mighty name of Jesus Christ.
21) O Lord, do not let my destiny stop prematurely, but I must prosper until your appointed time is fulfilled in my life, in the mighty name of Jesus Christ.
22) O Lord, do not let me chase my helpers away with my tongue, but attract my helpers to assist me through my storms, in the mighty name of Jesus Christ.
23) O Lord, let my tongue become a blessing and not a curse to me, in the mighty name of Jesus Christ.

24) O Lord, let my life never be the same after this storm, in the mighty name of Jesus Christ.
25) O Lord, let me dwell in the glory of your only begotten son from today, in the mighty name of Jesus Christ.
26) I declare that I am completely healed and delivered from this storm today, by the stripes of our Lord Jesus Christ, in the mighty name of Jesus Christ.
27) I declare that I shall increase while my enemies decrease, in the mighty name of Jesus Christ.
28) Almighty God, I declare by your authority today, let there be light upon me and my household, in the mighty name of Jesus Christ.
29) I declare that I shall not weep again, because my afflictions are over, in the mighty name of Jesus Christ.
30) I declare that everything that is causing me sorrow shall be uprooted from today, in Jesus's mighty name.
31) I declare that the joy of the Lord shall be my strength, in the mighty name of Jesus Christ.
32) I declare that I shall not know poverty and poverty shall not know me again forever, in the mighty name of Jesus Christ.
33) O Lord, release unlimited blessings and returns to me today, in Jesus's name.
34) O Lord, flush out every satanic alien in my home today, by the blood of Jesus Christ, in the name of Jesus Christ.
35) O Lord, open my eyes to see and receive your blessings today, in the mighty name of Jesus Christ.
36) I command all darkness in my life to be removed now, in the mighty name of Jesus Christ.
37) I declare that all my sorrows shall turn to joy, in Jesus's name.
38) Lord, I receive your faith to increase my faith today, in the mighty name of Jesus Christ.
39) Lord, do not let me ever stammer spiritually in speaking with you, in the mighty name of Jesus Christ.
40) Almighty God, release divine health to me while in your presence now, in the mighty name of Jesus Christ.

41) I declare that my joy is full from today, in Jesus's name.
42) I declare that from today, suffering in the midst of plenty shall not be my portion, in the mighty name of Jesus Christ.
43) I declare that every rain held back against my blessings is released upon me today, in the mighty name of Jesus Christ.
44) Arise, O Lord, and fix every broken area of my life today, in the mighty name of Jesus Christ.
45) Arise, O Lord, and fix every afflicted area of my body today, in the mighty name of Jesus Christ.
46) I command every broken part of my body to receive divine healing, in the mighty name of Jesus Christ.
47) I command every confused part of my mind to receive a divine solution, in the mighty name of Jesus Christ.
48) I command every strange voice in my ears to receive divine fire, in the mighty name of Jesus Christ.
49) I command every missing portion of my peace to return to me today, in the mighty name of Jesus Christ.
50) I command every storm in my life that could cause me to miss heaven to die off, in the mighty name of Jesus Christ.
51) I command every storm in my life that may hinder my breakthrough to die, in the mighty name of Jesus Christ.
52) I command every storm in my life blowing away my financial blessings to die, in the mighty name of Jesus Christ.
53) I command every storm blowing upon my life to keep me stagnant to die by fire, in the mighty name of Jesus Christ.
54) I command every storm in my life written against my victory to die, in the mighty name of Jesus Christ.
55) I command every storm in my children's lives, written against their destinies, to die, in the mighty name of Jesus Christ.
56) I command every storm directing problems to my life to die, in the mighty name of Jesus Christ.
57) I command all storms in my life to be still, in Jesus's name.

58) I command all evil storms in my life to return to their senders, in the mighty name of Jesus Christ.
59) I command all my spiritual Red Seas to become dry today, in the mighty name of Jesus Christ.
60) I resurrect all my buried treasures by the resurrection power of Jesus Christ, in the mighty name of Jesus Christ.
61) I declare that I shall have good success where others have failed, in the mighty name of Jesus Christ.
62) I command all mud in my life to be washed off by the blood of Jesus Christ.
63) I am more than a conqueror through Christ Jesus, in Jesus's name.
64) O Lord, let my life bear good fruits for you, in Jesus's name.
65) Lord, I declare that your light in me shall overshadow every situation in my life, in the mighty name of Jesus Christ.
66) I declare that all hidden darkness in my life must receive divine illumination now, in the mighty name of Jesus Christ.
67) I declare that every stubborn storm in my life must receive divine annulment, in the mighty name of Jesus Christ.
68) I declare that I shall be full of wisdom, knowledge, and understanding at the end of my breakthrough, so I may give God's children godly counsel.
69) I declare that I shall discover and possess all my treasures that were buried in my storms, in the mighty name of Jesus Christ.
70) I declare that no storm in my life shall be greater than the power of Christ in me.
71) I declare that where others failed and crashed in their storm, I will sail through and be victorious, in the mighty name of Jesus Christ.
72) I challenge every storm in my life to remain still forever, in the mighty name of Jesus Christ.
73) I declare that I am the head over all my storms, and my storms are beneath me, in the name of Jesus Christ.

74) O Lord, give me supernatural power and authority to calm down my raging seas, in the mighty name of Jesus Christ.
75) You, storm that swallowed my blessings, I challenge you by the fire of the Holy Ghost to vomit them back now, in the mighty name of Jesus Christ.
76) You, architect of deadly storms in my life, I command you to die by fire, in the name of Jesus Christ.
77) You, instruments of deadly storms in my life, I withdraw you from my life today and return you back to your owners now, in the mighty name of Jesus Christ.
78) I declare that I shall go through all phases of my life with the peace of God, in the name of Jesus Christ.
79) Almighty God, make me a winner and not a loser in the phases of my life, in the name of Jesus Christ.
80) Almighty God, do not let me disappoint you or my family because of the crisis in my life, in the mighty name of Jesus Christ.
81) O Lord Jesus, arise and take away the crisis of my life from me, in the mighty name of Jesus Christ.
82) O Lord Jesus, arise and remove agitators and instigators of the crisis of my life from me forever, in the mighty name of Jesus Christ.
83) Almighty God, arise and illuminate my life to your glory, in the mighty name of Jesus Christ.
84) I declare that my life shall experience the peace of God from today, in the mighty name of Jesus Christ.
85) I declare that I shall have sound wisdom and judgment concerning my life from today, in the mighty name of Jesus Christ.
86) I declare that my life shall overcome all the obstacles of death set against my destiny, in the mighty name of Jesus Christ.
87) I declare that I am made to succeed and I must succeed and be established, in the mighty name of Jesus Christ.

88) Whether in the storm or out of the storm, I declare that my destiny must be fulfilled in Christ Jesus.
89) O Lord, give me the strength to live and mentor all who need your wisdom through my experiences in life, in the mighty name of Jesus Christ.
90) I am covered by the blood of Jesus Christ forever.
91) Thank you, Lord, for answering all my prayers, in the mighty name of Jesus Christ. Amen.

25

Victory over Unsound Minds

SOMEONE WITH A sound mind will definitely have self-control. When we are not able to control ourselves, we start doing whatever our emotions tell us to do. Uncontrolled emotions can lead to suicide, adultery, fornication, stealing, murder, abuse, destruction, curse, slander, lies, and so forth. God has given each one of us the ability to choose good or evil, to do right or wrong, and to turn from evil or continue with evil. The ability to make the right choice centers on our emotional state of the moment. Self-control makes us choose the right path at that split second so we can avoid a lifetime of regret and guilt. This is why God did not give us the spirit of fear, but that of love, power, and a sound mind. What a blend of emotions to have in our palms. With this, everyone should be at peace with one another. With this, there should be no trouble in the world. Yet we see the opposite in our real world: brother turning against brother, and family turning against family. We now see people reacting like untamed animals over a little issue that could be resolved by a handshake. We see people divorcing daily because of minor misunderstandings in their relationships. We see people killing each other over little misunderstandings instead of taking control and finding lasting solutions to their problems.

The devil knows very well that we can snap out of our sound minds anytime, any day, and any minute. So he shoots arrows into our minds to cause confusion and instability in our ability to reason with sound judgment and take control of our situations. These arrows can be bitter words, offenses, or whatever device the devil thinks will throw your emotions off-balance. The instrument the devil uses can be your spouse, child, friend, boss, or coworker, or situations such as sickness, financial hardship, death, greed, etc. It doesn't matter whether you are rich or poor, tall or short, young or old, etc.; the devil will scheme to throw you off-balance with an unsound mind when you are not praying and enriching your soul with the word of God.

The following prayer points will help you regain a sound mind and get back on track to live a fulfilled life in Christ Jesus.

SCRIPTURAL REFERENCES

2 Timothy 1:6–8 Therefore I remind you to stir up the gift of God which is in you through the laying on of my hands. For God has not given us a spirit of fear, but of power and of love and of a sound mind. Therefore do not be ashamed of the testimony of our Lord, nor of me His prisoner, but share with me in the sufferings for the gospel according to the power of God.

Romans 12:1–2 I beseech you therefore, brethren, by the mercies of God, that you present your bodies a living sacrifice, holy, acceptable to God, which is your reasonable service. And do not be conformed to this world, but be transformed by the renewing of your mind, that you may prove what is that good and acceptable and perfect will of God.

Ezekiel 36:24–27 For I will take you from among the nations, gather you out of all countries, and bring you into your own land. Then I will sprinkle clean water on you, and you shall be clean; I will cleanse you from all your filthiness and from all your idols. I will give you a new heart and put a new spirit within you; I will take the heart of stone out of your flesh and give you a heart of flesh. I will put My Spirit within you and cause you to walk in My statutes, and you will keep My judgments and do them.

PRAYER POINTS

1) Start your prayers with praise and worship.
2) Ask our Lord Jesus to forgive you for all your sins.
3) Receive Him into your life and ask Him to dwell in you permanently.

4) Almighty God, make me appear teachable and submissive before you and before your leaders, in the mighty name of Jesus Christ.
5) Almighty God, incubate the fruits of the Holy Spirit in me, in the mighty name of Jesus Christ.
6) I challenge my life to prosper and be in good health, in the mighty name of Jesus Christ.
7) My life, I challenge you to have self-control alongside the systems of this world, in the mighty name of Jesus Christ
8) My life, I challenge you to have a sound mind and renounce the spirit of confusion, in the mighty name of Jesus Christ.
9) My life, receive divine fire and let it burn the spirit of autism away forever, in the mighty name of Jesus Christ.
10) I declare that my children are free from autism and its effects, in the mighty name of Jesus Christ.
11) I challenge attention disorder in my life to die forever, in the name of Jesus Christ.
12) Holy Spirit, let your fire consume and destroy attention deficit disorder for my family, my children, and myself, in the name of Jesus Christ.
13) I destroy the spirit of obsessive compulsion in my life, and I flush my mind with the precious blood of Jesus Christ.
14) I declare that I shall continue to make sound decisions all the days of my life, in the mighty name of Jesus Christ.
15) I denounce all association with all evil spirits manipulating my mind and actions, in the mighty name of Jesus Christ.
16) Dear Holy Spirit, take control of my mind and emotions, in the mighty name of Jesus Christ.
17) Fire of God, fall upon me now and sanitize my destiny to the glory of God, in the mighty name of Jesus Christ.
18) Fire of God, consume and destroy every mental disease in my bloodline, in the mighty name of Jesus Christ.
19) Every evil bank containing my financial blessings, I command you to open and release them now to me, in the mighty name of Jesus Christ.

20) Fire of God, arise with thunder and destroy every evil altar that harbors my blessings, in the mighty name of Jesus Christ.
21) Fire of God, burn to ashes every evil bank that contains my financial blessings, in the mighty name of Jesus Christ.
22) You, foundation of evil handwriting in my life, be uprooted and be cast into fire, in the mighty name of Jesus Christ.
23) Almighty God, wake me up from the sleep of death, in the mighty name of Jesus Christ.
24) Almighty God, deliver me and wake me up from the sleep of poverty, in the mighty name of Jesus Christ.
25) Almighty God, deliver me and wake me up from the sleep of laziness and inactivity, in the mighty name of Jesus Christ.
26) Almighty God, deliver me and wake me up from spiritual sleep, in the mighty name of Jesus Christ.
27) Almighty God, deliver me and wake me up from the sins of my father's house, in the mighty name of Jesus Christ.
28) Almighty God, deliver me and wake me up from the sins of my mother's house, in the mighty name of Jesus Christ.
29) Almighty God, command every evil mountain standing before me to become plain after the order of Zerubbabel, in the mighty name of Jesus Christ.
30) Almighty God, help me complete every good thing I lay my hands to build, in the mighty name of Jesus Christ.
31) Almighty God, help me build on the foundation of every good thing in my life, in the mighty name of Jesus Christ.
32) Almighty God, help me plant a good foundation in everything I do in my life, in the mighty name of Jesus Christ.
33) Almighty God, demolish every evil foundation laid against me and my family, in the mighty name of Jesus Christ.
34) O Lord of host, send your angels with blessings to come and bless me now, in the mighty name of Jesus Christ.
35) O Lord of host, anoint me for great miracles, signs, and wonders for this generation, in the mighty name of Jesus Christ.
36) O Lord of host, anoint your word in my mouth for this generation, in the mighty name of Jesus Christ.

37) O Lord of host, let your fire of healing burn unceasingly in me for this generation, in the mighty name of Jesus Christ.
38) O Lord of host, I command all impossible situations to become possible in my life for this generation, in the mighty name of Jesus Christ.
39) O Lord of host, I command all impossible healings to become possible in my life for this generation, in the mighty name of Jesus Christ.
40) O Lord of host, favor me with supernatural powers to perform great wonders on the earth, in the mighty name of Jesus Christ.
41) O Lord of host, expel every satanic thief stealing my blessings into the abyss, in the mighty name of Jesus Christ.
42) O Lord of host, let your fountain of blessings channel all your blessings into my life, in the mighty name of Jesus Christ.
43) Almighty God, from today I command that every fountain carrying my blessings shall not flow into a basket, in the mighty name of Jesus Christ.
44) Every satanic basket used in collecting my blessings, be consumed by fire to ashes, in the mighty name of Jesus Christ.
45) Every container leaking my blessings away, be replaced by the hand of Christ forever, in the mighty name of Jesus Christ.
46) Every satanic traffic officer directing my blessings away, be struck down by lightning and by thunder, in the mighty name of Jesus Christ.
47) I declare that God has not given me the spirit of fear but that of love, power, and a sound mind, in the name of Jesus Christ.
48) I receive power to overcome fear and the spirit of fear today, in the name of Jesus Christ.
49) I declare that my emotions shall remain stable from today, in the name of Jesus Christ.
50) I reject the spirit of emotional outbursts and embrace the peace of God forever in my life, in the name of Jesus Christ.
51) I denounce and cast out every wicked spirit making me cause trouble with other people, in the name of Jesus Christ.

52) I command the spirit of destruction to come out of my life today, and I cast it into the abyss, in the name of Jesus Christ.
53) You, spirit of rebellion and disobedience, come out of my life now and die by fire, in the name of Jesus Christ.
54) You, spirit of stupidity and wrong decisions, come out of me and be consumed by the fire of the Holy Spirit.
55) You, spirit of anger and offense, come out of my life now and die by fire, in the name of Jesus Christ.
56) You, spirit of anxiety and frustration, I command you to come out of my life now and be cast into the abyss, in the name of Jesus Christ.
57) Almighty God, arise and destroy every demonic spirit causing agitation and anxiety in my life, in the name of Jesus Christ.
58) I bind the spirit of rejection and sentence it to divine death, in the name of Jesus Christ.
59) I bind the spirit of depression and cast it into fire, in the name of Jesus Christ.
60) I declare that I am free from any and all mind-controlling spirits and drugs, in the mighty name of Jesus Christ.
61) Holy Spirit, fill me with your glory and help me to grow in your anointing, in the name of Jesus Christ.

26

Take Back Your Destiny by Fire

EVERY MAN WAS created with purpose and placed on this earth by our God to represent Him. No birth, be it through marriage, in wedlock or otherwise, is without purpose. Every man has to find that purpose for which he was created in order to be fulfilled in life. In every case, God is in the process and working to ensure that our destinies, or the purposes for which we were created, are fulfilled.

God told Jeremiah that before he was formed in his mother's womb, He knew him. Before he was born from his mother's womb, He already sanctified and ordained him a prophet to the nations (Jeremiah 1:5). In this case, Jeremiah's prophetic purpose or destiny on the earth was already established by God before he was born. God might have attached other ancillary purposes to Jeremiah's destiny, but his dominant and primary purpose was to be God's prophet to Israel. We are all destined in this manner, because no man is born into this world without God's knowledge and purpose. A person who claims that he does not believe in his Creator is plain ignorant and in denial of his origin and existence.

Satan was created by God just like we were created by God. God also gave him a purpose or destiny in heaven: to lead worship. He served God in that capacity until he felt that he needed to be exalted above God. He was cast out of heaven into this world with a third of the angels who supported him. Ever since, he has vowed to destroy every man's destiny by making him rebel and denounce God just as he did. Satan continues go after God and fight man, who desires to fulfill his destiny. Satan uses manipulation, curses, spells, lies, afflictions, sicknesses, diseases, poverty, addictions, sexual immorality, and many other devices to destroy man's destiny.

Many lives and destinies have been prematurely terminated because of the vices of the wicked one. Some still live on, but their destinies have been traded away in the spirit world to the highest bidders. By enchantments, divinations, and spiritual summons, many have lost their destinies. By occult and witchcraft practices, many destinies have been destroyed. By pure wickedness and lack of financial resources, many destinies have been aborted.

As you pray the following prayer points with authority and power, the power of God will break demonic resistance against your destiny and set you free to repossess your purpose and destiny.

SCRIPTURAL REFERENCES

Jeremiah 1:4–5 *Then the word of the Lord came to me, saying: "Before I formed you in the womb I knew you; Before you were born I sanctified you; I ordained you a prophet to the nations."*

Romans 8:2 8–30 *And we know that all things work together for good to those who love God, to those who are the called according to His purpose. For whom He foreknew, He also predestined to be conformed to the image of His Son, that He might be the firstborn among many brethren. Moreover whom He predestined, these He also called; whom He called, these He also justified; and whom He justified, these He also glorified.*

Proverbs 13:22 *A good man leaves an inheritance to his children's children, But the wealth of the sinner is stored up for the righteous.*

2 Samuel 5:19 *So David inquired of the Lord, saying, "Shall I go up against the Philistines? Will you deliver them into my hand?" And the Lord said to David, "Go up, for I will doubtless deliver the Philistines into your hand."*

Matthew 11:12 *And from the days of John the Baptist until now the kingdom of heaven suffers violence, and the violent take it by force.*

John 10:10 *The thief does not come except to steal, and to kill, and to destroy. I have come that they may have life, and that they may have it more abundantly.*

1 Samuel 30:8–14 *So David inquired of the Lord, saying, "Shall I pursue this troop? Shall I overtake them?" And He answered him, "Pursue, for you shall surely overtake them and without fail recover all." So David went, he and the six hundred men who were with him, and came to the Brook Besor, where those stayed who were left behind. But David pursued, he and four hundred men; for two hundred stayed behind, who were so weary that they could not cross the Brook Besor.*

PRAYER POINTS

1) Start this prayer session with praise and worship.
2) Ask the Lord to forgive all your sins and those of your father, mother, and ancestors.
3) Plead for the blood of Jesus Christ over you and your family now.
4) Start your prayer now with power and authority.
5) O Lord Jesus, empower me at this hour to take back my destiny from my enemies, in the name of Jesus Christ.
6) I challenge every strongman in my life by fire and command him to surrender my destiny back to me now, in the name of Jesus Christ.
7) You, satanic power holding down my destiny, be erupted by the terrible anger of the Lord.
8) You, powers of the night trading my destiny in satanic circles, catch fire, catch fire, catch fire, in the name of Jesus Christ.
9) You, household enemy tying my destiny down, I challenge you by the fire of the Holy Ghost to untie my destiny now, in the mighty name of Jesus Christ.
10) You, household wickedness that swallowed my destiny in the past and present, I command you to vomit my destiny

now and be crushed to ashes by the rock of ages, in the name of Jesus Christ.
11) Every witch or wizard stirring my destiny in your evil pots, I command your pots to shatter into pieces and release my destiny now, in the mighty name of Jesus Christ.
12) You, territorial powers monitoring my destiny using energies drawn from the sun, moon, and stars, receive divine judgment and die forever, in the name of Jesus Christ.
13) I take back my destiny by force, in the name of Jesus Christ.
14) I claim back right now all heavenly and earthly things that are mine from you, Satan, by the power of Jesus Christ, in the name of Jesus Christ.
15) You, agents of darkness, I command you to let go of my blessings by thunder and by fire, in the name of Jesus Christ.
16) I declare now with authority in the name of Jesus Christ, Holy Ghost fire [repeat twelve times], consume every stubborn enemy that has refused to release my destiny and let me go, in the name of Jesus Christ.
17) I erase all generational curses from my family affecting my destiny, by the blood of Jesus Christ.
18) Every generational curse that affected my parents that is now affecting me, I command you to be nullified by the blood of Jesus Christ.
19) Every satanic decree that was written against me in my family line, be nullified now, in the name of Jesus Christ.
20) Every evil gene planted in my DNA that is expressing curses in my life now, die by fire, in the name of Jesus Christ.
21) Every satanic eye watching my progress and slowing down my destiny, be blinded by the arrow of heaven, in the name of Jesus Christ.
22) Every satanic serpent wrapping around my destiny and holding my destiny captive, be destroyed by heavenly kerosene, in the name of Jesus Christ.

23) You, spirit of addiction fighting against my destiny, die, die, die, in the name of Jesus Christ.
24) You, spirit of manic psychosis troubling my life, die, die, die, in the mighty name of Jesus Christ.
25) You, spirit of depression and delusion troubling my destiny, die, die, die, in the name of Jesus Christ.
26) You, spirit of fear and anxiety troubling my destiny, die, die, die, in the name of Jesus Christ.
27) You, spirit of sexual perversion troubling my destiny, die, die, die, in the name of Jesus Christ.
28) You, spirit of cancer and HIV/AIDS troubling my destiny, die, die, die, in the name of Jesus Christ.
29) You, spirit of organ malfunction and dysfunction in my body troubling my destiny, die, die, die, in the name of Jesus Christ.
30) You, spirit of blindness, muteness, and deafness troubling my destiny, die, die, die, in the name of Jesus Christ.
31) You, spirit of lack and poverty, financial destroyer troubling my destiny, die, die, die, in the name of Jesus Christ.
32) You, spirit of wastefulness and leaking pockets troubling my destiny, die, die, die, in the name of Jesus Christ.
33) You, evil powers of my father's house troubling my destiny, die, die, die, in the name of Jesus Christ.
34) All rituals and sacrifices offered against me to destroy my destiny, backfire against your ritualist now. Backfire, backfire, backfire now, in the name of Jesus Christ.
35) Every evil bird flying for my sake and flying for my destiny's sake, fall down and die, fall down and die, fall down and die, in the name of Jesus Christ.
36) Lord Jesus, pull down all strongholds in my mind and take every thought working against me captive.
37) Holy Ghost fire, fall upon me, fall upon me now, fall upon me now, fall upon me now, in the name of Jesus Christ.
38) Every evil traffic signal stopping my blessings from coming to me, be shattered by the rock of ages now, in the mighty name of Jesus Christ.

39) Every red light positioned to delay God's purpose in my destiny, be smashed to pieces by the thunder of God, in the mighty name of Jesus Christ.
40) Every satanic register containing my blessings in the spirit world, be consumed by the fire of God to ashes, in the mighty name of Jesus Christ.
41) Every carrier of frustration in my life, in the name of Jesus Christ, fall down and die.
42) Every carrier of financial failure in my life, in the name of Jesus Christ, I command you to fall down and die.
43) Every carrier of premature death in my destiny, I bring you down by Christ's flaming sword, in the mighty name of Jesus Christ.
44) My life, I command you to experience supernatural breakthrough in the mighty name of Jesus Christ.
45) My life, I command you to receive divine favor, in the mighty name of Jesus Christ.
46) My life, I command you to receive divine wealth and riches, in the mighty name of Jesus Christ.
47) My life, I command you to receive divine prosperity, in the mighty name of Jesus Christ.
48) My life, I command you to receive divine grace to excel, in the mighty name of Jesus Christ.
49) From today, I decree that I shall remain above my enemies and not below them, in the mighty name of Jesus Christ.
50) From today, I command that my enemies shall remain below me forever and ever, in the mighty name of Jesus Christ.
51) You, unrepentant enemy seeking my life to destroy, sleep and do not wake up again, in the mighty name of Jesus Christ.
52) You, religious strongman tying down my destiny, I command you to lose my destiny by fire and by thunder, in the mighty name of Jesus Christ.
53) You, satanic strongman sitting on my destiny, I command you to stand up from my destiny, and to begin to sleep but not wake up, in the mighty name of Jesus Christ.

54) You, arrow of affliction attacking my destiny, break forever in the mighty name of Jesus Christ.
55) You, arrow of affliction attacking my life, in the name of Jesus Christ, return to your sender.
56) Every evil altar incubating my destiny, I command you to collapse upon your priest and smash him into pieces, in the mighty name of Jesus Christ.
57) You, satanic priest chanting incantations against my destiny, I command you to make mistakes that will advance my cause, in the mighty name of Jesus Christ.
58) I decree that the Lord has blessed me; therefore no man shall curse me or stop me from prospering, in the mighty name of Jesus Christ.
59) I decree that there shall be no divination against me and no sorcery against my family.
60) I decree that I am a winner and not a loser.
61) Today I command that the Lord has blessed the work of my hands; therefore I am prosperous.
62) I decree that my God shall supply all my needs according to His riches in glory by Christ Jesus.
63) I command every satanic load upon my life to shatter, in the mighty name of Jesus Christ.
64) I command every satanic whistleblower in my life to die by the fire of the Almighty, in the mighty name of Jesus Christ.
65) I declare that my destiny is not for sale, and I claim it back from whomever it was spiritually sold to, in the name of Jesus Christ.
66) You, sword of affliction, I command you to return to your sender now, in the mighty name of Jesus Christ.
67) Where is the Lord God of Elijah? Arise and consume every satanic prophet in my life by fire, in the name of Jesus Christ.
68) I claim back by thunder and by fire every blessing that was stolen from me in the past, in the mighty name of Jesus Christ. Amen.
69) I release the arrow of blackout into the camp of all my destiny destroyers, in the name of Jesus Christ.

70) You, dream stealers and spoilers, be crushed to ashes forever, in the name of Jesus Christ.
71) I declare that I am blessed and shall remain promoted forever and ever, in the name of Jesus Christ.
72) Thank you, Lord, for restoring my destiny and blessings to me, in Jesus's mighty name. Amen.

27

Uproot Satanic Yokes from Your Destiny

THE DEVIL HAS the ability to carefully study your life to determine your weaknesses and strengths, in order to design strategies to destroy those strengths and enhance the weaknesses. The devil's interference with our strengths and his subsequent enhancement of our weaknesses eventually result in major burdens and yokes we Christians see today. In order to weaken his victim, the enemy mounts his devices (yokes and burdens) upon the victim and escalates them to unbearable thresholds, thus forcing his victim to give up easily, prematurely, and to lose focus and interest in life. Once the devil succeeds with his evil schemes, he takes control of the victim's life and forces him to make and implement regrettable decisions: to go into drugs and alcohol to ease his pains, to commit all sorts of crimes, to tell lies, to run away from commitments. He may commit suicide and miss his destiny, unless by God's intervention.

Knowing the severity of evil burdens and yokes upon our lives, Jesus persuaded us to come to Him with our burdens and yokes. We are to take our situations to Christ, surrender our lives to Him, release our weaknesses to Him, and let Him use our strengths to empower us and glorify His name. The enemy's plan is simply to stop you from moving on to achieve your destiny. He knows that his destiny was aborted, and he wants yours to be equally so. He may use money, fame, men, women, wealth, riches, and even bad situations to set you up to become his victim. You must be freed from satanic yokes and burdens, and the only way is to take it to Jesus at the cross. These prayer points will lead you to that desired freedom, in Jesus's mighty name. Amen.

SCRIPTURAL REFERENCES

Matthew 11:28–29 Come to Me, all you who labor and are heavy laden, and I will give you rest. Take My yoke upon you and learn from Me, for I am gentle and lowly in heart, and you will find rest for your souls.

Isaiah 10:27 It shall come to pass in that day That his burden will be taken away from your shoulder, And his yoke from your neck, And the yoke will be destroyed because of the anointing oil.

Colossians 2:13–15 And you, being dead in your trespasses and the uncircumcision of your flesh, He has made alive together with Him, having forgiven you all trespasses, having wiped out the handwriting of requirements that was against us, which was contrary to us. And He has taken it out of the way, having nailed it to the cross. Having disarmed principalities and powers, He made a public spectacle of them, triumphing over them in it.

Galatians 3:13–14 Christ has redeemed us from the curse of the law, having become a curse for us (for it is written, "Cursed is everyone who hangs on a tree"), that the blessing of Abraham might come upon the Gentiles in Christ Jesus, that we might receive the promise of the Spirit through faith.

PRAYER POINTS

1) This is a spiritual warfare session. Start this prayer session with worship and praise.
2) Ask God to forgive all your sins, as well as your father's and forefathers'.
3) Ask the Lord to cover you with the blood of Jesus Christ.
4) Ask God to build a hedge of protection around you and your family at this time.

5) Start your prayer now.
6) I command every satanic burden upon my shoulders to be lifted off and be placed upon the owner's shoulders, in the mighty name of Jesus Christ.
7) I command every demonic yoke upon my neck to scatter into pieces, in the mighty name of Jesus Christ.
8) I dismantle every witches' coven casting evil yokes upon my life, in the mighty name of Jesus Christ.
9) You, carriers of evil load, now carry your load back to your sender, in the mighty name of Jesus Christ.
10) Every satanic load sitting on my breakthrough, catch fire, catch fire, catch fire, in the mighty name of Jesus Christ.
11) Every household strongman tying me down to stagnation, fall down and die [repeat three times], in the mighty name of Jesus Christ.
12) I refuse to carry any evil load, in the mighty name of Jesus Christ.
13) I shall not die but shall live to declare the works of the Lord in my life, in the mighty name of Jesus Christ.
14) You, power of darkness in my life, I command you to receive God's divine destruction today, in the mighty name of Jesus Christ.
15) I command all darkness in my life to receive God's divine light and glory, in the mighty name of Jesus Christ.
16) My soul, I command you to resist the devil and let him flee, in the mighty name of Jesus Christ.
17) My flesh, I command you to be broken for Jesus Christ, in the mighty name of Jesus Christ.
18) Almighty God, arise and destroy every evil tongue casting spells upon my life, in the mighty name of Jesus Christ.
19) Almighty God, do not let me walk away from your divine gospel, in the mighty name of Jesus Christ.
20) Almighty God, as your word is purified, so purify my tongue to declare your works in my life, in the mighty name of Jesus Christ.
21) Almighty God, let those who look for you find you in me, in the mighty name of Jesus Christ.

22) Out of my mouth shall flow rivers of living waters, in the mighty name of Jesus Christ.
23) I command my body, soul, and spirit to align with the will of Christ, in the mighty name of Jesus Christ.
24) I receive power from the Holy Spirit to overcome my enemies, in the mighty name of Jesus Christ.
25) I reject failure and receive victory into my life, in the mighty name of Jesus Christ.
26) I shall manifest the fruits of the spirit and discard pride of life and lust of the flesh, in the mighty name of Jesus Christ.
27) My life shall be a blessing to the kingdom of God, in the mighty name of Jesus Christ.
28) Whoever blesses me shall be blessed and whoever curses me shall be cursed, in the mighty name of Jesus Christ.
29) Almighty God, turn me into a fertile ground that I may bear much fruit in the coming seasons of my life, in the mighty name of Jesus Christ.
30) I rebuke the spirit of barrenness in my life, and I declare that I shall bear much fruit from now on, in the mighty name of Jesus Christ.
31) I command the fire of the Holy Spirit to consume all barrenness in my life to ashes, in the mighty name of Jesus Christ.
32) Lord Jesus, release your rain into all dry ground in my life, in the mighty name of Jesus Christ.
33) Almighty God, water every dry area of my life with your blessing, in the mighty name of Jesus Christ.
34) Lord Jesus, thank you for answering all my prayers and signing your signature on them all, in the mighty name of Jesus Christ.
35) Lord Jesus, let all the blessings of Abraham fall upon my life and family now, in the name of Jesus Christ.
36) I am set free from the curse of the law forever, in the name of Jesus Christ.

37) O Lord, arise and disarm every principality and power fighting against my destiny and cast them all into your fire, in the name of Jesus Christ.
38) I am justified and redeemed from every spiritual curse forever, in the name of Jesus Christ.
39) O Lord, I declare that my tongue shall speak of your righteousness in all the earth and to the ends of the age, in the mighty name of Jesus Christ.
40) I declare that my family is free from all spiritual curses forever, in the name of Jesus Christ.
41) Almighty God, you have shown me great and severe troubles. My God, revive me again and bring me up from the depths of the earth into a rich fulfillment, in the name of Jesus Christ.
42) Almighty God, arise and increase my greatness, and comfort me on every side from today, in the name of Jesus Christ.
43) I know, O Lord, that you have brought me out of my distress into a rich fulfillment in Christ. Let me never be moved out of your will again, in the name of Jesus Christ.
44) I declare that I shall flourish in the abundance of peace, until the moon is no more, in the name of Jesus Christ.
45) I declare that my children and family are covered by the blood of Jesus Christ, and they shall flourish like the tree planted by the rivers of water, in Jesus's mighty name.
46) O Lord Jesus, remember me and save me. I am the tribe of your inheritance, which you have redeemed. Let me never be put to shame.
47) O Lord Jesus, turn the axes and the hammers of my enemies against themselves and save me from all their troubles.
48) Lord Jesus, you are my king from the beginning of times. Arise and fight for your son/daughter and save me from all my troubles.

49) O Lord Jesus, the dark places of the earth are full of the haunts of cruelty. Do not deliver the life of your turtledove to the wild beast of the earth, in the name of Jesus Christ.
50) O Lord Jesus, let all the activity of the wicked against my destiny be stopped forever, in the name of Jesus Christ.
51) O Lord Jesus, do not let the wicked that oppress me escape from your rod. Pursue them, overtake them, and put them to shame because of me, in the name of Jesus Christ.
52) O Lord Jesus, arise and cut off the horns of the wicked by your sword of fire, and establish my horns in the earth, in the name of Jesus Christ.
53) Almighty God, you are the God who does wonders. Arise and perform wonders in my case. Arise and redeem me again, in the name of Jesus Christ.
54) As you parted the Red Sea, arise, O Lord, and part my Red Seas away, so I may go through life with peace and prosperity, in the name of Jesus Christ.
55) Dear Holy Spirit, hide my footsteps from my enemies and keep all my affairs from their knowledge, in the name of Jesus Christ.
56) I declare that I shall set my hope in God. O Lord, when I call to you, hear my prayers from your holy heaven, in the name of Jesus Christ.
57) Lord Jesus, thank you for uprooting satanic yokes from my destiny, and for breaking the rod of the wicked against my life into pieces, in your precious, mighty name. Amen.

28

Lord, Restore My Wasted Years

MANY OF US have wasted so much time pursuing career opportunities we thought were part of our destinies. However, on completion, we discovered that these opportunities were not part of our calling. Millions of people have obtained several academic degrees and never practiced in any of those respective fields of study. There are many others who never went to school and still found themselves delayed by generational curses that run in their families. Many are also delayed by poverty, sickness, hardship, death in the family, business loss, curses, bewitchments, natural phenomena, disobedience to God, rebellion against God, satanic temptations, and an inability to make good choices in life.

The prayer points below are designed to bring back into your life divine breakthrough and restoration. The Lord will restore your wasted years and command His blessings on you again as you pray them through.

SCRIPTURAL REFERENCES

Job 42:7–16 And so it was, after the Lord had spoken these words to Job, that the Lord said to Eliphaz the Temanite, "My wrath is aroused against you and your two friends, for you have not spoken of Me what is right, as My servant Job has. Now therefore, take for yourselves seven bulls and seven rams, go to My servant Job, and offer up for yourselves a burnt offering; and My servant Job shall pray for you. For I will accept him, lest I deal with you according to your folly; because you have not spoken of Me what is right, as My servant Job has."

So Eliphaz the Temanite and Bildad the Shuhite and Zophar the Naamathite went and did as the Lord commanded them; for the Lord had accepted Job. And the Lord restored Job's losses when he prayed for his friends. Indeed the Lord gave Job twice as much as he had before. Then all his brothers, all his sisters, and all those who had been his acquaintances before, came to him and ate food with him in his house; and they consoled him and comforted him for all the adversity that the Lord had brought upon him. Each one gave him a piece of silver and each a ring of gold.

Now the Lord blessed the latter days of Job more than his beginning; for he had fourteen thousand sheep, six thousand camels, one thousand yoke of oxen, and one thousand female donkeys. He also had seven sons and three daughters. And he called the name of the first Jemimah, the name of the second Keziah, and the name of the third Keren-Happuch. In all the land were found no women so beautiful as the daughters of Job; and their father gave them an inheritance among their brothers.

After this Job lived one hundred and forty years, and saw his children and grandchildren for four generations. So Job died, old and full of days.

PRAYER POINTS

1) O Lord Jesus, thank you for your presence with me at this hour of prayer.
2) Thank you for granting me favor to be in your presence at this time.
3) Thank you for lifting me up from spiritual slumber and weakness from my enemies.
4) I ask you to forgive all my sins and wash me with your precious blood.
5) I confess that you are the Christ, the son of the Living God.
6) I confess that you died and rose again from the dead, and ascended to heaven.
7) I invite you at this hour to take possession of my body, soul, and spirit, in the mighty name of Jesus Christ.

8) I declare that I am free from the law of sin and death, and Satan has no hold over my life and destiny, in the mighty name of Jesus Christ.
9) O Lord Jesus, from this day forward, transform my wasted years into productive years for the rest of my life, in the mighty name of Jesus Christ.
10) Lord Jesus, go into my past and erase my name from satanic registers in which my blessings were recorded and withheld, in the mighty name of Jesus Christ.
11) Lord Jesus, arise and destroy every satanic checkpoint that has brought delay to my breakthrough in life, in the mighty name of Jesus Christ.
12) I command every evil red light in my destiny to shatter by fire, in the mighty name of Jesus Christ.
13) I declare that every evil stop sign in my life and family be shattered to ashes by the rock of ages, in the mighty name of Jesus Christ.
14) Almighty God, arise and let all enemies of my destiny be scattered today, in the mighty name of Jesus Christ.
15) I receive divine victory and restoration into my life today, in the mighty name of Jesus Christ.
16) I declare that I have received double anointing to prosper from today, in the mighty name of Jesus Christ.
17) I pronounce this day that I have received anointing to prosper in double proportions wherever I go, in the mighty name of Jesus Christ.
18) I declare that anointing to increase productivity shall come upon my life starting now, in the mighty name of Jesus Christ.
19) I declare that anointing to increase from minimum to maximum shall come upon my life starting from this moment, in the mighty name of Jesus Christ.
20) I declare that I shall have breakthrough and success in all my business deals, in the mighty name of Jesus Christ.
21) I declare that I am healed from the top of my head to the soles of my feet, in the mighty name of Jesus Christ.

22) My life, receive divine promotion today, in the mighty name of Jesus Christ.
23) My life, receive the master key to open every door in your destiny from today, in the name of Jesus Christ.
24) I unlock every door of financial prosperity that was shut against me, in the name of Jesus Christ.
25) I receive divine authority to advance forward and not backward again, in the name of Jesus Christ.
26) I challenge the spirit of backwardness in my life to die by the fire of the Holy Spirit, in the mighty name of Jesus Christ.
27) I condemn every tongue that has risen against my life and destiny to remain paralyzed forever, in the mighty name of Jesus Christ.
28) Holy Spirit, arise and consume by your fire every evil tongue that has pronounced curses over my destiny, and sanctify my life by the precious blood of Jesus Christ, in the mighty name of Jesus Christ.
29) Almighty God, remove all unfriendly friends from my life and restore to me all helpers that walked away from my life in the past, in the mighty name of Jesus Christ.
30) I declare that I shall live an abundant and fulfilled life starting this year, in the mighty name of Jesus Christ.
31) I declare that I shall continue to prosper in health and even as my soul prospers, in the mighty name of Jesus Christ.
32) I pronounce that I shall receive a double portion of blessings from heaven today for the shame of my past, in the mighty name of Jesus Christ.
33) I declare that I shall continue to bear good fruits and become a blessing to my family, in the mighty name of Jesus Christ.
34) I declare that I shall leave a good inheritance for my children and their children from generation to generation, in the mighty name of Jesus Christ.
35) I command every waster spirit to receive divine judgment by fire, in the mighty name of Jesus Christ.

36) I command every satanic conspiracy over my life to be exposed and blown away by the east wind of God, in the mighty name of Jesus Christ.
37) I declare that I am the head and not the tail, in the mighty name of Jesus Christ.
38) I command every unrewarded effort in my past to become rewarded from this moment on in my life, in the mighty name of Jesus Christ.
39) I challenge every good eye that was closed against my recommendation to receive promotion to be opened today and recommend me for my promotion and advancement in my career, in the mighty name of Jesus Christ.
40) Holy Spirit, expand my territory after the order of Jabez, in the mighty name of Jesus Christ.
41) Lord Jesus, keep me connected to the vine so I may continue to bear fruits according to your will, in the mighty name of Jesus Christ.
42) Lord Jesus, as you let Job prosper in the last days, let me and my family prosper the same way today, in the mighty name of Jesus Christ.
43) Almighty God, as I wake up tomorrow morning from my bed, let your blessings rise up with me, in the mighty name of Jesus Christ.
44) Every power that swore that I shall remain stagnant and barren for life, I command your curses to backfire today, in the mighty name of Jesus Christ.
45) I nullify every pronounced curse and spell against my life by the blood of Jesus Christ, in the mighty name of Jesus Christ.
46) I erase by the blood of Jesus Christ every generational curse in my life and family keeping me backward, in the mighty name of Jesus Christ.
47) I declare that I am delivered and healed from evil powers of my father's house, in the mighty name of Jesus Christ.
48) Almighty God, lift me up from the slums of poverty and put me on the path of restoration and recovery, in the mighty name of Jesus Christ.

49) O Lord Jesus, show me your glory and help me dwell in your presence forever, in the mighty name of Jesus Christ.
50) You, arrows of poverty in my life, I command you to backfire to your senders now, in the mighty name of Jesus Christ.
51) You, arrows of affliction in my life, I command you to backfire to your senders now, in the mighty name of Jesus Christ.
52) You, satanic messengers shooting death arrows into my destiny, be consumed by the fire of the Holy Spirit, in the mighty name of Jesus Christ.
53) Almighty God, increase my years and help me fulfill your will in my life, in the mighty name of Jesus Christ.
54) My life, I command you to increase in God's favor, in the mighty name of Jesus Christ.
55) Holy Spirit, draw me closer to you and increase my days from minimum to maximum, in the mighty name of Jesus Christ.
56) Holy Spirit, arise and erase the mistakes of my past by the precious blood of Jesus Christ.
57) Holy Spirit, blow away the storm of affliction attached to my past and present, in the mighty name of Jesus Christ.
58) Almighty God, you are mighty in battle. Arise and fight for me now, in the mighty name of Jesus Christ.
59) Almighty God, command your angels to come down from heaven and be my helpers, in the mighty name of Jesus Christ.
60) Almighty God, send your ministering angels to come and minister to my bank accounts and pull me out of poverty, in the mighty name of Jesus Christ.
61) I destroy every monitoring device placed upon my life to monitor my progress and render me stagnant, in the mighty name of Jesus Christ.
62) Holy Spirit, shut down and destroy every satanic door through which my blessings are transported away from my life, in the mighty name of Jesus Christ.
63) I denounce any known and unknown association with the occult, past, present, and future, in the mighty name of Jesus Christ.

64) My life, I command you to experience tremendous financial breakthrough this year, in the mighty name of Jesus Christ.
65) My health, I command you to experience tremendous prosperity this year by God's speed, in the mighty name of Jesus Christ.
66) Holy Spirit, sanitize my life and destiny by your fire, in the mighty name of Jesus Christ.
67) I command every power fighting to pull me down each time I come up for promotion to die by fire, in the name of Jesus Christ.
68) I declare that my name must change from failure to victory, in the mighty name of Jesus Christ.
69) Any wicked power positioned in my life to push wrong buttons to instigate or agitate me to manifest bad habits, be consumed by fire, in the mighty name of Jesus Christ.
70) I challenge every family deity holding me backward to die by fire, in the mighty name of Jesus Christ. Amen.

29

Lord, Turn My Mourning into Dancing

SO MANY PEOPLE are full of regrets due to involvement in the occult, witchcraft, sin, abortion, stealing, cheating, and all forms of evil works. On the other hand, there are many who have become afflicted by the enemy, by poverty, by death, by curses, and by many other situations, and they have decided to live their lives in pain, suffering, and regrets. Some have lost their homes and become homeless; some have lost all their investments, businesses, jobs, and pensions. Many have been married for years without children because their wombs were blocked or bewitched to prevent them from having children.

Whatever situation you find yourself in today, know that God is turning your mourning into dancing after praying the following prayers points. Start with aggressive praise and worship and proceed to prayers.

SCRIPTURAL REFERENCES

Psalm 30:10–12 Hear, O Lord, and have mercy on me; Lord, be my helper! You have turned for me my mourning into dancing; you have put off my sackcloth and clothed me with gladness, To the end that my glory may sing praise to you and not be silent. O Lord my God, I will give thanks to you forever.

John 16:20–22 *Most assuredly, I say to you that you will weep and lament, but the world will rejoice; and you will be sorrowful, but your sorrow will be turned into joy. A woman, when she is in labor, has sorrow because her hour has come; but as soon as she has given birth to the child, she no longer remembers the anguish, for joy that a human being has been born into the world. Therefore you now have sorrow; but I will see you again and your heart will rejoice, and your joy no one will take from you*

PRAYER POINTS

1) Start this prayer session with praise and worship
2) Father, I thank you for this hour of victory in my life and family.
3) Lord, I repent of all my sins and ask for your forgiveness.
4) Wash me today with your precious blood, the blood of Jesus Christ.
5) I declare that you are the Son of God, my Lord and my Savior from today.
6) Father, I thank you for healing me and setting me free from all oppression of the wicked.
7) I thank you, Lord, for blessing me in season and out of season.
8) Lord, I thank you for divine protection and countless interventions for my life and family.
9) Holy Spirit, thank you for being my guardian and carrier of my blessings.
10) Holy Spirit, thank you for turning my mourning into dancing.
11) Lord Jesus, thank you for turning my sorrows into joy.
12) I declare that my joy shall be complete in you, O Lord, in the mighty name of Jesus Christ.
13) I declare that my freedom has come upon me today, in the mighty name of Jesus Christ.
14) I declare that your peace shall be upon my life and my family, in the mighty name of Jesus Christ.

15) Almighty God, speak to my situation so that it will surrender to your command, and lift me up from my predicament by your right hand, in the mighty name of Jesus Christ.
16) I command every evil power contending against my victory to receive divine termination, in the mighty name of Jesus Christ.
17) I command every evil power contending against my breakthrough to receive divine judgment by fire, in the mighty name of Jesus Christ.
18) I declare that I shall continue to prosper in health as my soul prospers, in the mighty name of Jesus Christ.
19) I declare that I shall not be moved by fear of the unknown because my God is my undertaker, in the mighty name of Jesus Christ.
20) I command the spirit of sorrow in my life to die by fire, in the mighty name of Jesus Christ.
21) O Lord, shut every door against the spirit of panic and confusion in my life, and I declare that your peace shall follow me and go before me all the rest of my life, in the mighty name of Jesus Christ.
22) You, agent of sorrow fighting against my happiness, be consumed to ashes by the fire of God, in the mighty name of Jesus Christ.
23) You, agent of sorrow fighting against my family, be shattered by the rock of ages, in the mighty name of Jesus Christ.
24) My life shall receive a divine solution in every situation facing me, in the mighty name of Jesus Christ.
25) My life shall experience divine harvest and multiple blessings in the earth, in the mighty name of Jesus Christ.
26) I command every desert spirit in my life to die and vanish away, in the mighty name of Jesus Christ.
27) O Lord Jesus, send your lifting power to lift me up from poverty starting today, in the mighty name of Jesus Christ.
28) O Lord Jesus, resurrect all my buried blessings today by your resurrection power, in the mighty name of Jesus Christ.
29) Arise, O Lord, and let all my enemies be scattered, in the mighty name of Jesus Christ.

30) I declare that the joy of the Lord shall be my strength forever, in the mighty name of Jesus Christ.
31) I declare that the goodness and mercy of the Lord shall follow me and my family wherever we go, in the mighty name of Jesus Christ.
32) Holy Spirit, remove the burden of depression from my life today, in the mighty name of Jesus Christ.
33) Holy Spirit, remove the burden of depression from my family today, in the mighty name of Jesus Christ.
34) Holy Spirit, make me the head and not the tail, in the mighty name of Jesus Christ.
35) I declare that I shall harvest all my past blessings this year, in the mighty name of Jesus Christ.
36) As a woman who does not remember the pains of her labor after birth, O Lord, do not let me remember the pains of my past, in the mighty name of Jesus Christ.
37) I declare that I am restored in every area of my life, in the mighty name of Jesus Christ.
38) I pronounce from this day that my enemies will not take my joy from me again, in the mighty name of Jesus Christ.
39) O Lord, I pronounce that I shall not be displaced from my throne of prosperity, in the mighty name of Jesus Christ.
40) Lord Jesus, as I enter your prosperity for my life, shut every door against all my devourers, in the mighty name of Jesus Christ.
41) I declare that I shall not be seen in the company of people that may bring sorrows into my life, in the mighty name of Jesus Christ.
42) I declare that in my prosperity, I shall never be moved, in the mighty name of Jesus Christ.
43) I declare that I shall be in good health and prosperity as long as I live on this earth, in the mighty name of Jesus Christ.
44) O Lord Jesus, by your favor I shall be favored in every way all the days of my life.
45) O Lord Jesus, by your favor I am healed and shall remain healed, in the mighty name of Jesus Christ.

46) O Lord Jesus, by your favor I am delivered and shall remain delivered, in the mighty name of Jesus Christ.
47) O Lord Jesus, by your favor I will be discovered for greatness this year, in the mighty name of Jesus Christ.
48) O Lord Jesus, by your favor I will be promoted to the top this year, in the mighty name of Jesus Christ.
49) O Lord Jesus, by your favor I will be established in this city this year, in the mighty name of Jesus Christ.
50) O Lord Jesus, by your favor I shall not lack good things all the years of my life, in the mighty name of Jesus Christ.
51) O Lord Jesus, by your favor I shall be employed and stay employed, in the mighty name of Jesus Christ.
52) O Lord Jesus, by your favor my horn shall be exalted, in the mighty name of Jesus Christ.
53) O Lord Jesus, by your favor I shall flourish in your favor, in the mighty name of Jesus Christ.
54) O Lord Jesus, by your favor I shall leap over my enemies, in the mighty name of Jesus Christ.
55) O Lord Jesus, by your favor my joy shall be full, in Jesus's name.
56) O Lord Jesus, by your favor all my sorrows shall be no more, in the mighty name of Jesus Christ.
57) O Lord Jesus, by your favor my business shall prosper, in the mighty name of Jesus Christ.
58) O Lord Jesus, by your favor I shall make profitable investments in all my business dealings.
59) O Lord Jesus, by your favor my life shall become a blessing to many in your kingdom, in the mighty name of Jesus Christ.
60) Lord Jesus, do not let me ever become a disappointment to you, in the mighty name of Jesus Christ.
61) O Lord Jesus, turn my mourning into dancing from today, in the mighty name of Jesus Christ.
62) O Lord Jesus, turn my sorrows into joy from today, in the mighty name of Jesus Christ.

63) Almighty God, arise and anoint me with the oil of joy and gladness, in the mighty name of Jesus Christ.
64) Almighty God, arise and give me double honor for my shame, in the mighty name of Jesus Christ.
65) Almighty God, by your favor I shall eat the riches of the gentiles, in the mighty name of Jesus Christ.
66) Almighty God, instead of confusion, let me rejoice in your blessings from this year, in the mighty name of Jesus Christ.
67) Almighty God, let me receive and possess double blessings in all my work, in the mighty name of Jesus Christ.
68) Almighty God, bestow your wisdom and understanding into my soul so I shall be upright, in the mighty name of Jesus Christ.
69) Almighty God, give me the spirit of excellence in the order of Daniel, in the mighty name of Jesus Christ.
70) My life, receive a divine solution to every problem today, in the mighty name of Jesus Christ.
71) My life, receive divine direction to your destiny, in the mighty name of Jesus Christ.
72) O Lord, make me a carrier of good news from today, in the mighty name of Jesus Christ.
73) O Lord, make me a minister of finance on the earth from today, in the mighty name of Jesus Christ.
74) Thank you, Lord Jesus, for answering all my prayers today, in the mighty name of Jesus Christ.

30

O Lord, Let My Giants Become Grasshoppers before Me

OUR GOD IS more than able to fight our battles and give us victory any day, anytime, and any moment. When the enemy comes against you as a flood, His Spirit will always raise a standard against them, always. Without Jesus Christ in our lives, Satan would have defeated us a long time ago. The Lord has lifted you and me above all our enemies and turned them into grasshoppers before us. If you have not surrendered your life to Christ, you must do so immediately to secure God's protection, grace, and mercy for your life and family. Letting Christ be Lord and Savior of your life empowers you to crush all your enemies and their powers under your feet. Spiritual victory will always be yours once you are in Christ Jesus.

The following prayer points will move you from the bottom to the top and put your enemies under your feet.

SCRIPTURAL REFERENCES

Numbers 13:26–33 Now they departed and came back to Moses and Aaron and all the congregation of the children of Israel in the Wilderness of Paran, at Kadesh; they brought back word to them and to all the congregation, and showed them the fruit of the land. Then they told him, and said: "We went to the land where you sent us. It truly flows with milk and honey, and this is its fruit. Nevertheless the people who dwell in the land are strong; the cities are fortified and very large; moreover we saw the descendants of Anak there. The Amalekites dwell *in the land of the South; the Hittites, the Jebusites, and the Amorites dwell in the mountains; and the Canaanites dwell by the sea and along the banks of the Jordan."*

Then Caleb quieted the people before Moses, and said, "Let us go up at once and take possession, for we are well able to overcome it." But the men who had gone up with him said, "We are not able to go up against the people, for they are stronger than we." And they gave the children of Israel a bad report of the land which they had spied out, saying, "The land through which we have gone as spies is a land that devours its inhabitants, and all the people whom we saw in it are men of great stature. There we saw the giants (the descendants of Anak came from the giants); and we were like grasshoppers in our own sight, and so we were in their sight."

PRAYER POINTS

1) Start this prayer session with praise and worship.
2) Lord, thank you for listening and answering all my prayers in this session.
3) Lord, thank you for keeping me rooted in your word
4) Thank you, Lord, for being my strong tower and defender.
5) I shall declare your glory over all the earth, for you are my rock and my salvation.
6) I declare that my giants shall become grasshoppers before me starting from today, in the mighty name of Jesus Christ.
7) I declare that every giant contending against my blessings must die by fire, in the mighty name of Jesus Christ.
8) I declare that every generational giant in my family must die by fire, in the mighty name of Jesus Christ.
9) I declare that I shall be the head over my giants and my giants shall remain the tail forever, in the mighty name of Jesus Christ.
10) I declare that I shall trample upon my giants and over all their powers, and nothing by any means shall hurt me, in the mighty name of Jesus Christ.

11) I declare that my giants have become grasshoppers and I have become the giant over them, in the mighty name of Jesus Christ.
12) I declare that I shall not be afraid of my giants again because they have become my grasshoppers before me from today, in the mighty name of Jesus Christ.
13) Holy Spirit, arise and destroy all my giants by your fire, in the mighty name of Jesus Christ.
14) Holy Spirit, let your fire fall and consume every household giant that has refused to let me become a giant in my family, in the mighty name of Jesus Christ.
15) Holy Spirit, pursue every stubborn giant in my family into the abyss, in the mighty name of Jesus Christ.
16) Holy Spirit, arise and pull me out of spiritual slumber and from my giant's den, in the mighty name of Jesus Christ.
17) Holy Spirit, pursue, overtake, and recover all my blessings from the hands of my giants, in the mighty name of Jesus Christ.
18) Almighty God, arise and feed my giants with their own wickedness and restore health back to me, in the mighty name of Jesus Christ.
19) I command my giants to be cast into the abyss and to be consumed by the fire of the Holy Ghost, in the mighty name of Jesus Christ.
20) Almighty God, I demand a millionfold compensation from my giants today, and I pronounce that they must pay back all they have stolen from my treasury, in the mighty name of Jesus Christ.
21) O God, let all my giants kneel before your face and be eternally condemned from your presence, in the mighty name of Jesus Christ.
22) Holy Spirit, let your fire consume the hands of my giants from my bank accounts, in the mighty name of Jesus Christ.
23) Almighty God, crush all my giants into ashes by the rock of ages, in the mighty name of Jesus Christ.

24) Almighty God, because you are Jehovah Sabaoth, arise and defend me against my giants, in the mighty name of Jesus Christ.
25) Almighty God, arise and displace every giant from my throne today, in the mighty name of Jesus Christ.
26) Almighty God, you know all my giants in this city. Arise and war against them and cast them into the pit, in the mighty name of Jesus Christ.
27) My life shall flourish with great blessings that my God shall release upon me, in the mighty name of Jesus Christ.
28) I command the giant of poverty in my life to die by fire, in the mighty name of Jesus Christ.
29) I command the giant of sickness and disease in my body to die by fire, in the mighty name of Jesus Christ.
30) I command the giant standing against my breakthrough to die by fire and release it back to me, in the mighty name of Jesus Christ.
31) Almighty God, arise and destroy every threat of the giant against my life, in the mighty name of Jesus Christ.
32) Almighty God, by the saving strength of your right hand, save me and my family from our giant's oppression, in the mighty name of Jesus Christ.
33) I shall be above only and my giants shall be beneath me, in the mighty name of Jesus Christ.
34) Almighty God, move my giant out of the way so I may advance and prosper, in the mighty name of Jesus Christ.
35) Almighty God, arise and reduce my giants to grasshoppers before me, in the mighty name of Jesus Christ.
36) I declare that I am transformed from being a grasshopper to a giant, in the mighty name of Jesus Christ.
37) I nullify with the blood of Jesus Christ every curse upon my life by my giant, in the mighty name of Jesus Christ.
38) Holy Spirit, enlarge me today from minimum to maximum, in the mighty name of Jesus.
39) Holy Spirit, let me receive promotion today while my giants receive demotion in the mighty name of Jesus.

40) I cancel and destroy every spirit of the tail from my life, in the mighty name of Jesus.
41) Almighty God, do not let me ever reject you, in the mighty name of Jesus.
42) Lord Jesus, help me to give you all the glory for saving me and my family.
43) Lord Jesus, thank you for putting all my giants under my feet so I can crush them, in the mighty name of Jesus.
44) Lord Jesus, condemn every giant speaking death sentences upon my life, in the mighty name of Jesus.
45) I reverse every death sentence upon my life back to its sender, in the mighty name of Jesus.
46) Let all the arrows of my giants return to their senders, in the mighty name of Jesus.
47) I command every giant that has trampled upon me to be trampled forever, in the mighty name of Jesus.
48) O Lord, as my giants curse, you bless me, in the mighty name of Jesus.
49) I neutralize every curse of the giant against my family by the blood of Jesus Christ, in the mighty name of Jesus.
50) O Lord, paralyze all my giants from the tops of their heads to the soles of their feet, in the mighty name of Jesus.
51) O Lord, let my life become exceedingly blessed, that my giants will be dumbfounded, in the mighty name of Jesus.
52) Almighty God, bring me to the land full of milk and honey in the seasons ahead, in the mighty name of Jesus.
53) Lord Jesus, let my giants become like ants before me forever, in the mighty name of Jesus.
54) I paralyze and flush out the spirit of fear at my giants, in the mighty name of Jesus.
55) O Lord, empower and equip me to spiritually face my giants until they are no more, in the mighty name of Jesus.
56) I command all my giants to surrender and be crushed to ashes, in the mighty name of Jesus.
57) Lord, I receive freedom and power over all my giants from you today, in the mighty name of Jesus.

58) I declare that I shall not be oppressed again by the devil, in the mighty name of Jesus.
59) O Lord, release your arrow of fire and destroy every stubborn giant refusing to surrender in my life, in the mighty name of Jesus.
60) I declare that my victory is sealed today by the blood of Jesus Christ.
61) I declare that my blessings are released back to me from every quarter today, in the mighty name of Jesus.
62) Thank you, Lord, for answering all my prayers, in the mighty name of Jesus.

31

My Angels Must Work for Me

WHEN WAS THE last time you asked your angel to do something for you? The fact is that God created angels to worship Him, and we have also seen that He uses them as spiritual beings to send errands to us, to protect us and fight for us. Angels are given lots of supernatural powers that can be used to defend us in spiritual battles, bless us in times of need, console us when we are troubled, heal us when we are sick, and even save us in the midst of trouble. However, we need to ask them to help us, work for us, and attend to us. I believe that God's angels who are assigned to walk with us do find themselves bored around us because we do not engage them in our daily struggles or ask them to be part of our daily battles. Remember, if you don't ask, you cannot receive. God's angels are always standing ready and willing to battle for us. Know that they are our friends and not our enemies.

The following prayer points are designed to put your angels to work for you and help you get to your destiny at God's appointed time. Your angels have the power to fight for you and turn your situation around for good, in the name of Jesus Christ.

SCRIPTURAL REFERENCES

Exodus 33:1–3 Then the Lord said to Moses, "Depart and go up from here, you and the people whom you have brought out of the land of Egypt, to the land of which I swore to Abraham, Isaac, and Jacob, saying, 'To your descendants I will give it.' And I will send My Angel before you, and I will drive out the Canaanite and the Amorite and the Hittite and the Perizzite and the Hivite and the Jebusite. Go up to a land flowing with milk and honey; for I will not go up in your midst, lest I consume you on the way, for you are a stiff-necked people."

Matthew 1:18–21 *Now the birth of Jesus Christ was as follows: After His mother Mary was betrothed to Joseph, before they came together, she was found with child of the Holy Spirit. Then Joseph her husband, being a just man, and not wanting to make her a public example, was minded to put her away secretly. But while he thought about these things, behold, an angel of the Lord appeared to him in a dream, saying, "Joseph, son of David, do not be afraid to take to you Mary your wife, for that which is conceived in her is of the Holy Spirit. And she will bring forth a Son, and you shall call His name Jesus, for He will save His people from their sins."*

Matthew 4:11 *Then the devil left Him, and behold, angels came and ministered to Him.*

PRAYER POINTS

1) Start this prayer session with praise and worship
2) Thank you, Lord, for this is the day you have made and I will be glad in it.
3) Thank you for saving me and my household from the hand of the wicked one.
4) Thank you for answering all my prayers by a yes and amen.
5) Thank you for giving me the strength to attend this prayer meeting now.
6) Arise, O Lord, and let all my enemies be scattered, in the mighty name of Jesus Christ.
7) O God, arise and send your angels to drive out all my enemies from my life, in the mighty name of Jesus Christ.

8) O God, arise and destroy every satanic power fighting against the angels you have assigned to protect me and my family, in the mighty name of Jesus Christ.
9) Almighty, let every angel you have assigned to help me locate me today, in the mighty name of Jesus Christ.
10) Almighty God, let all your angels carrying my blessings find me and bless me at this house of prayer, in the mighty name of Jesus Christ.
11) I bind every principality and power stopping my angel from reaching me, and I command them to be roasted by the fire of the Holy Spirit, in the mighty name of Jesus Christ.
12) O God, arise and empower your angel to fight and subdue all my enemies today, in the mighty name of Jesus Christ.
13) Almighty God, do not let my angels turn against me all the days of my life, in the mighty name of Jesus Christ.
14) Almighty God, issue a command to your angels to arise and perform the words I have spoken concerning my destiny today, in the mighty name of Jesus Christ.
15) Lord Jesus, destroy every satanic angel positioned to oppose your angels carrying my breakthrough, in the mighty name of Jesus Christ.
16) Lord Jesus, I declare that I shall prosper in the abundance of your riches for me forever and ever, in the mighty name of Jesus Christ.
17) Lord Jesus, send your angels to watch over me and my family in all the watches of the day and night, in the mighty name of Jesus Christ.
18) I declare that all the warring angels assigned to protect me must pursue, overtake, and destroy all satanic agents assigned to every department of my life, in the mighty name of Jesus Christ.
19) O Lord Jesus, send your angels to minister to my spiritual and physical needs, in the mighty name of Jesus Christ.
20) Lord Jesus, unite your angels to walk with me in every step that I take, in the mighty name of Jesus Christ.

21) Almighty God, let your presence go with us wherever we go, in the mighty name of Jesus Christ.
22) Let your angels become our bodyguards and protect us from the attacks of the evil one, in the mighty name of Jesus Christ.
23) Lord, send your ministering angels to come and administer healing and deliverance to me this day, in the mighty name of Jesus Christ.
24) Lord Jesus, send your ministering angels to come and administer financial blessings to me at this hour, in the mighty name of Jesus Christ.
25) Lord Jesus, send your ministering angels to come and administer protection and guidance to me and my family, in the mighty name of Jesus Christ.
26) Lord Jesus, send your ministering angels to come and administer strength to me when I am weak physically and spiritually.
27) Lord Jesus, position your angels to guard my boundaries on the north, south, east, and west from satanic intrusion, in the mighty name of Jesus Christ.
28) Lord Jesus, equip all my angels with the swords of fire to destroy every demonic agent fighting against my life and prosperity, in the mighty name of Jesus Christ.
29) Almighty God, let every angel carrying answers to my petitions find me today, in the mighty name of Jesus Christ.
30) Almighty God, let every angel carrying the solutions for my breakthrough locate me now, in the mighty name of Jesus Christ.
31) Almighty God, as your angels ministered to you, send them to minister to me today, in the mighty name of Jesus Christ.
32) I declare that the presence of the Lord shall remain with me always, whether sitting or standing, and whether sleeping or awaking, in the mighty name of Jesus Christ.
33) I declare that the angels of the Lord shall surround me at all times and protect me and my family by fire, in the mighty name of Jesus Christ.

34) Almighty God, send your angels to bring me good news today, in the mighty name of Jesus Christ.
35) Almighty God, let your angels direct me in the path that you desire for me, in the mighty name of Jesus Christ.
36) I declare that my angels shall assist me in my daily affairs so I may have good success, in the mighty name of Jesus Christ.
37) I declare that I shall prosper in everything I set my hands to do, because the angel of the Lord shall be my helper.
38) I declare that my angels shall locate good financial sources and draw me to them, in the mighty name of Jesus.
39) I declare that God's minister of finance shall begin to supernaturally transfer huge financial blessings into my life, in the mighty name of Jesus.
40) I declare that as the Lord blessed Abraham with wealth and riches, so shall I be blessed.
41) I declare that as the angel of the Lord brought Abraham good news, so shall I be brought good news, in the mighty name of Jesus.
42) Thank you, Lord Jesus, for answering all my prayers today, in your mighty, precious name. Amen.

32

Holy Ghost Fire, Destroy Them

THE FIRE OF the Holy Spirit is one of the most powerful weapons that destroys the enemy besides the word of God, the name of Jesus Christ, and the blood of Jesus Christ. The fire of the Holy Spirit, or Holy Ghost fire, is known to be fierce and powerful. No demon can withstand the fire of God. No human can withstand the fire of God. For this reason, no power or principality can withstand the fire of God. Naturally, fire is a burning or consuming element that denatures the integrity of any substance. Once a substance is exposed to fire, the rest is history. Water and a few chemicals can extinguish the natural fire, but no known substance can quench the fire of the Holy Spirit, or Holy Ghost fire. As a child of God, you are to be baptized by water and by fire (that is to say, you are to receive the baptism of the Holy Spirit). Jesus received His full power on earth after being baptized with water and by the Holy Spirit. Immediately after this encounter with John the Baptist at the River Jordan, Jesus's ministry took off with power and authority, as evidenced by all the miracles, signs, and wonders, including uncountable healings and deliverances.

One of the functions of the Holy Ghost fire is to be a sign of authority and power provided by God for His children. It is a healing instrument deployed by the Holy Spirit to destroy demons and satanic oppressors in the lives of God's people. It also has the ability to function as a spiritual radiation therapy for the children of God suffering from sickness, disease, and satanic afflictions. The fire of the Holy Ghost is also a weapon of spiritual warfare used by the children of God to fight against their enemies. It is a strong weapon of deliverance in times of captivity. In addition, Holy Ghost fire is equally used by God to show His supremacy over His creation and His people. When God's people turn to serve other gods, their idolatrous acts induce God's anger against them, and they suffer from His righteous judgment because He is a jealous God and a consuming fire.

The fire of God is a purifying instrument that exposes all our blind spots by living nothing hidden behind. When God puts us through character tests, wilderness tests, or any kind of test, our experiences in the process are usually comparable to being tried in the fire, because the process is always difficult to go through. The fire will truly reveal your integrity by exposing your weaknesses and strengths, and by rendering you approved or disapproved after the test. As a child of God, you will never reach your full potential with power and authority until you are baptized by fire (Acts 16:16). The sign of this baptism is speaking with tongues, as evidenced on the day of Pentecost in the Upper Room (Acts 2:1–2).

SCRIPTURAL REFERENCES

Matthew 3:11 *I indeed baptize you with water unto repentance, but He who is coming after me is mightier than I, whose sandals I am not worthy to carry. He will baptize you with the Holy Spirit and fire.*

Acts 2:1–4 *When the Day of Pentecost had fully come, they were all with one accord in one place. And suddenly there came a sound from heaven, as of a rushing mighty wind, and it filled the whole house where they were sitting. Then there appeared to them divided tongues, as of fire, and one sat upon each of them. And they were all filled with the Holy Spirit and began to speak with other tongues, as the Spirit gave them utterance.*

Psalm 104:4 *Who makes His angels spirits, His ministers a flame of fire.*

Jeremiah 20:6–9 *O Lord, you induced me, and I was persuaded; you are stronger than I, and have prevailed. I am in derision* daily; Everyone mocks me. For when I spoke, I cried out; I shouted, "Violence and plunder!" Because the word of the Lord was made to me A reproach and a derision daily. Then I said, "I will not make mention of Him, Nor speak anymore in His name." But His word was in my heart like a burning fire Shut up in my bones; I was weary of holding it back, And I could not.

Hebrews 12:28–29 Therefore, since we are receiving a kingdom which cannot be shaken, let us have grace, by which we may serve God acceptably with reverence and godly fear. For our God is a consuming fire.

Deuteronomy 4:23–24 Take heed to yourselves, lest you forget the covenant of the Lord your God which He made with you, and make for yourselves a carved image in the form of anything which the Lord your God has forbidden you. For the Lord your God is a consuming fire, a jealous God.

2 Kings 1:7–17 Then he said to them, "What kind of man was it who came up to meet you and told you these words?" So they answered him, "A hairy man wearing a leather belt around his waist." And he said, "It is Elijah the Tishbite." Then the king sent to him a captain of fifty with his fifty men. So he went up to him; and there he was, sitting on the top of a hill. And he spoke to him: "Man of God, the king has said, 'Come down!'" So Elijah answered and said to the captain of fifty, "If I am a man of God, then let fire come down from heaven and consume you and your fifty men." And fire came down from heaven and consumed him and his fifty. Then he sent to him another captain of fifty with his fifty men. And he answered and said to him: "Man of God, thus has the king said, 'Come down quickly'" So Elijah answered and said to them, "If I am a man of God, let fire come down from heaven and consume you and your fifty men." And the fire of God came down from heaven and consumed him and his fifty. Again, he sent a third captain of fifty with his fifty men. And the third captain of fifty went up, and came and fell on his knees before Elijah, and pleaded with him, and said to him: "Man of God, please let my life and the life of these fifty servants of yours be precious in your sight. Look, fire has come down from heaven and burned up *the first two captains of fifties with their fifties. But let my life now be precious in your sight."* And the angel of the Lord said to Elijah, *"Go down with him; do not be afraid of him."* So he arose and went down with him to the king. Then he said to him, *"Thus says the Lord: 'Because you have sent messengers to inquire of Baal-Zebub, the god of Ekron, is it because there is no God in Israel to inquire of His word? Therefore you shall not come down from the bed to which you have gone up, but you shall surely die.'"* So Ahaziah died according to the word of the Lord which Elijah had spoken. Because he had no son, Jehoram became king in his place, in the second year of Jehoram the son of Jehoshaphat, king of Judah.

1 Kings 18:36–40 *And it came to pass, at the time of the offering of the evening sacrifice, that Elijah the prophet came near and said, "Lord God of Abraham, Isaac, and Israel, let it be known this day that you are God in Israel and I am your servant, and that I have done all these things at your word. Hear me, O Lord, hear me, that this people may know that you are the Lord God, and that you have turned their hearts back to you again."*

Then the fire of the Lord fell and consumed the burnt sacrifice, and the wood and the stones and the dust, and it licked up the water that was in the trench. Now when all the people saw it, they fell on their faces; and they said, "The Lord, He is God! The Lord, He is God!"

And Elijah said to them, "Seize the prophets of Baal! Do not let one of them escape!" So they seized them; and Elijah brought them down to the Brook Kishon and executed them there.

PRAYER POINTS

1) Start this prayer session with praise and worship
2) Thank you, Lord, for your word is fulfilled in my life this day.
3) Thank you, Holy Spirit, for being in my life from my birth.
4) Holy Spirit, baptize me today by your fire.
5) Holy Spirit, fill us with your joy.
6) Holy Spirit, make me experience your presence in my life and show me a sign for good, in the mighty name of Jesus Christ.

7) Holy Ghost fire, arise and consume every hindrance in my life and destiny, in the mighty name of Jesus Christ.
8) Holy Ghost fire, consume and destroy every curse and affliction in my life, in the mighty name of Jesus Christ.
9) Holy Ghost fire, sanitize me today and remove every impurity from my life, in the mighty name of Jesus Christ.
10) Holy Ghost fire, breathe the peace of God into my life, in the mighty name of Jesus Christ.
11) Holy Ghost fire, I receive you as a sign of authority and power in my life, in the mighty name of Jesus Christ.
12) Holy Ghost fire, burn and destroy every sickness in my body today, in the mighty name of Jesus Christ.
13) Holy Ghost fire, burn and destroy every cancer in my body today, in the mighty name of Jesus Christ.
14) Holy Ghost fire, burn and destroy all arthritis in my body today, in the mighty name of Jesus Christ.
15) Holy Ghost fire, burn and destroy high blood pressure in my body today, in the mighty name of Jesus Christ.
16) Holy Ghost fire, burn and destroy every infection in my body today, in the mighty name of Jesus Christ.
17) Holy Ghost fire, burn and destroy all oppression in my body today, in the mighty name of Jesus Christ.
18) Holy Ghost fire, burn and destroy every oppressor in my body today, in the mighty name of Jesus Christ.
19) Holy Ghost fire, burn and destroy all opposition to my breakthrough today, in the mighty name of Jesus Christ.
20) Holy Ghost fire, burn and destroy all sickness in my body today, in the mighty name of Jesus Christ.
21) Holy Ghost fire, burn and destroy every evil altar fighting against my destiny today, in the mighty name of Jesus Christ.
22) Holy Ghost fire, burn and destroy every spirit of poverty in my life today, in the mighty name of Jesus Christ.
23) Holy Ghost fire, burn and destroy every Goliath of my life, in the mighty name of Jesus Christ.
24) Holy Ghost fire, burn and destroy every desert spirit in my life, in the mighty name of Jesus Christ.

25) Holy Ghost fire, burn in every part of my body today, in the mighty name of Jesus Christ.
26) Holy Ghost fire, burn in every part of my destiny today, in the mighty name of Jesus Christ
27) Holy Ghost fire, burn and destroy all sickness in my body today, in the mighty name of Jesus Christ.
28) Holy Ghost fire, burn in every part of my decision-making process from today, in the mighty name of Jesus Christ.
29) Holy Ghost fire, burn and destroy all my burdens today, in the mighty name of Jesus Christ.
30) Holy Ghost fire, burn and destroy all weakness in my life from today, in the mighty name of Jesus Christ.
31) Holy Ghost fire, burn and destroy every prophet of Baal in my life from today, in the mighty name of Jesus Christ.
32) Holy Ghost fire, burn and destroy every witch doctor in my life from today, in the mighty name of Jesus Christ.
33) Holy Ghost fire, burn and destroy every marine bewitchment of my destiny, in the mighty name of Jesus Christ.
34) Holy Ghost fire, burn and destroy every satanic manipulation of my life from today, in the mighty name of Jesus Christ.
35) Holy Ghost fire, consume and destroy every instrument of bewitchment used by satanic agents against me and my family, in the mighty name of Jesus Christ.
36) Holy Ghost fire, burn and destroy all opposition to my ministry, in the mighty name of Jesus Christ.
37) Holy Ghost fire, burn and destroy all powers using the energy from the sun, moon, and stars against my destiny, in the mighty name of Jesus Christ.
38) Holy Ghost fire, burn and destroy all powers using the energy from the earth, the heavens above, and the heavens below against my destiny, in the mighty name of Jesus Christ.
39) Holy Ghost fire, burn and destroy all powers using the energy from the wind, the water, the forest, the fire, the light, the elements, and darkness against my destiny, in the mighty name of Jesus Christ.

40) Holy Ghost fire, burn and destroy all powers transferring evil spirits into my life and my family, in the mighty name of Jesus Christ.
41) Holy Ghost fire, burn and destroy all principalities and powers releasing curses into my life and destiny, in the mighty name of Jesus Christ.
42) Lord, cut off every satanic rope pulling down my blessings from my life, in the mighty name of Jesus Christ.
43) Lord, cut off every satanic rope pulling away my blessings to the burial ground, in the mighty name of Jesus Christ.
44) O Lord, disconnect and destroy every satanic chain holding my promotion in stagnation, in the mighty name of Jesus Christ.
45) O Lord, let your fire burn down every evil altar erected in the earth against my life, in the mighty name of Jesus Christ.
46) O Lord, let your fire burn down and destroy every satanic altar erected in the heavens against my life, in the mighty name of Jesus Christ.
47) O Lord, let your fire burn down every satanic altar erected in the seas and oceans against my life, in the mighty name of Jesus Christ.
48) O Lord, let your fire pursue, overtake, and destroy every household power contending against my blessings, in the mighty name of Jesus Christ.
49) O Lord, let your fire pursue, overtake, and burn down all satanic structures housing my blessings, but leaving my blessings safe, in the mighty name of Jesus Christ.
50) I pronounce that the fire of God will become a hedge of protection around me and my family, in the mighty name of Jesus Christ.
51) O Lord, arise and illuminate my path by your fire, in the mighty name of Jesus Christ.
52) O Lord, arise and strengthen my destiny by your fire, in the mighty name of Jesus Christ.

53) O Lord, empower me to declare your word by your fire, and let your fire become a spiritual weapon from my mouth today, in the mighty name of Jesus Christ.
54) O Lord, let your fire expose all my blind spots and illuminate my life to your glory, in the mighty name of Jesus Christ.
55) Holy Ghost fire, burn and destroy the spirit of anger in my life today, in the mighty name of Jesus Christ.
56) Holy Ghost fire, burn and destroy the spirit of pride in my life today, in the mighty name of Jesus Christ.
57) Holy Ghost fire, burn and destroy the spirit of worry in my life today, in the mighty name of Jesus Christ.
58) Holy Ghost fire, burn and destroy the spirit of judgment and gossip in my life today, in the mighty name of Jesus Christ.
59) Holy Ghost fire, burn and destroy the spirit of divorce and separation in my life today, in the mighty name of Jesus Christ.
60) Holy Ghost fire, burn and destroy the spirit of unfaithfulness in my life today, in the mighty name of Jesus Christ.
61) Holy Ghost fire, burn and destroy the spirit of jealousy and betrayal in my life today, in the mighty name of Jesus Christ.
62) Holy Ghost fire, burn and destroy the spirit of destruction in my life today, in the mighty name of Jesus Christ.
63) Holy Ghost fire, burn and destroy the spirit of frustration in my life today, in the mighty name of Jesus Christ.
64) Lord Jesus, baptize me by your fire and empower me with heavenly authority and power to cast out demons and heal diseases, in the mighty name of Jesus Christ.
65) Holy Spirit, anoint me with your fire so I can walk and perform miracles, signs, and wonders, in the mighty name of Jesus Christ.
66) Thank you, Lord, for answering all my prayers today, in Jesus's name.

33

Be Delivered from Evil Contracts in Your Entertainment Career

ALL OVER THE world, many entertainers in the industry have been trapped by entertainment contracts that were not spiritually or physically beneficial to them. We have received several requests from famous entertainers to pray and break evil contracts they entered into while entering their careers without knowing the consequences. Thank God that He has set them free and released their souls from the manipulation and deception of the wicked.

The devil is quite interested in the soul of any man. He will do anything to gain your soul once you allow him the slightest opportunity. The devil comes with the promise of fame, money, sex, and power in this industry in exchange for the souls of those he finds in it. He initiates them into occult practices and uses the occult to push his agenda on them. Before the victims realize what is happening, it is already too late. Several prominent lives and destinies have been wasted because of satanic deception and manipulation in the entertainment industry. Those who continue in the occult do not last long, as they die prematurely and their careers are terminated before they have a chance to turn to Jesus Christ for deliverance and freedom.

If you are a victim of an evil contract, these prayer points will restore you to Christ and put your enemies under your feet to crush.

SCRIPTURAL REFERENCES

Mark 16:16–21 *He who believes and is baptized will be saved; but he who does not believe will be condemned. And these signs will follow those who believe: In My name they will cast out demons; they will speak with new tongues; they will take up serpents; and if they drink anything deadly, it will by no means hurt them; they will lay hands on the sick, and they will recover.*

Luke 10:18–19 *And He said to them, "I saw Satan fall like lightning from heaven. Behold, I give you the authority to trample on serpents and scorpions, and over all the power of the enemy, and nothing shall by any means hurt you."*

Luke 9:1–2 *Then He called His twelve disciples together and gave them power and authority over all demons, and to cure diseases. He sent them to preach the kingdom of God and to heal the sick.*

Also read **Psalms 35, 69, and 91**, *aggressively.*

PRAYER POINTS

1) Start with aggressive praise and worship, giving thanks to the Lord.
2) Repent for all your sins and ask Jesus Christ to forgive your sins and come into your life now.
3) Ask Him to wash away all your sins with His precious blood.
4) Confess that He alone is Lord over all the heavens and the earth.
5) Tell Jesus Christ that you will serve Him from today for the rest of your life and pray the following prayer points aggressively.
6) O Lord God, I thank you in advance for answering my prayers in this prayer session, in the mighty name of Jesus Christ.
7) O Lord God, purify my tongue with the blood of Jesus Christ, in the mighty name of Jesus Christ.

8) Almighty God, I command my enemies to fall like lightning from heaven and shatter into irreparable pieces, in the mighty name of Jesus Christ.
9) I take authority from Christ Jesus and trample upon my enemies and their powers today and crush them to ashes, in the mighty name of Jesus Christ.
10) I claim victory over all the evil powers of my father's house troubling my career, in the mighty name of Jesus Christ.
11) I claim authority and destroy all the evil powers of my mother's house troubling my career, in the mighty name of Jesus Christ.
12) O Lord, release famine into the camp of my spiritual enemies and starve them to death forever, in the mighty name of Jesus Christ.
13) I command that as my enemies wander from sea to sea and from north to south, they shall not find me, in the mighty name of Jesus Christ.
14) O Lord, destroy every evil poison I have ever taken and cleanse my body with the blood of Jesus Christ.
15) O Lord, let my enemies and my foes stumble and fall before my face, in the mighty name of Jesus Christ.
16) O Lord, neutralize with the precious blood of Jesus Christ every satanic substance that has been administered to me knowingly and unknowingly during my entertainment career.
17) Almighty God, untangle every demonic affliction in my life and return it back to its sender, in the mighty name of Jesus Christ.
18) Almighty God, I command every witch's pot cooking my blessings to explode into pieces, in the mighty name of Jesus Christ.
19) Almighty God, seal, shut, and scatter every corrupt tongue binding my progress in the entertainment industry, in the mighty name of Jesus Christ.
20) I reject every satanic gift I have received and return them to their givers now, in the mighty name of Jesus Christ.

21) I reject every evil gift of my dreams and return them to their senders now, in the mighty name of Jesus Christ.
22) My voice is not for sale, in the name of Jesus Christ. I claim back my voice from wherever it was sold, in the mighty name of Jesus Christ.
23) From today, I dedicate my voice to my Lord Jesus Christ, and no weapon formed against me shall prosper, in the mighty name of Jesus Christ.
24) I refuse to give my soul to Satan in exchange for fame and riches, in the mighty name of Jesus Christ.
25) In the name of Jesus, I cancel and nullify every contract knowingly and unknowing signed by me with the devil, in the mighty name of Jesus Christ.
26) From today, I receive and declare that Jesus Christ is my Lord and Savior, in the mighty name of Jesus Christ.
27) From today, I will only use my voice to sing to glorify Jesus Christ, in the mighty name of Jesus Christ.
28) From today, I dedicate my singing or acting career to my Lord and Savior Jesus Christ, and I declare that I am covered by His precious blood.
29) I command every satanic agent misleading me into satanic traps to fall down and die by fire, in the mighty name of Jesus Christ.
30) I command all deception and manipulation of satanic agents in my life to loose their hold, in the mighty name of Jesus Christ.
31) O Lord Jesus, destroy every satanic contract in my life and cast their agents into the abyss, in the mighty name of Jesus Christ.
32) O Lord Jesus, erase every satanic seal in my life by your precious blood, in the mighty name of Jesus Christ.
33) O Lord Jesus, break and shatter every satanic altar calling my name for evil, in the mighty name of Jesus Christ.
34) O Lord Jesus, take me, own me, and protect me by fire, in the mighty name of Jesus Christ.

35) O Lord Jesus, I cover my soul with your precious blood, and I declare that I shall make it to heaven, in the mighty name of Jesus Christ.
36) O Lord Jesus, set every contract existing between me and Satan ablaze with your fire, in the mighty name of Jesus Christ.
37) Almighty God, I surrender my destiny to you for the price of the blood of Jesus Christ, in the mighty name of Jesus Christ.
38) I declare and decree that my music and acting career shall be free from all satanic bondage, in the mighty name of Jesus Christ.
39) By the word of God I sanitize my mind and soul of every satanic lyric, in the mighty name of Jesus Christ.
40) Holy Ghost fire, arise, destroy, and consume to ashes every mind-controlling demon attached to my career, in the mighty name of Jesus Christ.
41) I denounce all involvement and association with any occultism in my life and career, in the mighty name of Jesus Christ.
42) It is written, "It shall come to pass in that day; That a great panic from the Lord will be among them" (Zech. 14:13). I declare that there shall be a great panic from the Lord in the camp of my enemies today, in the mighty name of Jesus Christ.
43) It is written, "How you are fallen from heaven, O Lucifer, son of the morning! How you are cut down to the ground, you who weakened the nations" (Isa.14:12). Almighty God, let Lucifer and his agents be cut down to the ground from my life and my music/acting career, in the mighty name of Jesus Christ.
44) O God, arise and cut down every agent of Satan plaguing my life and career, in the mighty name of Jesus Christ.
45) O God, arise and set on your fire every mind-controlling demon in my life, in the mighty name of Jesus Christ.
46) O God, arise and frustrate the enterprise of the wicked against my life, in the mighty name of Jesus Christ.

47) O God, arise and fill me with your Holy Spirit at this hour, in the mighty name of Jesus Christ.
48) Jesus said, "I saw Satan fall like lightning from heaven" (Luke 10:18). O God, arise and let Satan fall like lightning from my life and career, in the mighty name of Jesus Christ.
49) Almighty God, let my enemies bow down to me with their faces to the earth, and let them lick up the dust of my feet in Hollywood, in the mighty name of Jesus Christ.
50) Almighty God, because I wait for you, do not let me be ashamed because of my enemies, in the mighty name of Jesus Christ.
51) Almighty God, have mercy upon me according to your loving kindness and tender mercy, in the mighty name of Jesus Christ.
52) Almighty God, I want all of you and none of Satan. Arise and save me from the deception of Satan in Hollywood, in the name of Jesus.
53) Almighty God, today I receive my salvation through our Lord Jesus Christ, and I ask for mercy and grace to set me free from my sins and from the power of Satan, in the mighty name of Jesus Christ.
54) It is written, "Therefore thus says the Lord of hosts concerning the prophets: Behold, I will feed them with wormwood, And make them drink the water of gall; For from the prophets of Jerusalem Profaneness has gone out into all the land" (Jer. 23:15). Almighty God, I command every satanic prophet troubling my life to be fed with wormwood and made to drink the water of gall, in the mighty name of Jesus Christ.
55) It is written, "That I will break the Assyrian in My land, And on My mountains tread him underfoot. Then his yoke shall be removed from them, And his burden removed from their shoulders" (Isa. 14:25). O God, arise and break my enemies and evil powers in my life, and on your mountain tread them underfoot, in the mighty name of Jesus Christ.
56) O God, arise and remove every satanic yoke from my neck and his burden from my shoulders, in the mighty name of Jesus Christ.

57) It is written, "Yet you shall be brought down to Sheol, To the lowest depths of the Pit" (Isa. 14:15). Almighty God, I decree that all mind-controlling agents in my life shall be brought down to Sheol, and to the lowest depths of the pit, in the mighty name of Jesus Christ.
58) I nullify every evil contract I entered into by ignorance or by sound mind today, by the blood of Jesus Christ.
59) I set every satanic contract binding my music/acting career ablaze with the fire of the Holy Ghost, in the mighty name of Jesus Christ.
60) As I write, produce, and direct my songs and movies, I declare that I shall be led by the Holy Spirit and not the devil, in the name of Jesus.
61) All evil money paid to me in order to exchange my soul for fame, I set you ablaze with the fire of the Holy Ghost today, in the name of Jesus Christ.
62) Lord Jesus, use me in Hollywood to declare your glory through my songs and films, in the mighty name of Jesus Christ.
63) Almighty God, let my fame come from you and not from Satan, in the name of Jesus Christ.
64) Dear Holy Spirit, I dedicate my gifts and talents to you because you gave them to me and not Satan, in the mighty name of Jesus Christ.
65) I declare that no weapon formed against the gifts of God in my life shall prosper, in the mighty name of Jesus Christ. Amen.

34

Be Delivered from Demonic Powers and Curses in Your Entertainment Career

Part 1

IN CHAPTER 33, we dealt with evil contracts that exist in the entertainment industry. In this chapter, we are going to deal with all demonic curses, spells, divinations, enchantments, bewitchments, and afflictions that Satan uses in trapping you in the coven. Many have entered into blood covenants or some form of evil covenants and received threats of death if and when they attempted to opt out of the coven. Once initiated, it is hard to come out and remain free without being under the Lordship of our Savior, Jesus Christ.

Only aggressive prayers will break satanic oppression and demonic resistance. The following prayer points come with the power and authority to break every evil blood covenant, curse, and affliction that is associated with the occult in the entertainment industry.

SCRIPTURAL REFERENCES

Isaiah 49:24–26 Shall the prey be taken from the mighty, Or the captives of the righteous be delivered? But thus says the Lord: "Even the captives of the mighty shall be taken away, And the prey of the terrible be delivered; For I will contend with him who contends with you, And I will save your children. I will feed those who oppress you with their own flesh, And they shall be drunk with their own blood as with sweet wine. All flesh shall know That I, the Lord, am your Savior, And your Redeemer, the Mighty One of Jacob."

Ephesians 6:10–13 Finally, my brethren, be strong in the Lord and in the power of His might. Put on the whole armor of God, that you may be able to stand against the wiles of the devil. For we do not wrestle against flesh and blood, but against principalities, against powers, against the rulers of the darkness of this age, against spiritual hosts of wickedness in the heavenly places. Therefore take up the whole armor of God, that you may be able to withstand in the evil day, and having done all, to stand.

Also read **Psalms 69 and 91**

PRAYER POINTS

1) Start with prayer session with praise and worship
2) Lord, forgive me of all my sins and cleanse me with the blood of Jesus Christ.
3) Lord, I give my life to you, and I ask you to come into my life and take total possession of my life and destiny, in the name of Jesus Christ.
4) Dear Holy Spirit, surround me with your fire at this hour and continue to build a hedge of protection around me forever, in the name of Jesus Christ.
5) Almighty God, thank you for setting me free from the depths of Sheol, and from the bottomless pit, in the name of Jesus Christ.
6) I challenge my singing and acting career with the fire of the Holy Spirit, and I declare that I am free from the claws of Satan, in the mighty name of Jesus Christ.
7) I claim authority over satanic oppression in my acting or singing career and I challenge by the fire of the Holy Spirit every demonic priest calling my name for evil, in the name of Jesus Christ.

8) You, demons of destruction pursuing my singing career, be struck down by the lightning fire of God, in the name of Jesus Christ.
9) Holy Ghost fire, consume and destroy every satanic priest working against my life, in the name of Jesus Christ.
10) I retrieve my singing and acting contract from the altar of Satan and present it to Jesus Christ in His most holy temple, in the mighty name of Jesus Christ.
11) I command that every singing or acting contract between me any occult group be washed off by the blood of Jesus Christ.
12) I command all entertainment pharaohs in my entertainment career to die by the fire of the Holy Spirit, in the name of Jesus Christ.
13) Holy Ghost fire, burn to ashes all satanic priests sitting on the throne of my entertainment career, in the name of Jesus Christ.
14) I denounce and reject any involvement with any entertainment cult, in the name of Jesus Christ.
15) I rededicate my voice to Jesus Christ, and I command my voice to sing the Lord's song without fear, in Jesus's name.
16) I withdraw myself from every conscious and unconscious involvement with satanic priests and demons, in the name of Jesus Christ.
17) I declare that I shall live my life now to please my Lord and Savior Jesus Christ and not Satan, in the name of Jesus Christ.
18) I plead for the blood of Jesus Christ over my life, and I claim divine protection from the Almighty God in Jesus's mighty name.
19) I surround myself with the fire of the Holy Spirit and claim the Lord's hedge of protection by fire, in the name of Jesus Christ.
20) The name of Jesus Christ is a strong tower, and those who run to it are saved. I decree that I am saved and protected in the name of Jesus Christ.

21) In the name of Jesus Christ, every demon and satanic agent contending against my singing/acting career must bow to me, and every tongue that rises up against me in judgment and condemnation is hereby condemned to death by the fire of God.
22) I command every human agent working with Satan against me to repent and accept Jesus Christ or be consumed by the eternal fire of the Holy Spirit, in Jesus's mighty name.
23) O God, arise and exchange the soul of every stubborn human agent representing Satan in my case and let his soul become the sacrificial soul in their coven instead of mine, in the name of Jesus Christ.
24) Because they have refused to let me go but are bent on destroying my life, let their souls become the sacrificial souls in their coven instead of mine, in the name of Jesus Christ.
25) O God of Elijah, arise and consume them with your fire, those who pursue my soul for destruction, in the name of Jesus Christ.
26) O Lord Jesus, increase my popularity through your name and make my singing or acting career rise to the top, in the mighty name of Jesus Christ.
27) I am a winner and not a loser in my entertainment career. Thank you, Jesus, for taking me to the top of my career, in Jesus's mighty name.
28) I shall be the head and not the tail in my entertainment career, in the name of Jesus Christ.
29) I am free from any satanic manipulation of an accident against my life, in the name of Jesus Christ.
30) I command every satanic chain holding my singing and acting career captive to break into pieces, in the name of Jesus Christ.
31) I declare that I shall not be forced into drug addiction by wicked powers of the entertainment industry, in the name of Jesus Christ.
32) I command every meeting held against me in cultic circles to start with confusion and end with confusion, in the name of Jesus Christ.

33) Anything buried under the earth by anyone that is dragging my family down, die in the name of Jesus Christ.
34) Anything buried under the sea or water by anyone that is dragging my name down in Hollywood, Bollywood, or Nollywood, etc., die in the name of Jesus Christ.
35) O Lord, send your lifting power to lift me up from evil entertainment circles, in Jesus's mighty name.
36) Collective captivity that is affecting my singing/acting career, die in the name of Jesus Christ.
37) You, powers that have swallowed my voice and style, vomit them now in Jesus's mighty name.
38) Occult powers calling my name and my children's names for evil, die in the name of Jesus Christ.
39) Every witches' coven entertaining my case, catch fire in the name of Jesus Christ.
40) Every power of the occult order fighting against me and my children, I challenge you to die by the fire of the Holy Spirit and by the thunder fire of God, in the name of Jesus.
41) Every power of the occult order fighting to initiate me and my children into your cult, I command you to die in Jesus's name.
42) From today, I denounce any association or affiliation with the occult order directly or indirectly in my life, in Jesus's name.
43) From today, I and my children shall operate under the Lordship of our Lord Jesus Christ.
44) I surrender my life from today to the Lordship of Jesus Christ.
45) I cover myself and my children with the blood of Jesus Christ.
46) From today, I decree and declare that Jesus Christ is Lord of my life. Jesus Christ is Lord. Jesus Christ is Lord to the glory of God the Father.
47) I and my children will not die but live to declare the good works of the Lord in our lives, in Jesus's mighty name.
48) You, arrow of affliction fired from occult circles into my life and my children's lives, backfire, backfire, backfire, in the name of Jesus.
49) Where is the Lord God of Elijah? Arise and kill every satanic prophet assigned to my life, in Jesus's mighty name.

50) Bondage of my father and mother's house, what are you waiting for? Die in the name of Jesus Christ.
51) Where is the Lord God of Elijah? Arise and increase my speed to prosperity and freedom.
52) Any power that wants my family to suffer, you are a liar. Die in the name of Jesus.
53) My father, release unto me the angels of power to destroy every demon assigned to position itself in my home, in Jesus's name.
54) Inherited battles from all occult circles, hear the word of the Lord. Die in the name of Jesus Christ.
55) Every law that needs to be suspended for me to have my breakthrough, what are you waiting for? Be suspended and cancelled in the name of Jesus Christ.
56) Every power that must die for me to have my breakthrough, what are you waiting for? Die in the name of Jesus Christ.
57) Every tongue that must be cut off for me to have my breakthrough, what is holding you back? Be cut off in the name of Jesus Christ.
58) I command all satanic manipulation targeted at me to backfire to the sender, in the name of Jesus Christ.
59) I neutralize every satanic scandal targeted at my singing and acting career, in the mighty name of Jesus Christ.
60) I condemn every conspiracy and lie of my enemies meant to shut me down, in the name of Jesus Christ.
61) I declare that all evil tongues rising against me in judgment must face divine judgment, in the name of Jesus Christ.
62) I declare that no tabloid conspiracy or lie shall have any effect on my singing/acting career, in the mighty name of Jesus Christ.
63) I cancel any untimely death sentence against my life in Hollywood, in the mighty name of Jesus Christ.
64) I cancel any programmed affliction against my body, soul, or spirit by evil powers of Hollywood, in the mighty name of Jesus Christ.

65) I erase my name from all satanic registers that show pending any program execution on a certain date and time, in the mighty name of Jesus Christ.
66) I declare that I shall not die but live to declare the works of God in my life, in the mighty name of Jesus Christ.
67) Holy Spirit, arise and raise a standard against any evil and mind-controlling power that may rise against me in Hollywood, in the mighty name of Jesus Christ.
68) I declare that I am free from the claws of Satan today, in the mighty name of Jesus Christ.
69) I declare that my sins are all forgiven by my Lord and Savior, Jesus Christ.
70) I declare that heaven and earth shall pass away, but the love of Christ for me shall never pass away, in Jesus's mighty, precious name.
71) I nullify all programmed death sentences against me in this life, in Jesus's mighty name. Amen.
72) I sanitize by soul with the blood of Jesus Christ, and I declare my soul unfit for satanic sacrifice, in the mighty name of Jesus.
73) I receive the mark of Jesus Christ upon my forehead, and I command that I shall be rejected for any satanic sacrifice wherever my enemies have taken me, in the mighty name of Jesus Christ.
74) I declare that all my birthdays shall be celebrated in peace and blessings, in the mighty name of Jesus Christ.
75) I declare that no physical or spiritual bullet shall penetrate my body or soul, in the mighty name of Jesus Christ.
76) I declare that every satanic weapon used against me shall become counterfeited, in the mighty name of Jesus Christ.
77) I declare that I shall experience tremendous success in my singing or acting career, in the mighty name of Jesus Christ.
78) I declare that I shall experience breakthrough in every facet of my singing and acting career, in the mighty name of Jesus Christ.

79) I declare that Jesus Christ is my singing and acting partner in Hollywood, in the mighty name of Jesus Christ.
80) I declare that what costs others their blood and soul to succeed shall not cost me anything but my life and soul given already to Jesus Christ.
81) I dedicate my entertainment career to my Lord and Savior, Jesus Christ, and I ask Him to render His divine protection upon me and my family and my career, in the mighty name of Jesus Christ.
82) Thank you, Lord Jesus Christ, for answering all my prayers today. Amen.

35

Be Delivered from Demonic Powers and Curses in Your Entertainment Career

Part 2

SCRIPTURAL REFERENCES

Luke 9:1–2 *Then He called His twelve disciples together and gave them power and authority over all demons, and to cure diseases. He sent them to preach the kingdom of God and to heal the sick.*

Isaiah 54:17 *"No weapon formed against you shall prosper, And every tongue which rises against you in judgment you shall condemn. This is the heritage of the servants of the Lord, And their righteousness is from Me," Says the Lord.*

PRAYER POINTS

1) O Lord Jesus, let all my attackers be put to shame and brought to dishonor who seek after my life, in the name of Jesus Christ.
2) Lord Jesus, deliver me from evil powers and destroy all manipulators who seek my hurt, in the name of Jesus Christ.
3) O Lord Jesus, arise and dismantle the council of Ahithophel against my life and destiny, in the name of Jesus Christ.

4) Every satanic conspiracy to force me out of my destiny, be crushed into dust, in the name of Jesus Christ.
5) Every evil conspiracy to render me useless and spiritually powerless, I nullify you today by the blood of Jesus Christ.
6) Every satanic conspiracy to silence my voice on the earth, I challenge you by the fire of the Holy Spirit, in the name of Jesus Christ.
7) Every household strongman conspiring against my breakthrough, be crushed into pieces by the Rock of Ages, in the mighty name of Jesus Christ.
8) You, family stronghold binding me with the chain of conspiracy, I command your chain to shatter into pieces, in the name of Jesus Christ.
9) O Lord Jesus, let your voice break every rod of affliction against my life, in the name of Jesus Christ.
10) Every conspiracy originated from unfriendly friends that is now affecting me, backfire, backfire, backfire to your senders, in the name of Jesus Christ.
11) I challenge all manipulation and conspiracy against my business success to backfire, in the name of Jesus Christ.
12) I command every power contending against my breakthrough in life to return to and destroy its sender, in the name of Jesus Christ.
13) Every witchcraft gathering against my happiness and advancement, be dissolved by the molten fire of God, in the name of Jesus Christ.
14) You, spirit of antagonism and jealousy projected against me and my family, be cut off forever, in the name of Jesus Christ.
15) O God, arise and silence every conspiracy against my marriage by demonic in-laws, in the name of Jesus Christ.
16) I command every conspiracy network against my progress and breakthrough to shatter into pieces, in the name of Jesus Christ.

17) I command every evil tongue risen against my health and prosperity to be cut off, in the name of Jesus Christ.
18) I command every workplace conspiracy by demonic spirits to hinder my promotion to receive divine arrows, in the name of Jesus Christ.
19) I command every satanic agent stationed at my workplace or on stage or on set causing confusion and manipulation against my progress and promotion to die, in the name of Jesus Christ.
20) O Lord, perfect the work of my hands and improve my progress while performing on stage, rehearsing, singing, or acting, in the name of Jesus Christ.
21) I stand against every negative and destructive accusation against my life and destiny, in the name of Jesus Christ.
22) I dismantle every witches' coven casting evil yokes upon my life, in the mighty name of Jesus Christ.
23) You, carriers of evil load, carry your load now in the mighty name of Jesus Christ.
24) Every satanic load sitting on my breakthrough, catch fire in the mighty name of Jesus Christ.
25) Every household strongman tying me down to stagnation, fall down and die, in the mighty name of Jesus Christ.
26) I refuse to carry any evil load on me, in the mighty name of Jesus Christ.
27) I reject any negative publicity that may destroy my destiny in my entertainment career, in the name of Jesus Christ.
28) I declare that I shall have a good marriage and be successful as an entertainer, in the mighty name of Jesus Christ.
29) I declare that I shall not die from any poison in my life, in the name of Jesus Christ.
30) I declare that my success and fame shall not be for a night, in the mighty name of Jesus Christ.
31) I shall not die but live to declare the works of the Lord in my life, in the mighty name of Jesus Christ.
32) You, power of darkness in my life, receive God's divine destruction, in the mighty name of Jesus Christ.

33) I command all darkness in my life to receive God's divine glory, in the mighty name of Jesus Christ.
34) My soul, I command you to resist the devil and let him flee, in the mighty name of Jesus Christ.
35) My flesh, I command you to be broken for Jesus Christ, in the mighty name of Jesus Christ.
36) Almighty God, arise and destroy every evil tongue casting spells upon my life, in the mighty name of Jesus Christ.
37) Almighty God, do not let me walk away from your divine gospel, in the mighty name of Jesus Christ.
38) Almighty God, as your word is purified, so use it to purify me, in the mighty name of Jesus Christ.
39) Almighty God, let those who look for you find you in me, in the mighty name of Jesus Christ.
40) Out of my mouth shall flow rivers of living waters, in the mighty name of Jesus Christ.
41) Lord Jesus, use me as a conduit to win souls for you in Hollywood.
42) I command my body, soul, and spirit to align with the will of Christ, in the mighty name of Jesus Christ.
43) I receiver power from the Holy Spirit to overcome my enemies today, in the mighty name of Jesus Christ.
44) I reject failure and receive victory into my life, in the mighty name of Jesus Christ.
45) I shall manifest the fruits of the spirit and discard pride of life and lust of the flesh, in the mighty name of Jesus Christ.
46) My life shall be a blessing to the kingdom of God, in the mighty name of Jesus Christ.
47) Whoever blesses me shall be blessed and whoever curses me shall be cursed, in the mighty name of Jesus Christ.
48) I command every melody produced from my mouth to bring glory only to our Lord Jesus Christ.
49) I command every satanic trading of my voice to terminate, and let the thunder fire of God destroy all evil merchants fighting against my destiny, in the name of Jesus Christ.
50) O Lord, let your living water flow out of my mouth and glorify your Holy name.

51) Thank you, Lord, for answering my prayer today.
52) Thank you, Lord, for setting me free from the powers of the occult.
53) Thank you, Lord, for delivering me from demonic and satanic captivity.
54) Thank you, Lord, for washing me with your blood and for breaking every known and unknown covenant I might have entered with Satan.
55) From today, I surrender my life totally to the Lordship of my savior, Jesus Christ.
56) I confess that Jesus Christ is my Lord and Savior forever.
57) I confess that Jesus Christ died and was resurrected for my sins.
58) I confess that Jesus Christ is the Son of God.
59) I confess that I am saved by His death and I have received His grace and favor in my life.
60) I confess that I shall only sing the Lord's song and not the devil's lyrics, in the name of Jesus Christ.
61) I confess that I bear on my body the mark of Jesus Christ, and I denounce the mark of Satan placed upon me and my entertainment career.
62) I confess that I shall only hear the voice of Jesus Christ in my head and not the voice of Satan.
63) I confess that many shall come to Christ because of my acting and singing, and it shall bring glory to God.
64) I confess that I shall not be ashamed of the name of Jesus Christ because in His name, Satan and his demons must flee.
65) I confess that I will not die but live to declare the good works of the Lord Jesus Christ in my life.
66) I shall live a meaningful life worthy of glory unto God.
67) I shall bear much fruit in my entertainment career, and all to the glory of God.
68) In my life I shall experience great joy as a child of God.
69) I shall be the head and not the tail in Hollywood.
70) I shall be above only and not beneath in Hollywood.
71) I shall be at the top and not at the bottom in Hollywood.

72) I shall be first and not last in Hollywood.
73) Holy Spirit, use me to the glory of my Father while in Hollywood, in the mighty name of Jesus Christ.
74) Almighty God, let me not be caught up in peer pressure in Hollywood, in the mighty name of Jesus Christ.
75) Lord Jesus, arise and anoint me by your fire so I may burn in Hollywood for you, in Jesus's mighty name. Amen, amen, amen.

36

Arise and Dwell in God's Glory Today

AS CHRISTIANS, WE must desire spiritual revival in our lives. Many Christians cannot pray, and when they do, they can't pray effectively. This is because we are not continuously dwelling in His glorious presence. We need the localized presence of the Holy Spirit in our lives, in our homes, in our prayer meetings, and in our churches. Once the glory of God shows up in our midst, revival prevails. It is the localized presence of the Holy Spirit or His Shekinah glory that starts a revival both physically and spiritually within us and among us. As you dwell in God's glory, your enemies shall be afraid of you. You will pray and witness miracles, signs and wonders taking place. It is the Lord's desire for you to be in His presence, where you will truly find peace, joy, and blessings.

As you pray the following prayer points, expect the Holy Spirit to revive you again spiritually, physically, and financially. Amen.

SCRIPTURAL REFERENCES

John 1:14 The Word became flesh, and dwelt among us, and we beheld His glory, glory as of the Only begotten from the Father, full of grace and truth.

Isaiah 37:16 O Lord of hosts, God of Israel, the One who dwells between the cherubim, you are God, you alone, of all the kingdoms of the earth. You have made heaven and earth.

John 17:22 *And the glory which you gave Me I have given them, that they may be one just as We are one: And what agreement has the temple of God with idols? For you are the temple of the living God. As God has said: "I will dwell in them And walk among them. I will be their God, And they shall be My people."*

PRAYER POINTS

1) Start this prayer session with praise and worship
2) Lord Jesus, I thank you for this prayer session today and I ask You to come and take Your rightful place with me, in the mighty name of Jesus Christ.
3) Dear Holy Spirit, have Your way in me and lead me to Your presence, in the mighty name of Jesus Christ.
4) O Lord Jesus, let my latter glory be greater than the former, in the mighty name of Jesus Christ.
5) O Lord Jesus, let Your light shine upon me and let Your glory be seen in my life from today, in the mighty name of Jesus Christ.
6) O Lord Jesus, let my heart become a dwelling place for Your glory, in the mighty name of Jesus Christ.
7) O Lord Jesus, do not take Your glory away from me, not today nor forever.
8) O God, arise and sanctify me with the blood of Jesus Christ.
9) O Lord Jesus, fasten Your glory to my heart and let it not depart from me, in the mighty name of Jesus Christ.
10) O Lord Jesus, let my heart become a glorious throne for you to dwell in, in the mighty name of Jesus Christ (Isa. 22:23).
11) O Lord Jesus, let Your glory manifest in our worship, in the mighty name of Jesus Christ.
12) I command any obstacle that may stop God's glory in my life to die by fire, in the mighty name of Jesus Christ.
13) I command every satanic veil covering God's glory in my life to be shredded into pieces, in the mighty name of Jesus Christ.

14) I reject every lifestyle that may rob me of God's glory, in the mighty name of Jesus Christ.
15) Almighty God, let your glory transform me into a well of living water, that I may become a fountain of life in Your kingdom, in the mighty name of Jesus Christ.
16) Almighty God, let Your wave of glory awake and blow upon me like the north and the south winds, in the mighty name of Jesus Christ (Sol. 5:16).
17) O Lord God, as Your glory dwells in Zion, so let Your glory dwell in my life (Ps. 135:21).
18) Almighty God, You who dwell between the cherubim, arise and shine forth in my life, in the mighty name of Jesus Christ.
19) Almighty God, because I am a carrier of Your glory, deliver me from evil men and preserve me from their violence, in the mighty name of Jesus Christ (Ps. 140:1).
20) Almighty God, because of Your glory in my life, let me not darken your counsel and partake in lies against you or anyone, in the mighty name of Jesus Christ (Job 38:2).
21) Arise, O Lord, and cover my house and family with Your glory, in the mighty name of Jesus Christ.
22) Arise, O Lord, and cover my marriage with Your glory, in the mighty name of Jesus Christ.
23) Arise, O Lord, and remove every ancestral sin from my destiny, in the mighty name of Jesus Christ.
24) Lord Jesus, purify my life with Your precious blood and make me whole again.
25) I shall live a righteous life in Christ Jesus.
26) I am made of incorruptible seed by the word of God through Christ Jesus.
27) I am of a holy nation, a royal priesthood, and a chosen generation in Christ Jesus.
28) I am called out of the darkness of this world into Christ's marvelous light (1 John 2:8).
29) The blood of Jesus Christ has washed away my sins; therefore I am holy.

30) I am divinely favored because the glory of God is upon my life, in the mighty name of Jesus Christ.
31) I no longer dwell in darkness but in the Shekinah presence of the Holy Spirit.
32) I am flourishing in great prosperity because of the overwhelming glory of God upon me today, in the mighty name of Jesus Christ.
33) I command any demonic spirit working against my glory to catch fire, in the mighty name of Jesus Christ.
34) I command any satanic stronghold obstructing the glory of God in my life to shatter by the rock of ages.
35) Holy Spirit, remove all unfriendly friends from my life, in the mighty name of Jesus Christ.
36) Almighty God, do not take your Holy Spirit away from me, in the mighty name of Jesus Christ.
37) Almighty God, arise and occupy Your merciful seat in my heart, in the mighty name of Jesus Christ.
38) O Lord Jesus, help me to forgive all who offend me, in the mighty name of Jesus Christ.
39) O Lord Jesus, let Your Shekinah glory shine upon my bank account.
40) O Lord Jesus, stand at the door of my heart and chase away every satanic intruder, in the mighty name of Jesus Christ.
41) O Lord Jesus, because of Your glory in my life, use me and keep me, in the mighty name of Jesus Christ.
42) I shall be first and not last, in the mighty name of Jesus Christ.
43) Lord Jesus, destroy all satanic manipulation in my life, in the mighty name of Jesus Christ.
44) Almighty God, remove every affliction of the second heaven from my life, in the mighty name of Jesus Christ.
45) Almighty God, destroy every satanic arrow shot at your seat of glory in my life, in the mighty name of Jesus Christ.
46) Almighty God, consume every satanic arrow shot into my life, in the mighty name of Jesus Christ.

47) Every wind of affliction blowing on my destiny, be blown away by the east wind of God, in the mighty name of Jesus Christ.
48) Almighty God, because my body is Your temple, take off every filthy garment from me, in the mighty name of Jesus Christ.
49) Almighty God, because my body is Your temple, rebuke every demonic intrusion in my life, in the mighty name of Jesus Christ.
50) Almighty God, because my body is Your temple, rebuke every type of addiction in my life, in the mighty name of Jesus Christ.
51) Almighty God, because my body is Your temple, rebuke every unholy sexual habit in my life, in the mighty name of Jesus Christ.
52) Almighty God, because my body is Your temple, remove every craving for immorality and close all doors against it, in the mighty name of Jesus Christ.
53) Almighty God, because my body is Your temple, remove every form of idolatry from my life, in the mighty name of Jesus Christ.
54) Almighty God, help me to have a broken and a contrite heart, and renew a rightful spirit within me, in the mighty name of Jesus Christ.
55) O Lord Jesus, increase my zeal for You, in the mighty name of Jesus Christ.
56) O Lord Jesus, because of Your glory, make me work in the spirit of compassion, in the mighty name of Jesus Christ.
57) Almighty God, for Your name's sake, lead me from glory to glory, in the mighty name of Jesus Christ.
58) Almighty God, let Your presence go with me to wherever you shall send us, in the mighty name of Jesus Christ.
59) Almighty God, let my life be filled with Your glory from the top of my head to the soles of my feet.
60) Almighty God, You are the shield for me, the glory and the lifter of my head, in the mighty name of Jesus Christ.

61) My life, you shall dwell in the glory of God, in the mighty name of Jesus Christ.
62) My life, you shall not depart from the glory of God, in the mighty name of Jesus Christ.
63) For my sake, O Lord, do not hold Your peace and do not rest until my righteousness goes forth as brightness and my salvation as a lamp that burns, in the mighty name of Jesus Christ (Isa. 62:1).
64) Almighty God, because of Your glory in my life, do not let me be termed forsaken, in the mighty name of Jesus Christ.
65) Almighty God, let me be a crown of glory in Your hand, in the mighty name of Jesus Christ (Isa. 62: 3).
66) Almighty God, because of Your glory, set watchmen over my life, in the mighty name of Jesus Christ.
67) Almighty God, as the bridegroom rejoices over the bride, so you shall rejoice over me, in the mighty name of Jesus Christ.
68) Lord Jesus, do not allot the portion of my inheritance to another, in the mighty name of Jesus Christ.
69) Lord Jesus, let Your glory draw all heavenly blessings into my life, in the mighty name of Jesus Christ.
70) Lord Jesus, let my life become a celebration to you always, in the mighty name of Jesus Christ.
71) Lord Jesus, let Your glory fill my house always.
72) Lord Jesus, let Your glory fill my life always.
73) Lord Jesus, let Your glory fill my children always.
74) Thank you, Lord, for answering all my prayers today, in the mighty name of Jesus Christ.

37

Victory over Repeated Problems

Part 1

THE LORD HAS given us power and authority to destroy every stubborn problem in our lives. Through prayer we are able to set the fire of God on our problems and cast them all into the abyss. The enemy wants to perpetually oppress God's children, and to constantly stop them from advancing forward to get their breakthrough and receive victory. For those Christians who do not pray, the enemy goes after them with discouragement by making them experience the same problems over and over again. A person who has been healed from arthritis may continue to feel arthritic pains though the arthritis has been healed. The devil could be instigating problems in a marriage and causing the couple to constantly argue and quarrel for no just reason. A person could get pulled over and receive a traffic ticket every time he or she was about to have a little savings put away for a rainy day. Many people have had to constantly fix their cars over and over again because they could not afford a new one.

In so many cases, the enemy has used the same or similar situations to manipulate God's children into frustration in order to make them doubt God and possibly question God's loyalty and faithfulness to them. If you are one of these people, the following prayer points will break satanic and repeated cycles of problems in your life and give you great victory. Amen.

SCRIPTURAL REFERENCES

Revelation 12:7–12 *And war broke out in heaven: Michael and his angels fought with the dragon; and the dragon and his angels fought, but they did not prevail, nor was a place found for them in heaven any longer. So the great dragon was cast out, that serpent of old, called the Devil and Satan, who deceives the whole world; he was cast to the earth, and his angels were cast out with him. Then I heard a loud voice saying in heaven, "Now salvation, and strength, and the kingdom of our God, and the power of His Christ have come, for the accuser of our brethren, who accused them before our God day and night, has been cast down. And they overcame him by the blood of the Lamb and by the word of their testimony, and they did not love their lives to the death. Therefore rejoice, O heavens, and you who dwell in them! Woe to the inhabitants of the earth and the sea! For the devil has come down to you, having great wrath, because he knows that he has a short time."*

Romans 8:36–37 *As it is written: "For your sake we are killed all day long; We are accounted as sheep for the slaughter." Yet in all these things we are more than conquerors through Him who loved us.*

Psalm 44:21–22 *Would not God search this out? For He knows the secrets of the heart. Yet for your sake we are killed all day long; We are accounted as sheep for the slaughter.*

1 Corinthians 15:56 *The sting of death is sin, and the strength of sin is the law. But thanks be to God, who gives us the victory through our Lord Jesus Christ.*

PRAYER POINTS

1) Start this prayer session with praise and worship
2) Lord Jesus, I thank you for covering me with Your precious blood at this hour of prayer.
3) Forgive me of my sins today, in the mighty name of Jesus Christ.
4) I confess that You are the Son of God, and that You died for me on the cross.
5) I receive You into my life today.

6) I thank you for saving me by forgiving all my sins through your death on the cross.
7) Thank you for Your sustaining grace upon me and my family.
8) Thank you for Your blessings and favor upon my home and family.
9) There is now therefore no condemnation for me and my family, in the mighty name of Jesus Christ.
10) Thank you, Lord, for setting me and my family free from the law of sin and death.
11) Holy Spirit, do not let me set my mind on things of the flesh, but make me set my mind on things of the spirit.
12) Holy Spirit, help me to be spiritually minded so I may have abundant life and peace.
13) Holy Spirit, help me to please You so I may enter the fullness of God's blessings for my life.
14) O Lord, deliver me from the bondage of corruption of this world into the glorious liberty of the sons of God.
15) I command every repeated problem in my life to face the wrath of God, in the mighty name of Jesus Christ.
16) I command every demonic stronghold in my life to receive heavenly destruction, in the mighty name of Jesus Christ.
17) I command all inherited bondage in my life to be flushed out by the blood of Jesus Christ.
18) I command every strong root of poverty in my life to be uprooted and cast into fire, in the mighty name of Jesus Christ.
19) I command all ancestral bondage in my life to receive divine termination, in the mighty name of Jesus Christ.
20) I command every form of deity and any idolatrous presence in my family to be consumed by fire, in the mighty name of Jesus Christ.
21) Holy Spirit, destroy every stubborn problem in my life forever, in the mighty name of Jesus Christ.
22) Every demonic tree planted against my life that has refused to die, be uprooted by the resurrection power of Christ, in the mighty name of Jesus Christ.

23) Holy Spirit, intercede with groaning that cannot be uttered for my sake, and uproot and destroy every stubborn problem in my life today, in the mighty name of Jesus Christ.
24) Holy Spirit, arise and pull me out of all my weaknesses and bring restoration to every area of my life, in the mighty name of Jesus Christ.
25) I command that no power or principality shall bring any charge against me or my family, in the mighty name of Jesus Christ.
26) Holy Spirit, arise and cast out every authority that shall try to separate me from your love, in the mighty name of Jesus Christ.
27) Almighty God, root out and pull down every strongman and repeated problem in my life, in the mighty name of Jesus Christ.
28) Almighty God, destroy and throw down every generational pharaoh in my life, in the mighty name of Jesus Christ.
29) Almighty God, build and plant your prosperity and righteousness in my life, in the mighty name of Jesus Christ.
30) Almighty God, erect a bronze wall against all stubborn problems and afflictions in my life, in the mighty name of Jesus Christ.
31) Almighty God, empower me to face every giant in my life and destroy them to your glory, in the mighty name of Jesus Christ.
32) I command all marine witchcraft bewitching my life to die by fire, in the mighty name of Jesus Christ.
33) I command every marine temple manipulating my destiny to receive a divine earthquake, in the mighty name of Jesus Christ.
34) I break the powers of satanic betting over my life, in the mighty name of Jesus Christ.
35) I command every satanic remote control over my finances to shatter to pieces, in the mighty name of Jesus Christ.
36) O Lord Jesus, send a rain of blessings to fall upon my life now, in the mighty name of Jesus Christ (Zech. 10:1).

37) O Lord Jesus, command your flashing clouds to bring showers of rain and victory into my life, in the mighty name of Jesus Christ.
38) Thus says the Lord God, come from the four winds, O breath of life, and breathe on my finances today, that I may become exceedingly prosperous in this city, in the mighty name of Jesus Christ (Ezek. 37:9).
39) I declare that I am an overcomer and shall continue to remain so until Jesus comes, in the mighty name of Jesus Christ.
40) Holy Spirit, command victory into every area of my life and destiny today, in the mighty name of Jesus Christ.
41) Holy Spirit, arise and destroy every programmed and excessive spending habit from my life, in the mighty name of Jesus Christ.
42) Holy Spirit, arise and destroy every repeated habit and lifestyle from my destiny today, in the mighty name of Jesus Christ.
43) Holy Spirit, arise and show me your glory today, in the mighty name of Jesus Christ.
44) I refuse and reject stubborn spirits from my life forever, in the mighty name of Jesus Christ.
45) I command the spirit of failure and frustration to die out of my life, in the name of Jesus Christ.
46) I uproot constant loss of income and employment from my life, in the mighty name of Jesus Christ.
47) I nullify every accusation and destroy every marriage destroyer in my home by fire, in the mighty name of Jesus Christ.
48) Holy Spirit, thank you for answering all my prayers today, in the mighty name of Jesus Christ. Amen.

38

Victory over Repeated Problems

Part 2

SCRIPTURAL REFERENCES

Revelation 12:10–12 Then I heard a loud voice saying in heaven, "Now salvation, and strength, and the kingdom of our God, and the power of His Christ have come, for the accuser of our brethren, who accused them before our God day and night, has been cast down. And they overcame him by the blood of the Lamb and by the word of their testimony, and they did not love their lives to the death. Therefore rejoice, O heavens, and you who dwell in them! Woe to the inhabitants of the earth and the sea! For the devil has come down to you, having great wrath, because he knows that he has a short time."

Romans 8:36–37 As it is written: "For your sake we are killed all day long; We are accounted as sheep for the slaughter." Yet in all these things we are more than conquerors through Him who loved us.

Psalm 44:21–22 Would not God search this out? For He knows the secrets of the heart. Yet for your sake we are killed all day long; We are accounted as sheep for the slaughter.

1 Corinthians 15:56 The sting of death is sin, and the strength of sin is the law. But thanks be to God, who gives us the victory through our Lord Jesus Christ.

PRAYER POINTS

1) Start this session with praise and worship
2) Dear Holy Spirit, thank you for exposing every stubborn problem in my life.
3) Dear Holy Spirit, thank you for delivering me from all ancestral curses.
4) Dear Holy Spirit, that you for setting me free from the evil powers of my father's and my mother's houses.
5) Dear Lord Jesus, have your way in every area of my life.
6) Every evil power operating in my neighborhood against my progress, be cut off forever by the sword of fire, in the mighty name of Jesus Christ.
7) Every demonic agent directing sickness into my life, be cut off forever by the sword of fire, in the mighty name of Jesus Christ.
8) Every repeated cycle of insomnia in my life, be cut off forever by the sword of fire, in the mighty name of Jesus Christ.
9) Every demonic spirit fighting against my peace at night, I command you to sleep forever and do not wake up, in the name of Jesus.
10) Every repeated marital problem in my life, be cut off forever by the sword of fire, in the mighty name of Jesus Christ.
11) Every repeated financial failure in my business transactions, be cut off forever by the sword of fire, in the mighty name of Jesus Christ.
12) Every repeated miscarriage in my life, be cut off forever by the sword of fire, in the mighty name of Jesus Christ.
13) Every repeated disappointment in my life, be cut off forever by the sword of fire, in the mighty name of Jesus Christ.
14) Every repeated criminal tendency in my life, be cut off forever by the sword of fire, in the mighty name of Jesus Christ.
15) Every recurring infection in my body, hear the word of the Lord. Be cut off forever by the sword of fire, in the mighty name of Jesus Christ.

16) Every repeated cancer in my body, hear the word of the Lord. Be cut off forever by the sword of fire, in the mighty name of Jesus Christ.
17) Every repeated lung, liver, kidney, thyroid, and duodenal disease in my body, hear the word of the Lord. Be cut off forever by the sword of fire, in the mighty name of Jesus Christ.
18) All repeated high blood pressure, diabetes, arthritis, blood disease, asthma, COPD, emphysema, and nervous disease, hear the word of the Lord. Be cut off forever by the sword of fire, in the mighty name of Jesus Christ.
19) Every repeated head injury or nose, mouth, ear, or eye problem in my life, hear the word of the Lord. Be cut off forever by the sword of fire, in the mighty name of Jesus Christ.
20) Every repeated episode of divorce in my life, hear the word of the Lord. Be cut off forever by the sword of fire, in the mighty name of Jesus Christ.
21) Every repeated addiction plaguing my life, hear the word of the Lord. Be cut off forever by the sword of fire, in the mighty name of Jesus Christ.
22) Every repeated territorial affliction against my family, hear the word of the Lord. Be cut off forever by the sword of fire, in the mighty name of Jesus Christ.
23) Every returning demonic animal moving around for my sake, hear the word of the Lord. Be cut off forever by the sword of fire, in the mighty name of Jesus Christ.
24) Every returning satanic insect and bird flying for my sake, hear the word of the Lord. Be cut off forever by the sword of fire, in the mighty name of Jesus Christ.
25) All repeated incantations and sorcery spoken against my life, hear the word of the Lord. Be cut off forever by the sword of fire, in the mighty name of Jesus Christ.
26) Every repeated spell and curse spoken against my destiny, hear the word of the Lord. Be cut off forever by the sword of fire, in the mighty name of Jesus Christ.

27) Today I declare that my God is for me, and my enemies shall not stand against me forever and ever, in the mighty name of Jesus Christ.
28) I command every dry area of my life to receive a divine flood.
29) I command every difficult situation in my life to receive a divine solution, in the mighty name of Jesus Christ.
30) Dear Lord Jesus, groan for me and restore everything that the enemy stole from me (John 11:38).
31) Dear Lord Jesus, take away the stone of all captivities and oppression from my life, in the name of Jesus Christ (John 11:43).
32) You, satanic powers fighting against my destiny, hear the words of Jesus Christ: "Loose me and let me go," in the name of Jesus Christ.
33) Dear Lord Jesus, command my blessings to come forth.
34) O Lord Jesus, speak life into every dead area of my life, after the order of Lazarus.
35) O Lord Jesus, bless me so I may be a blessing to others and your kingdom, in the mighty name of Jesus Christ.
36) O Lord Jesus, arise and command every repeated generational curse in my life to be broken forever.
37) Almighty God, you are my king, O God; command victories for me today, in the mighty name of Jesus Christ (Ps. 44:4).
38) O Lord Jesus, rebuke every evil power of my father's house to die and set me free, in the mighty name of Jesus Christ.
39) O Lord Jesus, rebuke every stubborn wind in my life to be calmed forever, in the mighty name of Jesus Christ.
40) I command every evil flood in my destiny to dry up forever, in the mighty name of Jesus Christ.
41) Lord Jesus, sanitize my life with your precious blood.
42) O Lord Jesus, breathe upon your blessings for me now, in the name of Jesus Christ.
43) O Lord Jesus, rebuke every evil power of my mother's house to die and set me free, in the mighty name of Jesus Christ.

44) Almighty God, arise and close all doors against any repeated problem in my life, in the name of Jesus Christ.
45) O Lord Jesus, let my prayer rise and come before you as a sweet sacrifice, pleasing to you.
46) Lord, I thank you for hearing and answering all my prayers at this hour, in the mighty name of Jesus Christ. Amen.

39

Receive Healing by Confessing the Word of God

Part 1

THE BEST FORM of prayer is to pray the word of God and activate the power embodied in the word to act for you. The word of God is living and powerful. The word of God is spirited and alive. It is the power in the word that heals, delivers, and convicts one to repentance and salvation. The devil cannot stand it when you speak the word of God from a pure heart. The devil will hate you for exercising your right to use the word of God in your prayer because he knows that the word will break his yoke and destroy his burden upon you. You will be healed by using the word of God in the name of Jesus Christ to challenge your sickness, cancer, disease, affliction, and demonic oppression.

No one should underestimate the power of God in His word. Words are powerful, as they can give or take a life. They can bless one or induce a curse. Words can build or destroy. The power that is in the word, whether it is of God or of man or of the devil, is unlimited. For this reason, God has given you the authority and power, through His word, to trample upon your enemy and over all his powers, to ensure that you are not hurt by him. Your healing will be activated by declaring the word of God in any situation in which you find yourself.

Healing is conditional, as there are several factors that may determine your healing from God. The greatest condition on healing is that God will heal whomever He wants to heal; otherwise, everyone seeking healing would be healed. However, our God is very compassionate and gracious. He is full of love and abounding in mercy. He will heal when He wants to and how He chooses to, and no one can make Him do otherwise. If God sees that the only reason you come to Him is to be healed, then He will delay your healing until you have changed the way you think and love Him first, then give you your healing afterward. This is called a "renewing of your mind." God is concerned about your healing but more so about your soul. You must seek first the kingdom of God and all its righteousness; then every other thing shall be added unto you, including your healing.

The following things will hinder you from receiving healing from God:

a. Lack of faith in God and in His word (Rom. 10:17, Heb. 11:6)
b. You are not in the presence of God.
c. Pride and arrogance
d. Unforgiveness in your heart
e. Not redeeming your vows to God
f. Ungratefulness to God
g. Being outside of faith (not believing in Christ)
h. A curse due to sin in your life
i. Having double standards
j. Being in sin (disobedience)
k. Lack of repentance
l. Rebellion against God
m. Selfishness

Read the following scriptures and pray the prayer points aggressively, and your healing will surely manifest.

SCRIPTURAL REFERENCES

Exodus 15:26 *And God said, "If you diligently heed the voice of the LORD your God and do what is right in His sight, give ear to His* commandments and keep all His statutes, I will put none of the diseases on you which I have brought on the Egyptians; For I am the LORD who heals you."

PRAYER POINTS

1) Start this prayer session with praise and worship
2) Lord Jesus, forgive me and my family for all our sins past and present, in the name of Jesus Christ.
3) Cleanse and cover me and my family with the blood of Jesus Christ.
4) Help me and my family to obey your word and to walk upright in your ways.
5) Almighty God, remove all disease and sickness from me and my family today, and bring restoration to our health, in the name of Jesus Christ.

Deuteronomy 32:39. Now see that I, even I, am He, And there is no God besides Me; I kill and I make alive; I wound and I heal; Nor is there any who can deliver from My hand.

6) Almighty God, you are the Lord of host. Kill and destroy all my diseases and afflictions, heal and make me alive, and deliver me from the hand of the wicked and from all his troubles, in the mighty name of Jesus Christ.
7) Almighty God, arise and let all my enemies be scattered forever

2 Chronicles 7:14. "If My people who are called by My name will humble themselves, and pray and seek My face, and turn from their wicked ways, then I will hear from heaven, and will forgive their sin and heal their land.

8) O Lord Jesus, hear my prayers today and forgive my sins and heal me and my family, in the mighty name of Jesus Christ.
9) I repent for my pride and arrogance before you today.

10) Fill me with your Holy Spirit and help me turn from my wicked ways to your ways, in the mighty name of Jesus Christ

Psalms 30:2 O LORD my God, I cried out to You, And You healed me.

11) O Lord Jesus, answer me and heal me as I cry to you,
12) Do not let my enemies rejoice over me in my distress.
13) Arise, O Lord, and put my enemies to shame by healing me and making me whole again, in the mighty name of Jesus Christ

Psalms 6:2. Have mercy on me, O LORD, for I am weak; O LORD, heal me, for my bones are troubled.

14) Almighty God, have mercy upon me, for I am weak. Heal my bones and muscles and make me strong, in the mighty name of Jesus Christ.
15) I declare that I am healed from every form of arthritis and pain in my body, in the mighty name of Jesus Christ.
16) I declare that I am healed from every joint and bone deformation in my body, in the mighty name of Jesus Christ.
17) I declare that I am healed today from all muscle weakness, lack of strength, and paralysis in my body, in the mighty name of Jesus Christ.
18) I refuse to remain wheelchair-bound from this day, in the mighty name of Jesus Christ.
19) I declare that I shall walk around painless, strong, and with boldness on my two feet, and will be able to run if I choose to, in the name of Jesus Christ.
20) I challenge my entire body with the fire of the Holy Ghost, and I command supernatural healing and transformation upon my body, soul, and spirit, in the mighty name of Jesus Christ (Ps. 103:1–4).
21) Almighty God, forgive all my iniquities, heal all my diseases, redeem my life from destruction, crown me with loving kindness and tender mercy, and restore all my strength and blessings, in the mighty name of Jesus Christ.

22) O Lord Jesus, as you heal me and take away my sickness this day, I shall continue to declare and proclaim your goodness before your congregation.
23) Lord Jesus, do not let me become ungrateful to you after healing me today.
24) Let me be as the one who returned to give you thanks for the ten you healed.
25) I challenge my soul to remember the goodness of the Lord from today in the land of the living.
26) Bless the Lord, O my soul, and all that is within me. I challenge you to bless His holy name forever and ever

Psalms 107:20. *He sent His word and healed them, And delivered them from their destructions.*

27) Almighty God, because of your word, heal me now and deliver me from my destruction.
28) Almighty God, arise and command victory for me today, in the name of Jesus Christ.
29) Almighty God, according to your word, I am healed from the top of my head to the soles of my feet, and so shall it be forever, in the mighty name of Jesus Christ.
30) Holy Ghost fire, consume and destroy every satanic agent casting spells of destruction against my life and my family, in the mighty name of Jesus Christ.
31) I challenge my cancer with the word of God and I command it to disappear from my body forever and ever, in the mighty name of Jesus Christ.
32) I challenge my body with the blood of Jesus Christ, and I command all my diseases to be flushed away by the blood of Christ, in the name of Jesus.
33) I challenge every infection in my body by Psalm 107:20, in the mighty name of Jesus Christ.
34) I declare that destruction shall not be my portion in this life, from body and soul to my spirit, in the mighty name of Jesus Christ

Psalms 147:3 *He heals the brokenhearted And binds up their wounds.*

35) Lord Jesus, my heart is broken due to my sickness and pain. Heal my entire body and bind up my wounds, in the mighty name of Jesus Christ.
36) Lord Jesus, I am tired of my pains. I cry to you day and night. Let Psalm 147:3 be my portion today, in the name of Jesus Christ
37) Lord Jesus, I cry to you and seek your face because I am in distress. I repent for only seeking your face when I am in distress. Forgive me of my selfishness and heal me from all my wounds, in the name of Jesus Christ.

Proverbs 3:7-8 *Do not be wise in your own eyes; Fear the LORD and depart from evil. It will be health to your flesh, And strength to your bones.*

38) O Lord Jesus, because I fear your holy name, release health to my life and strength to my bones, in the mighty name of Jesus Christ.
39) Lord Jesus, deliver me from the spirit of the Antichrist and doubt, in the mighty name of Jesus Christ.
40) I denounce every judgmental spirit in my life and declare that Jesus Christ is my Lord and Savior.
41) I fire the arrow of black out into the camp of all my enemies, in the name of Jesus Christ.
42) You, spirit of rebellion and the Antichrist, die out of my life by fire, in the mighty name of Jesus Christ.
43) I declare that God's wisdom shall guide me all the days of my life, in the name of Jesus Christ

Proverbs 4:20-22 *My son, give attention to my words; Incline your ear to my sayings. Do not let them depart from your eyes; Keep them in the midst of your heart; For they are life to those who find them, And health to all their flesh.*

44) Almighty God, help me pay attention to your word and believe it in my heart.
45) Increase the years of my life and help me live in good health, in the name of Jesus Christ.
46) Nourish my flesh with your word and heal me from all my afflictions, in the mighty name of Jesus Christ.
47) I declare that I am healed and will not die from my sickness again, in the mighty name of Jesus Christ

Isaiah 53:5 *But He was wounded for our transgressions, He was bruised for our iniquities; The chastisement for our peace was upon Him, And by His stripes we are healed.*

48) I receive my healing today because of the stripes of Jesus Christ on the cross.
49) I receive my healing today because He was wounded for my transgressions.
50) I receive my healing today because He was bruised for my iniquities.
51) I receive my healing today because the chastisement for our peace was upon Him.
52) Dear Lord Jesus, I receive my healing today because of your death on the cross.
53) Lord Jesus, I declare that I am healed right now because of your finished work on the cross.
54) I declare that I am healed today because I have entered into your rest because of the finished work on the cross

Isaiah 58:8 *Then your light shall break forth like the morning, Your healing shall spring forth speedily, And your righteousness shall go before you; The glory of the LORD shall be your rear guard.*

55) Almighty God, let your healing spring forth speedily before me.
56) Lord, let your glory be my undertaker and my rear guard, in the mighty name of Jesus Christ.

57) Let your light shine before me and radiate all my infirmities away, in the name of Jesus Christ.
58) I declare that I shall be made whole when I arise in the morning, in the name of Jesus Christ.
59) I declare that my blindness shall disappear as I awake in the morning, in the name of Jesus Christ.
60) I declare that the moon and the stars shall not smite me in the night, in the name of Jesus Christ.
61) I declare that my healing is fast and complete, in the name of Jesus Christ.
62) I command every obstacle to my healing to receive divine judgment by fire, in the name of Jesus Christ.
63) I issue an eviction notice to every sickness and all stubborn afflictions in my body, in the name of Jesus Christ.

Isaiah 61:1 *"The Spirit of the Lord GOD is upon Me, Because the LORD has anointed Me To preach good tidings to the poor; He has sent Me to heal the brokenhearted, To proclaim liberty to the captives, And the opening of the prison to those who are bound;*

64) Almighty God, let your spirit come upon me now and take over my life, in the name of Jesus Christ.
65) Holy Spirit, arise and repair every spiritual and physical wound in my life, in the name of Jesus Christ.
66) Holy Spirit, remove the spirits of depression and manic psychosis from me at this hour, in the name of Jesus Christ.
67) Holy Spirit, ignite your fire and consume every satanic priest manipulating my life for destruction, in the name of Jesus Christ.
68) Holy Spirit, arise and consume the spirit of attention deficit disorder from my life and that of my children, in the name of Jesus Christ.
69) I command attention deficit disorder with hyperactivity to die out of my children's lives forever, in the name of Jesus Christ.
70) Dear Holy Spirit, dwell in me and reside in me. Heal me and send me to heal others, in the mighty name of Jesus Christ.

71) I challenge my life with the fire of the Holy Spirit, and I command that no satanic weapon formed against me shall prosper, in the name of Jesus Christ.
72) Lord Jesus, heal me from the spirit of anxiety and panic attacks today, in the name of Jesus Christ.
73) Lord Jesus, heal me from the oppression of anorexia and bulimia and destroy their prophets by fire, in the name of Jesus Christ.
74) I break the chains of darkness tying me down, by the word of God, in the name of Jesus Christ.
75) Lord Jesus, arise and set me free from all captivities of the enemy, in the mighty name of Jesus Christ.
76) Holy Spirit, give me the spirit of boldness to pray always and to scatter the devices of the wicked against my life, in the mighty name of Jesus Christ.

Jeremiah 3:22 *"Return, you backsliding children, And I will heal your backslidings.""Indeed we do come to You, For You are the LORD our God.*

77) Almighty God, forgive me for backsliding and cheating on you.
78) Heal me and help me to be able to forgive myself, in the mighty name of Jesus Christ.
79) Show me a token for good and heal all my backslidings, in the name of Jesus Christ.
80) I repent for turning away from you and embracing my selfish desires.
81) Restore the son of your right hand to his glorious place, which you prepared for him from the beginning.
82) Let me see your awesome goodness and healing in my life now, in the mighty name of Jesus Christ. Amen, amen, amen.

40

Receive Healing by Confessing the Word of God

Part 2

SCRIPTURAL REFERENCES

Jeremiah 17:14 Heal me, O LORD, and I shall be healed; Save me, and I shall be saved, For you are my praise.

PRAYER POINTS

1) O Lord Jesus, heal me and I shall be healed; save me and I shall be saved, for you are my praise.
2) I declare that by the strength of your right hand, I am healed.
3) I declare that by the power in your word, I am healed.
4) I declare that by the authority in your name, I am healed.
5) I declare that at the mention of your name, I am healed.
6) I declare that I am healed in the name of Jesus Christ.
7) I declare that I am the healed of the Lord.
8) I declare that I am healed from all my sicknesses and demonic afflictions.
9) I declare that I am blessed; therefore, no sickness shall possess my body again.
10) I declare that I am healed from my high blood pressure and diabetes today.

11) I declare that I am healed from every heart problem and liver and kidney disease today.
12) I declare that I shall have twenty-twenty vision again, in the name of Jesus Christ.
13) I declare that I am free from evil powers of my father's house.
14) All sickness, satanic oppression, curses, and spells that affected my father or mother that are now trying to affect me, I command you to die by fire, die by fire, in the name of Jesus Christ.
15) I declare that I am washed and purified by the blood of Jesus Christ.
16) I release the axe of fire into the roots of all my ailments and cut them into irreparable pieces, in the name of Jesus Christ.

***Jeremiah 30:17** For I will restore health to you And heal you of your wounds,' says the LORD, 'Because they called you an outcast saying: "This is Zion; No one seeks her."*

17) Almighty God, restore my health according to your commandment and heal my wounds according to your promises, in the mighty name of Jesus Christ.
18) O Lord, deal with every ancestral pharaoh in my life after the order of the Red Sea, in the mighty name of Jesus Christ.
19) Lord Jesus, roast the tongue of all wicked strongmen who laugh at me by your holy fire, in the name of Jesus Christ

***Jeremiah 33:6** 'Behold, I will bring it health and healing; I will heal them and reveal to them the abundance of peace and truth.*

20) Almighty God, arise and bring health and healing to me, and reveal your abundance of peace and truth in me, in the mighty name of Jesus Christ.
21) Lord Jesus, restore healing and your peace in my home.
22) Lord Jesus, restore financial increase and prosperity in my home.

23) Lord Jesus, seal every leaking pocket in my life and saturate my life with abundant peace, joy, and happiness.
24) Lord Jesus, make me a lender and not a borrower.
25) Lord Jesus, make me a giver and not a taker.
26) Arise, O Lord, and destroy all financial destroyers in my life, in your precious name.
27) Arise, O Lord, and set the spirit of poverty in my life in your fire.

Hosea 6:1 *Come, and let us return to the LORD; For He has torn, but He will heal us; He has stricken, but He will bind us up.*

28) Almighty God, because I have come before you today, please heal me and bind me in your mercy, in the mighty name of Jesus Christ.
29) Dear Lord Jesus, I declare that my heart belongs to you and shall continue to be yours in all my days.
30) Do not punish me according to my sins but continue to forgive me as you have promised.
31) Heal all my wounds and afflictions and receive me into your righteous arms, in the mighty name of Jesus Christ.
32) Because you are merciful, show me great mercy and grace, in the name of Jesus Christ.

Hosea 14:4 *"I will heal their backsliding, I will love them freely, For My anger has turned away from him.*

33) Almighty God, let your anger turn away from me and let your peace reign in my life.
34) Heal me from all my iniquities and set me free from demonic oppression, in the mighty name of Jesus Christ.
35) Thank you for healing and loving me freely despite my backslidings.
36) I pronounce that you alone are my God and healer in all the earth.

37) I shall continue to praise you until the moon is no more, because you have healed me and comforted me on every side.

Malachi 4:2 *But to you who fear My name The Sun of Righteousness shall arise With healing in His wings; And you shall go out And grow fat like stall-fed calves.*

38) O Lord God, help me to fear your name, and let my healing come from the son of righteousness as He arises with healing in his wings.
39) The sun shall not smite me by day and the moon shall not smite me by night.
40) Any power using the energy drawn from the sun, the moon, and the stars against me and my family, die in the name of Jesus Christ.
41) Any power projecting sickness and affliction against my body from astral altars, I command you to fall down and crash into irreparable pieces, in the name of Jesus Christ.
42) I declare that I shall go out and grow fat like stall-fed calves, in the name of Jesus Christ.
43) I declare that I am healed and shall be in good health all the days of my life, in the name of Jesus Christ.
44) I declare that my children are healed and shall be in good health all the days of their lives, in the name of Jesus Christ

Matthew 4:23 *And Jesus went about all Galilee, teaching in their synagogues, preaching the gospel of the kingdom, and healing all kinds of sickness and all kinds of disease among the people.*

45) Lord Jesus, heal my diseases and sickness today, in your mighty, precious name.
46) Lord Jesus, I am suffering from [sickness]. I declare that I am healed according to Matthew 4:23.
47) Let your precious blood flush out all sickness and disease from my body at this moment, in the mighty name of Jesus Christ.

48) I pronounce that I have received my healing now and forever, from my Lord Jesus Christ.
49) I proclaim your healing now, Lord Jesus, for my children and for my loved ones, in your precious name.

Matthew 8:13 *Then Jesus said to the Centurion, "Go your way; and as you have believed, so let it be done for you." And his servant was healed that same hour.*

50) Lord Jesus, I receive my healing today after the order of the centurion.
51) As the centurion's servant was healed at the same hour, so let me be healed now. Let my family be healed at this same house, in the name of Jesus Christ.
52) I come to you by faith and I declare that my faith shall activate my deliverance and healing from you at this hour, in the name of Jesus Christ.

Matthew 8:16 *When evening had come, they brought to Him many who were demon-possessed. And He cast out the spirits with a word, and healed all who were sick,*

53) Lord Jesus, according to your word, cast out every evil spirit from my life, in the mighty name of Jesus Christ.
54) I command every demonic spirit in my life and in my home to catch fire and burn to ashes, in the mighty name of Jesus Christ.
55) I challenge every household satanic agent monitoring my recovery to fall down and die, in the name of Jesus Christ.
56) Every demon positioned in the four watches to afflict me with afflictions, die by fire, die by fire, in the name of Jesus Christ.
57) You, satanic agent injecting poverty into my life in exchange for my blessings, receive divine death, in the name of Jesus Christ.
58) You, evil powers causing chronic sickness in my body, I command you to uproot your chronic sickness and disease and return to your senders, in the mighty of Jesus Christ.

59) You, demonic stronghold that has refused to let me go, I cast you out of my life with the word of Jesus in Matthew 8:16.

Matthew 9:35 Then Jesus went about all the cities and villages, teaching in their synagogues, preaching the gospel of the kingdom, and healing every sickness and every disease among the people.

60) In the name of Jesus, I receive healing for every sickness and disease in my life today, in the mighty name of Jesus Christ.
61) I declare that I am healed from the top of my head to the soles of my feet.
62) I declare that my healing is complete today in Christ Jesus.

Matthew 10:1 And when He had called His twelve disciples to Him, He gave them power over unclean spirits, to cast them out, and to heal all kinds of sickness and all kinds of disease.

63) Lord Jesus, today I receive your power over all unclean spirits, allowing me to cast them out and to heal all kinds of sickness and disease in my body, in the mighty name of Jesus Christ.
64) I challenge every power contrary to your power in my life to receive divine judgment by fire, in the name of Jesus Christ.
65) I cast out all demonic spirits troubling my soul today, in the name of Jesus Christ.
66) I cast out every foul spirit that has taken possession of my loved one today, in the name of Jesus Christ.
67) I command you to come out of (person's name) now and surrender to the eternal fire of God, in the name of Jesus Christ.
68) Dear Holy Spirit, arise and take over my body and soul now, in the name of Jesus Christ.
69) Dear Holy Spirit, arise and take over my children's bodies and souls now, in the name of Jesus Christ.
70) I challenge all bewitchment and every witch doctor casting spells and curses into my life to receive judgment after the order of Pharaoh in Egypt, in the name of Jesus Christ.

Matthew 10:8 *"Heal the sick, cleanse the lepers, raise the dead, cast out demons. Freely you have received, freely give.*

71) Today I receive power to heal the sick, cleanse the lepers, raise the dead, and cast out demons, in the name of Jesus Christ.
72) I am healed and cleansed of all my infirmities, in the mighty name of Jesus Christ.

Matthew 12:22 *Then one was brought to Him who was demon-possessed, blind and mute; and He healed him, so that the blind and mute man both spoke and saw.*

73) Lord Jesus, I declare that I am healed from the afflictions of mute and blind spirits, in the name of Jesus Christ.
74) I command my blindness to disappear and let the light of God shine upon me and into my eyes again, in the name of Jesus Christ.
75) I receive back my voice and declare healing upon my vocal cords, in the name of Jesus Christ.
76) I challenge every mute and blind spirit in my life to die forever, in the name of Jesus Christ.
77) I declare the power of God into my tongue and as I speak let every blind and mute see and speak up, in the name of Jesus Christ.
78) O Lord Jesus, use me to heal the blind and the mute. Use me to heal the lame and the crippled, in the name of Jesus Christ.
79) Lord Jesus, as you have healed me, so use me to heal all who have suffered from afflictions similar to mine, in the name of Jesus Christ.

Matthew 14:14 *And when Jesus went out He saw a great multitude; and He was moved with compassion for them, and healed their sick.*

80) Lord Jesus, have mercy upon me and heal me, for I am in pain.
81) Show me your compassion and deliver me from the hand of the wicked.

82) Do not pass me by, for I am waiting for you to heal me.

Luke 6:19 *And the whole multitude sought to touch Him, for power went out from Him and healed them all.*

83) Allow me to touch you this hour, that I may receive my healing.
84) Let your power set me free from all my addictions today.
85) Let your lifting power lift me up from chronic stagnation and waywardness in life.
86) Arise and illuminate my life again with your glory, and fill me again with your fresh fire, in the name of Jesus Christ.

Luke 9:6 *So they departed and went through the towns, preaching the gospel and healing everywhere.*

87) Let many receive your healing as I preach your word to them.
88) Use me mightily to touch your people in this city.

Luke 10:8-9 *"Whatever city you enter, and they receive you, eat such things as are set before you. {9} "And heal the sick there, and say to them, 'The kingdom of God has come near to you.*

Luke 17:15 *And one of them, when he saw that he was healed, returned, and with a loud voice glorified God,*

89) Lord Jesus, I thank you for healing me this day
90) I vow that I shall declare your glory in the presence of your people and give thanks to you for healing me today.
91) I declare that I shall join hands with God's children to build your kingdom wherever I go.
92) Holy Spirit, make me whole today, in the name of Jesus Christ.
93) Holy Spirit, give me complete healing in my body, soul, and spirit, in the name of Jesus Christ.

94) Holy Spirit, let all my enemies be confounded and put to shame because I am healed and delivered from all their afflictions, in the name of Jesus Christ.

Acts 3:12 *So when Peter saw it, he responded to the people: "Men of Israel, why do you marvel at this? Or why look so intently at us, as though by our own power or godliness we had made this man walk?*
Acts 4:29-31 *"Now, Lord, look on their threats, and grant to Your servants that with all boldness they may speak Your word, "by stretching out Your hand to heal, and that signs and wonders may be done through the name of Your holy Servant Jesus."And when they had prayed, the place where they were assembled together was shaken; and they were all filled with the Holy Spirit, and they spoke the word of God with boldness.*

95) Lord Jesus, as I pray, let the foundation of my enemy's stronghold begin to shatter into pieces, in the name of Jesus Christ.
96) Lord, give me the spirit of boldness to confront the wicked with your word and destroy them all, in the name of Jesus Christ.
97) Arise, O Lord, and challenge every generational curse in my family to disappear into the abyss forever, in the name of Jesus Christ.

1 Corinthians 12:9 *"To another faith by the same Spirit, to another gifts of healings by the same Spirit,"*

98) Holy Spirit, increase your anointing in me. Raise me and heal me, in the mighty name of Jesus Christ.
99) Holy Spirit, you alone are the spirit who dwells in me. Multiply your gifts and anointing in my life. Make me become a praise in the earth, in the mighty name of Jesus Christ.

James 5:14-16 *Is anyone among you sick? Let him call for the elders of the church, and let them pray over him, anointing him with oil in the name of the Lord. {15} And the prayer of faith will save the sick, and the Lord will raise him up. And if he has committed sins, he will be forgiven. {16} Confess your trespasses to one another, and pray for one another, that you may be healed. The effective, fervent prayer of a righteous man avails much.*

100) Dear Lord Jesus, because of my sickness, I have come before you for help. Arise and heal me as I pray, and make me whole again.
101) Dear Holy Spirit, as your servant prays for me and anoints me with the oil, arise and sanctify me, heal me, deliver me, and set me free, in the name of Jesus Christ.
102) Lord Jesus, as I confess my sins before you, hear me and forgive me, and heal me from all my afflictions.
103) Lord Jesus, let my prayer come to you with faith, and use my mustard seed faith to activate my healing and deliverance today, in your precious, mighty name.
104) Lord Jesus, use my prayer of faith to save me and my family, and raise me up from my predicament, in your precious, mighty name.
105) Dear Holy Spirit, arise and make my prayers become effective before you, though I am weak. Let my prayers stand out to you and strengthen me despite my distresses, in the mighty name of Jesus Christ.

Revelation 22:2 *In the middle of its street, and on either side of the river, was the tree of life, which bore twelve fruits, each tree yielding its fruit every month. The leaves of the tree were for the healing of the nations.*

106) Almighty God, let me bear the fruit of healing in my life. Use me to heal all who are sick and afflicted, in the name of Jesus Christ.
107) I declare that I shall continue to bear good fruits all the days of my life, in the name of Jesus Christ.

108) Lord, use me to heal your nations and let the nations I do not know run to me to receive your healing and power, in the name of Jesus Christ.

Luke 8:47 *Now when the woman saw that she was not hidden, she came trembling; and falling down before Him, she declared to Him in the presence of all the people the reason she had touched Him and how she was healed immediately..*

109) Lord Jesus, because I have touched you with my prayers and supplications today, heal me and deliver me from all my infirmities.
110) Lord, cast all my infirmities away and restore strength to me.
111) I refuse to walk away from your presence empty-handed. Bless me and make me prosper, that those who mock me may know that you alone are Lord over all the earth.
112) Holy Spirit, give me the strength and boldness to testify about what Jesus Christ has done for me in the open.
113) Lord, do not let me become shy about the testimony of Jesus Christ in my life.
114) In the presence of all your people, let me become the mouthpiece of Christ, in the name of Jesus Christ.

Luke 8:48 *And He said to her, "Daughter, be of good cheer; your faith has made you well. Go in peace."*

115) Lord Jesus, thank you for healing me and sending me home with cheer and in peace.

Luke 5:17 *Now it happened on a certain day, as He was teaching, that there were Pharisees and teachers of the law sitting by, who had come out of every town of Galilee, Judea, and Jerusalem. And the power of the Lord was present to heal them.*
Psalms 34:17-18 *The righteous cry out, and the Lord hears, And delivers them out of all their troubles. The Lord is near to those who have a broken heart, And saves such as have a contrite spirit.*

116) Lord Jesus, I have cried out to you and you have heard me. Thank you for healing me and removing all my troubles from me, in the mighty name of Jesus Christ.
117) Thank you for being near to me.
118) Thank you for restoring me before you and making me strong again.
119) Thank you for giving me a broken and a contrite heart, and for saving me from all curses, sicknesses, and diseases.
120) I declare that I am healed, my children are healed, my family is healed, my business and my work are healed, and my church is healed, in Jesus's mighty name. Amen.

41

Defeat Obsessive-Compulsive Disorder and Receive Healing for Your Mind

OBSESSIVE-COMPULSIVE DISORDER IS a disease that makes you do the same things over and over again. It strips you of your ability to take control of your life. It is a curse that carries the spirit of repetition, which makes one incapable of refusing to obey compulsive commands. The word of God lets us understand that God has not given us the spirit of fear, but of power, love, and a sound mind. The term "sound mind" refers to "self-control," which is essential in this case. The spirit of obsession depletes the victims of self-control and renders them totally unable to function and respond normally to emotional, physical, psychological, and spiritual impulses.

The following prayer points will destroy the spirit of OCD and root them out of your life so you can regain your freedom, in Jesus's name. Amen.

SCRIPTURAL REFERENCES

2 Timothy 1:7 *For God has not given us a spirit of fear, but of power and of love and of a sound mind.*

Psalm 147:2–3 *The Lord builds up Jerusalem; He gathers together the outcasts of Israel. He heals the brokenhearted And binds up their wounds.*

Psalm 34:17–18 *The righteous cry out, and the Lord hears, And delivers them out of all their troubles. The Lord is near to those who have a broken heart, And saves such as have a contrite spirit.*

Psalm 41:1–4 *Blessed is he who considers the poor; The Lord will deliver him in time of trouble. The Lord will preserve him and keep him alive And he will be blessed on the earth; You will not deliver him to the will of his enemies. The Lord will strengthen him on his bed of illness; You will sustain him on his sickbed. I said, "Lord, be merciful to me; Heal my soul, for I have sinned against You."*

Jeremiah 17:14 *Heal me, O Lord, and I shall be healed; Save me, and I shall be saved, For You are my praise.*

Psalm 51:16–18 *For You do not desire sacrifice, or else I would give it; You do not delight in burnt offering. The sacrifices of God are a broken spirit, A broken and a contrite heart—These, O God, You will not despise. Do good in your good pleasure to Zion; Build the walls of Jerusalem.*

PRAYER POINTS

1) Start this prayer session with praise and worship.
2) Lord, I thank You for healing my mind and my spirit today.
3) Lord, I thank You for healing my body, soul, and spirit today.
4) Lord, I thank You for your sustaining grace in my life.
5) Lord, I thank You for delivering me from the circle and trap of the wicked.
6) Lord, heal me and I shall be healed. Lord, save me and I shall be saved.
7) Lord, take away every burden from my shoulders and remove every yoke from my neck because of Your anointing, in the name of Jesus Christ.
8) Lord, I receive the spirit of power, love, and a sound mind today.
9) I command all satanic intimidation in my life to roast by fire.
10) I reverse every curse against my life, against my family, and against my ministry, in the name of Jesus Christ.
11) I cancel every fear programmed into my life by satanic prophets, in the name of Jesus Christ.

12) I cancel every fear programmed into my life by religious strongmen, in the mighty name of Jesus Christ.
13) My family and I are covered by the blood of Jesus Christ.
14) I am covered by the blood of Jesus Christ.
15) O Lord, hear my cry and deliver me from all my troubles.
16) O Lord, oppose all opposition to my destiny, in the name of Jesus Christ.
17) O Lord, oppose all opposition to my mental stability, in the name of Jesus Christ.
18) O Lord, build up the walls of destiny and establish my life on a solid rock, in the name of Jesus Christ.
19) O Lord, save me and heal me from the afflictions of my enemy, in the name of Jesus Christ.
20) O Lord, cleanse my heart with Your precious blood and restore purity to my mind, in the name of Jesus Christ.
21) Arise, O Lord, and let my enemies be scattered, in the name of Jesus Christ.
22) O Lord, bless and keep me and my family alive to see the goodness of the Lord in the land of the living, in the name of Jesus Christ.
23) O Lord, heal and bind up every wound that the enemy has inflicted upon me, in the name of Jesus Christ.
24) O Lord, fill me with Your anointing so I can excel and prosper in your calling for my life, in the name of Jesus Christ.
25) O Lord, I shall not miss the mark of Your calling upon my life, in the name of Jesus Christ.
26) Almighty God, give me a broken spirit and a contrite heart to fear your name, in the name of Jesus Christ.
27) Almighty God, expose every wicked scheme of the enemy against my life, in the mighty name of Jesus Christ.
28) Almighty God, expose every wicked scheme of the enemy against my destiny, in the name of Jesus Christ.
29) Almighty God, remove every arrow of affliction from my heart and set me free from all forms of oppression, in the name of Jesus Christ.
30) Almighty God, establish me and set me apart for You in the name of Jesus Christ.

31) Lord Jesus, help me to fear and trust in the power of your name.
32) Lord Jesus, flush my heart with Your precious blood and put upon me a divine hunger and thirst for righteousness, in the name of Jesus Christ.
33) Thank you, Lord, for answering all my prayers, in the name of Jesus Christ.
34) Almighty God, destroy the spirit of obsessive-compulsive disorder in my life today, in the mighty name of Jesus Christ.
35) You, spirit of anxiety and fear in my life, I sentence you to death by fire, in the mighty name of Jesus Christ.
36) You, spirit of discouragement in my life, I command you to roast to ashes, in the mighty name of Jesus Christ.
37) You, spirit of instability and agitation, I command you to be evicted from my body by the fire of the Holy Spirit, in the mighty name of Jesus Christ.
38) I bind the spirit of compulsion and confusion in my life today, in the mighty name of Jesus Christ.
39) Almighty God, destroy the Goliath of compulsion in my life by the rock of ages, in the mighty name of Jesus Christ.
40) I challenge the spirit of intimidation and loneliness by fire of the Holy Spirit and command it to burn to ashes, in the mighty name of Jesus Christ.
41) O Lord Jesus, arise and cause all obsessive impulses in my body to melt by Your fire, in the mighty name of Jesus Christ.
42) I condemn the architect of compulsive disorder in my life to the abyss, in the mighty name of Jesus Christ.
43) Listen to me, Satan: I refuse to drink from your cup of affliction today, in the mighty name of Jesus Christ.
44) Almighty God, let my enemies be condemned and put to shame because you love me, in the mighty name of Jesus Christ.
45) I command victory and happiness into my life today, in the mighty name of Jesus Christ.

46) I bind the spirit of sadness and rejection in my life, in the mighty name of Jesus Christ.
47) I declare that from today I will not chase away my helpers, in the mighty name of Jesus Christ.
48) I rebuke every spirit responsible for loss of friends and loved ones in my life and command them to be roasted by fire, in the mighty name of Jesus Christ.
49) I paralyze the spirit of the tail and receive the spirit of the head, in the mighty name of Jesus Christ.
50) I am victorious through Christ Jesus and I declare that favor shall come upon me today, in the mighty name of Jesus Christ.
51) I declare that my life shall receive a major breakthrough from today, in the mighty name of Jesus Christ.
52) I command that I am free from the curse of my father's house, in the mighty name of Jesus Christ.
53) I declare that I am free from the curse of my mother's house, in the mighty name of Jesus Christ.
54) I rebuke every monitoring gadget monitoring my progress and advancement, and I command you to shatter into irredeemable pieces, in the mighty name of Jesus Christ.
55) You, spirit of compulsion in my life, take your disorder and come out of my mind forever and ever, in the mighty name of Jesus Christ.
56) You, unfriendly friends in my life, I reject you as my friends both physically and spiritually, in the mighty name of Jesus Christ.
57) Every tongue speaking judgment against me and my destiny, I command you to roast by fire, in the mighty name of Jesus Christ.
58) Every witchcraft network against my life at work, I challenge you by the fire of the Holy Spirit to take your hands off my life today, in the mighty name of Jesus Christ.
59) I call back all friendly friends into my life again, in the mighty name of Jesus Christ.
60) I call back all my displaced helpers into my life again, in the mighty name of Jesus Christ.

61) I call back all my shattered blessings into my life again, in the mighty name of Jesus Christ.
62) Thank you, Lord Jesus, for answering all my prayers today, in the mighty name of Jesus Christ. Amen.

42

Change Poverty Codes in Your Life to Blessings

POVERTY CODES ARE used by the enemy to deter God's children from physical and spiritual advancement, thereby causing abject poverty and stagnation in their lives and in their future progress. The good news is that Jesus Christ already wiped out the handwriting of requirement that was against you, which was contrary to your increase in blessings, prosperity, advancement in life, breakthrough in life, success, and expansion. Christians all over the world are millionaires and billionaires, while many are still living in abject poverty.

The majority of these codes are inherited through our bloodline. The information needed for continuous replication in our lives is embedded in our genes, our DNA. It is only the blood of Jesus Christ that is capable of flushing out these demonic codes so as to reverse the continuous replication and perpetuation of poverty in our lives and in the lives of the future generation.

Poverty codes are curses, and they originate from generational curses through our bloodline; satanic afflictions; bad business dealings; addictions; involvement in the occult; religious curses; stealing; bloodshed for wealth and riches; bewitchments; unwillingness to show kindness to the less privileged; oppression of the poor, the widowed, and the fatherless; and unwillingness to build and advance the kingdom of God. These codes are spirits, and their sole purpose is to perpetuate poverty in the family lineage such that the subsequent generations are not able to advance God's kingdom. Poverty codes will affect your personal life and spiritual and business life as well.

You will know that you are a carrier of poverty codes when you start seeing yourself in dreams living in dirty houses infested with roaches; picking around for pennies, nickels, dimes, and quarters; riding on rusted bicycles; driving rusted and old, beaten-up cars; riding in a truck or a car full of junk; seeing piles of your dirty or torn underwear or clothes; engaging in petty trading; and having no goods in your storehouse or warehouse.

You will also know that you are a carrier of poverty codes when in dreams people break into your home and loot or steal your property or personal belongings, when people break into your business and start stealing your goods, when you find yourself planting on desert-like soils, when you see yourself reaping or harvesting unripened fruits or bad (dead, lean) fruits or crops, or when you start seeing storms and bad weather conditions coming against you. God is faithful and will show you these afflictions as the enemy manipulates them into your life, so you can pray and take authority over them.

To overcome poverty codes, you must fast and pray, give to the poor, give to the needy, give to the fatherless, give to the widowed, give to the homeless, sow seeds for missionaries and missions, give generously to your local church and pastors, and give to God's people. God will use your generosity and kindness through giving to reverse poverty codes, and He will recode blessings into your life in Jesus's name. Amen.

SCRIPUTRAL REFERENCES

Colossians 2:11–15 In Him you were also circumcised with the circumcision made without hands, by putting off the body of the sins of the flesh, by the circumcision of Christ, buried with Him in baptism, in which you also were raised with Him through faith in the working of God, who raised Him from the dead. And you, being dead in your trespasses and the uncircumcision of your flesh, He has made alive together with Him, having forgiven you all trespasses, having wiped out the handwriting of requirements that was against us, which was contrary to us. And He has taken it out of the way, having nailed it to the cross. Having disarmed principalities and powers, He made a public spectacle of them, triumphing over them in it.

Proverbs 14:20–21 The poor man is hated even by his own neighbor, But the rich has many friends. He who despises his neighbor sins; But he who has mercy on the poor, happy is he.

Psalm 41:1–3 Blessed is he who considers the poor; The Lord will deliver him in time of trouble. The Lord will preserve him and keep him alive, And he will be blessed on the earth; you will not deliver him to the will of his enemies. The Lord will strengthen him on his bed of illness; you will sustain him on his sickbed.

PRAYER POINTS

1) Lord, thank You for making it possible for me to attend this prayer session, in the name of Jesus Christ.
2) I ask You to forgive all my sins and wash me with your precious blood.
3) I ask You to come into my life and be one with me.
4) Let all my prayers rise before You, Lord, at this hour, in the name of Jesus Christ.
5) Lord, decode evil marks of poverty from my blood and encode the marks of blessings, in the name of Jesus Christ.
6) By the stripes of Jesus Christ, I declare that all evil marks and codes in my bloodline are erased and healed.
7) Lord, reverse all satanic marks placed upon my life, by the blood of Jesus Christ.
8) I challenge every satanic mark in my life by the fire of the Holy Ghost, and I declare that I am free from the bondage of poverty, in the name of Jesus Christ.
9) Lord Jesus, break and destroy all genetic codes carrying poverty marks in my bloodline, in the name of Jesus Christ.

10) Lord Jesus, pull out and set all poverty codes in my life on fire, and let your fire consume them to ashes.
11) I declare that the spirit of poverty in my life must be flushed out by the blood of Jesus Christ.
12) I declare that the seed of poverty in my life must be crushed to ashes by the rock of ages, in the name of Jesus Christ.
13) As water cleanses and purifies a dirty cloth, so let the blood of Jesus Christ cleanse and purify my life from all effects of poverty, in the name of Jesus Christ.
14) Lord, tear down the stronghold of poverty in my life and set me free to receive my prosperity until the moon is no more, in the name of Jesus Christ.
15) I declare that the sins of my youth shall not become a curse for me, because I am forgiven in the name of Jesus Christ.
16) Almighty God, uproot the roots of poverty from my bloodline and cast them into your burning fire, in the name of Jesus Christ.
17) Father, pronounce the judgment of death upon all poverty manipulators in my life, in the name of Jesus Christ.
18) Lord, detangle all strands of poverty codes in my destiny and cast them into the abyss, in the name of Jesus Christ.
19) I command the spirit of poverty in my life to face divine destruction and execution now, in the name of Jesus Christ.
20) I command the spirit of poverty in my family to receive divine death, in the name of Jesus Christ.
21) Holy Spirit, flush my bloodline with the blood of Jesus Christ and restore all stolen blessings to us, in the name of Jesus.
22) Lord, thank you for wiping the handwriting of poverty from my life, in the name of Jesus Christ.
23) Lord, thank you for wiping the handwriting of poverty from my family, in the name of Jesus Christ.
24) Lord, thank you for erasing the curse of poverty from my family and restoring blessings to us, in the name of Jesus Christ.
25) Lord, thank you for removing poverty codes from my bloodline and replacing them with blessings, in the name of Jesus Christ.

26) Lord, help me to begin to do things that will attract blessings into my life, in the name of Jesus Christ.
27) Lord, bless me so I may begin to bless the poor and the widowed, in the name of Jesus Christ.
28) Lord, lead me to that individual that needs what I have to offer and let me be a blessing to him or her, in the name of Jesus Christ.
29) Lord, let me never be tired of using the resources in my life for the building of Your kingdom, in the name of Jesus Christ.
30) Lord Jesus, preserve and keep me alive so I may continue to give to the poor, the widowed, and the fatherless, in the name of Jesus Christ.
31) Lord Jesus, let me be that tree that never stops yielding good fruits, so those who come to me may benefit from me, in the name of Jesus Christ.
32) Lord, lead me and show me whom to bless this day, in the name of Jesus Christ.
33) Lord, as I support the poor and give to the building of your kingdom, let all spirits of poverty in my life disappear forever, in the name of Jesus Christ.
34) Lord, as I consider your poor and continue to support the needy, bless me and my family and deliver us in times of trouble, in the name of Jesus Christ.
35) I pronounce freedom and breakthrough upon every area of my life, in the name of Jesus Christ.
36) I pronounce increase and abundance upon my life and upon my children, in the name of Jesus Christ.
37) I declare that my hands shall never dry again, and I shall continue to experience prosperity all the days of my life, in the name of Jesus Christ.
38) O Lord Jesus, position helpers in my way to help me wherever I shall go all day long, in the name of Jesus Christ.
39) I pronounce the supernatural favor of God upon my life, my work, and my business, and declare that I shall not lack in any area of my life, in Jesus's mighty name.

40) I reverse every generational curse of poverty in my life and flush it out by the blood of Jesus Christ.
41) I reverse all generational curses in my bloodline by the blood of Jesus Christ, in the name of Jesus.
42) I plead for the blood of Jesus Christ over my family bloodline, and I loose and shatter every chain of poverty tying us down by the rock of ages, in the name of Jesus Christ.
43) O Lord, use Your battle-axe and cut off every link that exists between me and the spirit of poverty in my life, in the name of Jesus Christ.
44) O Lord, arise and destroy all evil covenants that were established by my forefathers in the past that are now responsible for poverty in my life, in the name of Jesus Christ.
45) O Lord, arise and remove every curse of poverty in my life that has come as a result of evil covenants instituted by my forefathers, in the name of Jesus Christ.
46) O Lord, forgive my parents of any sin committed in the past that has led to poverty in my life, in the name of Jesus Christ.
47) O Lord, forgive me and reverse every curse of poverty in my life that is due to my carelessness and wrong dealings with people, in the name of Jesus Christ.
48) I command all poverty codes planted in my life by the spirit of poverty to be uprooted now and cast into fire, in the name of Jesus Christ.
49) I command every poverty code planted in my life by dream demons to be uprooted and returned back to its sender, in the name of Jesus Christ.
50) I return all pennies, nickels, dimes, and quarters I might have collected and kept in my dreams back to their senders by fire, in the name of Jesus Christ.
51) I return all evil money in my possession due to normal business transactions back to its senders, in the name of Jesus Christ.
52) I cover all my money, cash and checks, with the blood of Jesus Christ.
53) O Lord, destroy all roach infestation and contamination in my life by Your fire, in the name of Jesus Christ.

54) I command all roach invasions in my dreams to be consumed by the fire of the Holy Spirit.
55) I remove every poverty rag put upon me in my dreams and I cast it into the fire, in the name of Jesus Christ.
56) I pursue, overtake, and recover all my stolen blessings from dream demons and agents, in the name of Jesus Christ.
57) I command all territorial spirits of poverty around me to die, in the name of Jesus Christ
58) I command every rusted plate, cup, spoon, fork, knife, and pot in my dreams to be removed and cast into the abyss, in the name of Jesus Christ.
59) I command every dirty and pest-infested house in my dreams to catch fire and burn down to ashes, in the name of Jesus Christ.
60) I declare that my spirit shall refuse any food, substance, or drinks served to me in dreams by people familiar and unfamiliar to me, in the name of Jesus Christ.
61) I command all food or drink I have eaten already in my dreams to be flushed out of my life by the blood of Jesus Christ.
62) I command every sickness in my body (cancer, AIDS, hypertension, diabetes, kidney or liver problems, heart problems, head problems, blood problems, eye problems, nerve problems, bone problems, etc.) caused by foods given to me in my dreams to be flushed out by the blood of Jesus Christ, from the top of my head to the soles of my feet, in the name of Jesus Christ.
63) I command every rusted or broken-down bicycle or car given to or ridden or driven by me in my dreams to catch fire now, catch fire now, in the name of Jesus Christ.
64) I destroy every foundation of satanic schooling in my dreams, and I command it all to be uprooted and shattered to pieces, in the name of Jesus Christ.
65) I erase every known and unknown signature of mine in covenants with poverty agents in my dreams, by the blood of Jesus Christ.

66) I command all evil birds carrying information about me from one place to another to fall down and die, in the name of Jesus Christ.
67) I command every evil altar entertaining my case with poverty curses to catch fire and burn down to ashes, in the name of Jesus Christ.
68) O Lord, arise and recall to You all money taken from me and placed on satanic altars, and return them to me, in the name of Jesus Christ.
69) I command the hand of every satanic agent handling my money to wither and melt by fire, in the name of Jesus Christ.
70) O Lord, arise and blind every eye watching my progress for evil, in the name of Jesus Christ.
71) O Lord, arise and release all my blessings from all satanic banks and warehouses and return them to me, in the name of Jesus Christ.
72) O Lord, take your explosive devices and explode every satanic bank and warehouse holding my blessings, in the name of Jesus Christ.
73) I declare that I shall not be made to pick pennies in my dreams, in the name of Jesus Christ.
74) O Lord, empower me to overcome all manipulation from my enemies in this world and in the spirit world, in the name of Jesus Christ.
75) Every household power fighting against my breakthrough, die by fire, in the name of Jesus Christ.
76) Every religious stronghold fighting against my breakthrough, be smashed into pieces in the name of Jesus Christ.
77) Every ancestral pharaoh refusing to set me free, die by fire in the name of Jesus Christ.
78) Every satanic rat and mouse eating up my blessings, be consumed by the fire of the Holy Ghost, in the name of Jesus Christ.
79) Every satanic roach infesting my business and the work of my hands, be eradicated by heavenly insecticides, in the name of Jesus Christ.

80) Every satanic snake wrapping my progress to stagnation, be destroyed by heavenly kerosene, in the name of Jesus Christ.
81) Every sickness in my household eating up my finances, I command you to die forever, in the name of Jesus Christ.
82) Everything belonging to me that is eating up my finances, be removed from my life, in the name of Jesus Christ.
83) Every poverty code seen and unseen fighting against my prosperity, I command you to die, in the name of Jesus Christ.
84) Let all bewitchments in my life receive divine death, in the name of Jesus Christ.
85) I command all bewitchments in my life to lose control and disappear forever, in the name of Jesus Christ.
86) I remove all money and property belonging to me that was nailed to any tree or buried in the ground with a curse and set it free, in the name of Jesus Christ.
87) I declare that no weapon formed against me shall prosper, in the name of Jesus Christ.
88) I sanctify and purify my home, my life, and my family of all satanic pollution and its effects, by the blood of Jesus Christ, in the name of Jesus.
89) Every power that says I shall not prosper, I command you to dry up and die, in the name of Jesus Christ.
90) I reverse all enchantment, divination, and bewitchment back to their senders, in the name of Jesus Christ.
91) I cover myself and my family with the blood of Jesus Christ.
92) I declare that I and my family are free from the effects of poverty, in the name of Jesus Christ.
93) I declare that I and my family are free from the spirit of poverty, in the name of Jesus Christ.
94) I declare that my children are free from the spirit of poverty, in the name of Jesus Christ.
95) I declare that we are disentangled and free from all poverty codes physically and spiritually, in the name of Jesus Christ.
96) I engage heavenly bulldozers to demolish any structure erected by the enemy physically or spiritually to store my blessings, in the name of Jesus Christ.

97) I command all satanic snails planted to drag me behind to be crushed by the rock of ages, in the name of Jesus Christ.
98) O Lord Jesus, arise and burn into ashes any snail spirit delegated to manipulating and delaying my life and destiny.
99) I command every crawling animal used by the enemy to stall my breakthrough to die, in the name of Jesus Christ.
100) O Lord Jesus, let all poverty rags, panties, and clothes used by the enemy to tie me down and invoke shame upon me to catch fire now, in the name of Jesus Christ
101) I uproot any crocodile or reptile spirit planted on my back to retard my progress and future to stagnation, in the name of Jesus Christ.
102) I release the arrow of blackout into the camp of turtle spirits assigned to put my life on hold, in the name of Jesus Christ.
103) I challenge every satanic prophet using the energy drawn from the sun, moon, and stars to manipulate my blessings to die by the sword of God, in the name of Jesus Christ.
104) I declare that the evil powers of my wife's father and mother's house will not become a stumbling block to my blessings and prosperity.
105) I declare that the evil powers of my wife's father and mother's house will not stop my progress and my breakthrough, in the name of Jesus Christ.
106) I declare that the evil powers of my husband's father and mother's house will not become a stumbling block to my blessings and prosperity, in the name of Jesus Christ.
107) I declare that the evil powers of my husband's father and mother's house will not stop my progress and breakthrough, in the name of Jesus Christ.
108) Thank you, Lord, for answering all my prayers at this hour, in the name of Jesus Christ. Amen, amen, amen.

References

1) *New King James Version Study Bible.* 2007. Thomas Nelson, Inc.

2) *New King James Version Bible.* 1982. Thomas Nelson, Inc.

3) *The Amplified Bible.* 1987. Lockman Foundation.

4) *God's Word Translation Bible.* 1995. God's Word to the Nations, Baker Publishing Group.

5) Olukoya, Dr. Daniel. *Prayer Passport, to Crush Oppression.*

6) "The Bible and Homosexuality," God's Holy Spirit Bible Site., http://www.godsholyspirit.com/chrisitan.../the_bible_and-homosexuality.htm.

About the Author

Pastor Dr. Elijah Akpan is Co-founder and General Overseer of the International Ministry of Salvation and Praise and the Healing House Ministries with his wife Pastor Inifiok Akpan, in Las Vegas, Nevada, USA.

In May of 2003, en route to Africa, an angel appeared to Pastor Elijah Akpan in a dream and shone a powerful, bright light toward him. As he tried running away, he found himself frozen and could not move. After about two minutes, the light ceased. Then he saw a huge, tall man standing about ten feet away from him. Pastor Elijah asked him, "What is your name?" He answered, "My name is Steven." Pastor Elijah was quickened in the spirit to know that he was Angel Steven. He then asked the angel again, "Where is the Father?" Suddenly, Steven appeared beside Pastor Elijah and stated that he should walk with him to go meet the Father.

When Pastor Elijah finally met the Father, He was sitting on a wooden chair with a wooden staff in His right hand. He knew He was the Father the moment he saw Him. Pastor Elijah lay prostrate on the ground and worshipped Him. The Father then asked him to stand up; as he stood up, His first words to him were, "It is time for you to do my work." The Father stood up and asked Pastor Elijah to walk with Him. As they walked side-by-side along a path, He gave him instructions on what needed to be done. When the Father finally departed with His angelic entourage, Pastor Elijah found himself healing the sick, preaching the word of God, and performing miracles to multitudes that appeared in front of him from nowhere.

When he returned from his trip abroad, Pastor Elijah's business began to gradually run downhill. Problems started with employees and scaled to investigations and the eventual loss of the business. He and his family then went through an intense five years of court cases from several lawsuits that left him and his wife with almost no penny to their names. Friends, some relatives, and business circles deserted them, except God and those He chose to comfort and pray with them. When the court cases ended, they went through an additional two years of financial hardship, which resulted in the loss of many properties and uncountable investments. It was during this time that the Lord showed up again and told Pastor Elijah with an audible voice to read (Isa. 61:6–11). That same night, the Lord also spoke to his wife, Pastor Ini Akpan, and told her to read (Isa. 60:18). From that night of reading came the name of their ministry, the International Ministry of Salvation and Praise.

On October 25, 2012, an Old Man appeared again to Pastor Elijah Akpan in a dream and said, "I will give you great riches no man can quantify if you choose to pursue a business career." His reply to the Old Man was, "No, I do not desire great riches anymore because I already made up my mind to serve God." The Old Man tried to force Pastor Elijah to accept His proposal and he resisted with passion. Immediately, the Old Man's face and His appearance changed. He appeared strong, tall, and healthy. Standing about seven feet away from Pastor Elijah, He declared with a loud voice, "I am the Lord. Now I know that you are ready to serve me. Come, that I must show you things to come." From then on, He took Pastor Elijah through stadium after stadium filled with people from all races. He finally brought him into His throne room and placed him on a platform below His throne. The force between the Lord and Pastor Elijah was so strong that Pastor Elijah could barely maintain his posture while standing. He felt love and peace in a way he had never experienced before.

As the Lord was talking to Pastor Elijah, He asked him to turn around and look to his right. On turning, there stood a Man in royal-purple or burgundy robes with a crown on His head, extending His two arms toward him. Pastor Elijah had the ability to know everything at that moment. By now, he already knew that He was Jesus Christ. He shouted, "Je-sussssssssss!" So he jumped and hugged Him, and refused to let go of Jesus just as Jesus was hesitant to let go of him. Then the Father said to him again, "Look to your right. There is someone here to see you." As Pastor Elijah turned to his right, his heart felt like it was dropping out of his chest. He saw a Man standing, dressed in a purplish, burgundy-colored robe. He knew He was the Holy Spirit. So he leapt with every power in him—shouting His name, "Holy Spir-iiit!"—to embrace Him. As he got to Him, he knelt down with tears running down from his eyes, soaking the Holy Spirit's feet. Then the Holy Spirit said to Pastor Elijah, "I heard when you called, and I was going to come." Then Pastor Elijah started singing to Him a song he had heard but for which he never knew the lyrics on earth.

Looking down from the throne room, Pastor Elijah said he could see an array of angels seated in perfect formations around the arena that appeared like a stadium. He saw some of them trying to look back to see what was going on inside the throne room. "As they tried to bend down to see us, they twisted their bodies and arched their wings, looking backward as though a great light was disturbing them from seeing us, though I did not see the light. The power of love held us and bonded us so strongly that I felt like exploding with love inside my heart. Then I woke up with tears soaking my pillows. God's love is truly the force that holds the universe together," Pastor Elijah stated.

On the following day, October 26, 2012, International Ministry of Salvation and Praise had a healing conference that lasted most of the evening hours. After the conference was over, a little boy went outside and quickly ran back inside and said, "Pastor, come and look, come and look." As other curious members and Pastor Elijah went out to see what it was, they saw the most beautiful rainbow surrounding the moon at about 9:15 p.m. Suddenly, the Holy Spirit spoke to Pastor Elijah and said, "I said I was going to come. This shall be a sign of covenant between Me and you from now on. I will always be with you wherever you go and wherever I send you. I will listen to you whenever you call to Me because you are My friend."

Due to the partnership of the Holy Spirit with our ministry, we have witnessed the power of God and His Shekinah glory like never before in our meetings. The majority of the time, the glory of God has come and filled our meeting rooms. Adults and children have seen angels all around us. We have seen great deliverance, healing, miracles, signs, and wonders in our gatherings. Hundreds have been delivered from demonic oppression. Hundreds have been set free from the powers of cancer, addiction, deities, and generational curses. Many have been healed from every form of sickness in the name of Jesus Christ. Our websites at www.the-healinghouse.com or www.theIMSP.com are bombarded with prayer requests on a daily basis, and a majority are receiving breakthrough because of the power of Jesus Christ.

Pastor Dr. Elijah Akpan is one of the highly anointed leaders in the kingdom of God today with a powerful gift of healing and deliverance. He attended the University of Southern California (USC) School of Pharmacy, Los Angeles, California, USA, where he obtained his doctorate degree in pharmacy. God has called Pastor Elijah Akpan into the Fivefold Ministry with a strong calling to Apostolic and Prophetic Evangelism. God has used Pastor Elijah Akpan to heal and deliver thousands of people from various diseases, infirmities, and demonic oppressions in the name of Jesus Christ around the world.

www.ingramcontent.com/pod-product-compliance
Lightning Source LLC
Chambersburg PA
CBHW032033150426
43194CB00006B/254